TORAH
FROM OUR
SAGES

Pirke Avot

A
New
American
Translation and Explanation
by

Jacob Neusner

illustrated
by

Mordechai Rosenstein

Chappaqua, New York

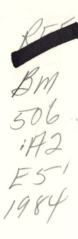

ACKNOWLEDGMENTS

The author and the publisher wish to thank Professor David Altshuler for serving as editor of the present volume. The vocalization used in the Hebrew text of Pirke Avot is that of Hanokh Yalon in the Albeck Mishnah *and is used here by permission of the copyright owners, the Bialik Institute and Dvir Co. Thanks are also due to Rabbi Miles B. Cohen, who supervised the typesetting of the Hebrew and English text.*

NOTES TO THE READER

The sixth chapter of Pirke Avot, called Perek Kinyan Torah, *was probably compiled to facilitate the study of Avot as part of the liturgy on six successive Sabbaths between Passover and Shavuot. The translation included in this volume was prepared by Howard Schwartz.*

While the explanation in all cases seeks to be egalitarian, the translation of Avot itself consciously makes use of the masculine and feminine referents as they appear in the original Hebrew, thus allowing the sages to speak in the authentic voice of their time.

Library of Congress Cataloging in Publication Data

Mishnah. Avot.
    Torah from our sages.

    Text in English and Hebrew; commentary in English.
    Includes bibliographical references.
    1. Mishnah. Avot—Commentaries. I. Neusner, Jacob,
1932-   . II. Mishnah. Avot. English. 1983.
III. Title. IV. Title: Pirke Avot.
BM506.A2E5 1983   296.1'2305   83-21295
ISBN 0-940646-05-6

© Copyright 1984 by Jacob Neusner
Illustrations © 1984 by Emes Editions, Ltd.
Hebrew vocalization © by The Bialik Institute and Dvir Co.
Published by Rossel Books
44 Dunbow Drive, Chappaqua, New York 10514

First Edition

Composition by Bet Sha'ar Press, Inc.

Manufactured in the United States of America.

Table of
Contents

PROLOGUE
WHY STUDY AVOT?

PROLOGUE
WHY STUDY AVOT?

Pirke Avot—"the lessons of the founders"—finds a place in the program of synagogue and school alike. It is the one classical Judaic text, besides the Siddur (prayer book) and the Hebrew Bible, that most Jews are likely to confront. Scholars without number study it. Through most of Jewish history, Jews paid their tribute in devotional and even careful reading. Why does it attract sustained attention in our own day, as much as in the past?

It would be easier to tell you why people might neglect this little tractate of the Mishnah than to explain why they have loved it so. The sayings which comprise it are unadorned, not set into the context of stories that might give the lessons color and life. No dramatic events provide a setting for the founders themselves. We are not told who the authorities are or why we should listen to them. So the didactic lessons of the founders come to us in a stark way. The statements are each expressed in a few simple words. They give instruction. They do not attempt to persuade. They tell us what to be and do, pure and simple.

Perhaps the very absence of rich and well-told historical tales, the simplicity of the setting, the focus of all light solely on what is said—these are what give the lessons of the founders their timeless quality. For if we do not know where and when a saying first was uttered and what personality stands behind it other than a name among unfamiliar names, we are free to use our own imaginations. We create for the sages' sayings a world much like our own. We make the sages' wisdom immediately relevant—because the framer did not try. If the stage is dark but for a beam of light, in our minds we see the scenery ourselves. Not knowing more than a name, we invent the character. Not hearing more than simple and universal truths, we create the context and impart our own detailed meanings.

Compare these timeless and eternally relevant sayings to other such collections, and the point is clear. Sayings of wisdom, whether deriving from ancient India or China or Israel or Mesopotamia or Egypt, have in common the power to come right to the point and to say only what urgently demands statement.

Some Historical Questions

At the outset, let us ask ourselves the necessary questions of authorship and context: Who wrote this book? How did it reach us?

The simple fact is that Pirke Avot does not contain the answers to these questions. We do not know the sources of the tractate, where the people who compiled the sayings got them, or how the sayings reached the final authorities who framed the tractate as we have it. We do not know where they did their work, though we assume it was in the Land of Israel. We do not know when they did it. The chronologically latest names to appear in the tractate generally are thought to have lived in the middle of the third century, about a generation beyond the publication of the Mishnah by Judah the Patriarch. Thus we may guess that the tractate was compiled some time afterwards, perhaps around 250–275 C.E.* But how did the people who composed the book know the sayings they put in it? And where did they get the names? We do not know the answers to these questions.

Nor are we the first to ask these questions. Indeed, others, for a long time, also answered them. The usual answer given is that there was a long process of tradition—handing down— that carried both the saying and the name of the person alleged to have spoken it from the beginning to the point at which, hundreds of years later, it was written down. This process of handing down through memorization and communication [called "oral tradition" since things were at first not written down] is certainly how the Mishnah of Judah the Patriarch was formulated and handed on for a while. But there is no conclusive evidence that the same way in which the completed

---

*Common Era: equivalent of Christian usage, A.D.

Mishnah was "published"—through oral formulation and oral transmission—is how everything prior to the formulation of the Mishnah also was preserved and handed on. We simply do not know anything at all about how things were formulated and placed into circulation. Writing was routine in Israelite culture for a long time, and the technology of writing goes back for more than 2,000 years before the time of the Mishnah. So people had to reject one form of long-term communication and take up another.

It seems clear they did so for a very special document, the Mishnah—until, in about 200 C.E., it was recorded. But how the framers of the Mishnah got their materials, including the sayings now collected and arranged in our tractate, we do not know. We cannot demonstrate from evidence that the picture of oral formulation and oral transmission drawn for Avot, and for the Mishnah of which it is part, is accurate for the period in which the sayings were made up and handed on. Rather than belabor the point, we have simply to admit we do not know how the people who compiled Avot knew the sayings they put into it, or where they got the names.

One fact is clear, as you will see in this book: The work of composition was done at the end. I mean, the labor of selecting and arranging sayings was not cumulative, carried on over a long time. Rather, the editorial authorship of the third-century masters imposed its ideas upon whatever material they had in hand. For the construction of chapters one, two and five of Avot shows that everything was put together in an artful way, with close attention to questions of form. Accumulations of wise sayings made over a long period of centuries do not magically fall into neat arrangements by threes, fives, twos, fours, sevens and the like. Since the sayings in these chapters do form patterns, we must conclude that we know much less about the origin and evolution of our tractate than we might like.

The Framers of Avot

The tractate consists of sayings attributed to important authorities. Who chose these authorities? Clearly, the framers who composed the tractate as a whole believed these authorities comprised a chain of instruction that could be traced all the way back to Moses at Sinai. They say so in the opening statement of Avot. The first authority cited is Simeon the Righteous who probably flourished in the third century B.C.E.* From his name onward, the list progresses in easy generations, through the second century, the first century, B.C.E.; then the first, second, and early third centuries C.E. In chapter two, the figures are not arranged chronologically, for we have two stems of the ancient tradition.

The Authorities of the Mishnah

Judah the Patriarch, the Jewish authority universally credited with the publication of the Mishnah, and there-fore also of Avot, was one of the two types of dominant Jewish leaders portrayed in our document, as you will see. Judah's title, "Patriarch," represents the Hebrew word nasi, *ruler of the Jewish nation. Judah flourished in the Land of Israel in the last part of the second century and the first part of the third. As patriarch and sage, he headed two establishments which were one.*

First, he was the ruler of the patriarchate the Romans set up for the Jews after the defeat of Bar Kokhba's messianic war, 132–135 C.E. The Romans' policy was to rule con-quered peoples through cooperative native authorities, so far as that was convenient. In the case of the Jews, that policy extended back to the time of Herod, nearly two hundred years earlier, and onward for yet another two centuries. In the aftermath of the tragic war, the Romans recognized the government of the Jewish nation in the Land of Israel that had begun to function before the war and put that government, and the family that headed it, back into power. So Judah the Patriarch headed the governing family that led the autonomous Jewish govern-ment. Since we generally suppose that the Mishnah as we know it was brought to closure and published around 200 C.E., and since all documents of the time attribute to the Mishnah the authority of the patriarch, we assume the

---

* Before the Christian Era: equivalent of Christian usage, B.C.

primacy of Judah the Patriarch in the sponsorship of the
Mishnah.

Second, Judah headed the sages, the other type of leader.
Judah did not do the work all by himself. He had at hand
a considerable body of learned scribes, bureaucrats, and
administrators of his government called sages (Hebrew:
hakhamim). *They drew upon the long traditions of their*
profession, on how the Scriptures were to be interpreted
and applied, and on how the Jewish community was to be
run in accord with the laws of Torah.

So, in all, the Mishnah derives from two sources: first, the
political authority and power of the patriarch; second, the
traditions of learning and proper administration of the
sages. Early on, you will see how these two distinct, but
cooperating, bodies combined their separate and distinct
ways of seeing things into a single document. Chapters
one and two of Avot in particular show us two lines of
tradition traced back to a single source, that is, two sets of
names, one of the patriarchal house, the other of the sages'
group, extending backward to a single authority—Moses
at Sinai. But I have moved far ahead of my story.

One is the stem represented by the name of Judah the
Patriarch and his two sons, hence, late-second- and early-
third-century c.e. authorities. Judah the Patriarch stands
behind the Mishnah as a whole. So he was one principal
figure.

The other stem lists Yohanan ben Zakkai and his disciples.
Yohanan ben Zakkai bridged the abyss from the time in which
the Temple stood to the aftermath of the Temple's destruction
in 70 c.e. and the founding of the sages' movement and school
at Yavneh.

So the purpose of chapter two was to link the two stems
of authority upon which the Mishnah as a whole rested—the
patriarch, on the one side; the sages, on the other. Chapters
three and four roughly follow what we believe to be the chronological order of their named authorities. But this is only a
surmise on our part. Chapter five for its part is not composed

of chains of names at all. It presents other kinds of constructions entirely. Accordingly, the several chapters are organized in diverse ways. The way in which a chapter is organized tells us the point important to the *framers* of the chapter. In due course, we shall explore in depth what that point was, case by case.

All of this explanation is meant to set Avot in context—and to explain why, in the end, we know less about even that context than we might wish. Yet that is a fact. It means that the framers did not want to give us history or biography. They composed Avot for some other purpose. When we ask historical questions—who were these named masters or sages of Avot? When did they live? What did they do?—we are asking inappropriate questions. But what questions do the framers of Avot address?

Generations of Jews knew. We may be sure of that fact, because generations of Jews have found the power to hear the framers of Avot, to grasp their questions, and to make those questions their own. Each generation must do this anew. The only facts are what the framers of Avot and the sayings they hand on to us have given us. Out of these facts, we have to locate other facts. By this I mean, from what people *do,* we have to investigate what they *intended.*

One of the things the framers of Avot do give us is the names of the authorities, even while they tell us little about who those people were, when they lived, what they did. Accordingly, we have to ask why the names were important, if the biographies and histories were not. The answer is that these names stand for something. They represent—as the framers will tell us—links in a chain of tradition extending from the time of the framers of the document in the middle of the third century C.E. backward to Sinai. Chapters one and two lay the foundations for this enormous allegation; and chapters three and four build that structure of authority that reaches to the time of the framers of Avot themselves. So each name was important not for itself, but for what it represented: a generation—the guarantee that each group, each age, had received from its teachers and handed on to its disciples precisely that Torah or teaching that had begun at Sinai.

What would you call this under other circumstances? If you were dealing with an aristocracy, you would call it genealogy—that which validates the claim of the present generation to its rightful place and position. In ancient Israel, it was the priests who validated their rights and privileges through genealogy. In our tractate's list of names, we have the method of the priests applied to the doctrines and beliefs of the sages—the scribes—of the Mishnah. In many ways, Avot thus captures in microcosm the trait of the Mishnah as a whole: the priests' interests and modes of thought, the scribes' methods and ways of interpreting and applying the law. Judaism as we know it in Avot combines the methods of the priests with the contents of the sages—hence, genealogy, but applied not to an aristocracy but to a spiritual family.

A Timeless Message

In fact, even though we do not know much about who made up these sayings and attached them to the names at hand, we know a great deal about the power of mind and imagination of the framers of the document. They were people with unusual powers of focusing upon the main theme. They chose with care and restraint to formulate and hand on accessible truths. They spoke in such a way that we, nearly eighteen hundred years later, wish to listen to them. So they had an extraordinary gift for insight into the ongoing and enduring condition of humanity. They wrote for all time, because they could transcend the cares and concerns of one time and place. If we can understand them, it is because they wrote in such a way as to make us want to understand them. They said things so as to make us able to enter into conversation with them. So in our hands is the work of sages of exceptional gifts of taste and judgment.

Still, if the traits of Avot as literature—simplicity and understatement of detail—win our admiration, as yet we do not know why we should listen to what the sages say, however well they say it. Let me list some reasons people study the words I translate in this book.

First, a work that is timeless always proves timely. What the founders say about the Torah applies also to their own writing: "Turn it over and over again, because everything is in it." You may not find every word equally suggestive for your life every moment of every day. But you are sure to find something aimed straight at your circumstance of heart and mind. That is the power of the document.

Second, you are not the first Jew in the world, nor are you going to be the last. True, here and now you make the critical decisions—but only because people before you decided things, too. So you must find relevant to your own condition as a human being not only what speaks to your private circumstance. Pertinent also is what Avot tells you about your situation as a Jew. As individual Jews, we deal with a Judaism "out there," an ongoing set of viewpoints and concerns and convictions held by many other Jews. The issues facing the individual Jew derive not only from personal experience, mine or yours. We do not create ourselves as Jews. We have to learn what other Jews know and feel. Thus we encounter the Jewish situation, what it means to be a Jew over time. The Judaism "out there" is a tradition we do not invent every morning; it is a faith we share with others. We who are American, British, and Canadian Jews, morever, with our powerful national traditions of independence and self-reliance, need to be reminded of this fact. Judaism stands for continuity and cooperation, experience that is shared and handed on, wisdom that we only partially discover individually, truth that abides.

When, therefore, a book of wisdom such as Avot comes into our hands, it speaks to each of us as an individual. But it addresses us in the name of the people Israel.

When we find something relevant to ourselves in Avot, the tractate, by definition, tells us that we, individually and privately, are relevant to Israel, the Jewish people as a whole. What we think is our own turns out to be public and broadly shared. So a document of Israel's heritage serves as the link between the private person, who studies the words as if spoken to him or her in particular, and the entire community and people of Israel, all the Jews, together.

Accordingly, we turn to Avot to find what is relevant to our situation. That is our personal motivation. But we turn out to discover how *we* are relevant to the Jewish situation, collectively and nationally. That is Israel's motivation. So, when Avot speaks to us, it speaks in the name of the whole of Israel, the Jewish people. When, in the privacy of our hearts, we listen to Avot, we ourselves then speak, out of our private being, to the whole of Israel, the Jewish people.

But what of the message? I said before that even though we appreciate Avot for its artful style of expression, we still do not know why we should listen to what the founders say. Just now I argued that there are solid reasons for listening to these founders. Yet I have not said what I think they have to say to us. And I shall not do so in advance. I prefer to stand back and speak only after the founders have spoken.

Any other role would be presumptuous and intrusive. It would presume that I can read, but you cannot. It would intrude my voice over the voice of the founders themselves. Stating in advance what to look for—as distinct from *how* to see and *why* to look at all—would impose my judgment upon yours, my perspective and capacity to observe and hear upon those of my companion, you, the reader. That I will not do.

Let me explain my way of presenting the sayings that comprise the Torah of our sages. This method involves two distinct tasks: first, rendering the Hebrew into English; and, second, explaining what the saying means.

My translation is easy to explain. I translate as literally as possible. I claim in no way to innovate in the selection of a word in English to serve as the counterpart—the translation—of a word in Hebrew. If there are conventions on these matters of word choice, I generally follow them. I lay out the translation, however, in a way that will be unfamiliar. I try to allow each complete and autonomous thought, or unit of thought, to stand by itself. That is why I have broken up long columns of undifferentiated words not only into sentences, but also into visually distinct units.

In this way the reader immediately sees the way in which the sentences are composed and then made to form complete thoughts, fully exposed ideas. So, for one thing, the grouping of ideas into patterns—triplets, for example—and the provision of secondary explanation or amplification of a primary sentence always come into clear focus. You, therefore, should be able to see not only *what* the sages say, but also *how* they say it. If I can clarify how the language works, how the sentences convey meaning, I can show you something critical to Avot. The lessons come in fact as poetry, not prose. The ideas not only are stated, they are framed with exquisite care into phrases and sentences. Nothing is random. Everything is closely and reflectively balanced. When *how* things are said matters as much as *what* is said, then you have poetry. And Avot is poetry.

The Individual and the Community

All of us come to study Judaism's great texts because something about ourselves, as individuals, makes us want to do so. We look for something relevant to our own lives, to the problems we have to work out, to the issues we confront from day to day. So we look in Avot for something to speak to our private concerns. But Avot addresses all Jews. If it tells you to do something, it tells the same thing to all of us—hence, by definition, Avot speaks to the Jews as a group, even though, to begin with, we come to Avot one by one, as individuals.

When Avot speaks to us as individuals, therefore, our capacity to hear and understand and appropriate that message signifies that we are not isolated individuals at all. The power to hear the message of Avot indicates that we share traits of heart and mind with the sages who speak through Avot. And that means we are not only radically isolated individuals, each with his or her own distinctive traits. We share in common traits as Jews. We hear a Jewish message because we have Jewish powers of understanding. Thus, whatever we find particular to ourselves— that is, meaningful to our own situation—turns out to define the least special characteristics about ourselves— that is, our Jewish traits, our sharing with other Jews the same concerns and the same values.

What seems to be individual turns out to mark us as part of a larger community of feeling and concern, caring and intellect. With that paradox in mind, what it means to take up and respond to a classic text of Judaism may be clearer.

My explanation ("commentary") of the Torah of our sages focuses upon groups of sayings. My perspective is upon what sayings mean when seen as a whole. What I believe I can tell you, which you may not have thought on your own, is how to see things from the angle of vision of the people who brought statements together and saw them whole. For the sayings one by one either speak to us directly and without need of mediation, or they fail. As I have stressed, their power is that they do not require much amplification or illustration. Short of preaching obvious sermons to you on the self-evident meanings the sages' sayings have for us, I can have no reason to tell you what you can see for yourself. But I can try to get at the perspective of those who framed the sayings into groups.

That is to say, I can try to explain what the person who put several sayings together in just this way accomplished. Why did an editor link opinion A with opinion B? Do these two opinions read differently when they are placed side by side from the way they read separately? Does the juxtaposition also present a contrast, for example? Or does it provide an emphasis somewhat different from the stress of a saying read all by itself? Does a set of five or ten sayings add up, when read all together, to something greater than the parts of the set seen one by one? This is what I mean by claiming to provide the perspective, the viewpoint, of the people who combined the sayings into the constructions now at hand. There is, then, the saying read all by itself. But there also is the saying seen in a larger context. The perspective of the one who took two or more sayings and grouped them as we now have them—that is the angle of vision I try to reveal.

This perspective on Avot will indicate what to me is Avot's surprising and radical character. For when we insist that we have more than merely random sayings, one thing after another, but a carefully crafted construction, we perceive a new dimension of meaning, a fresh message and judgment. Then we see the architecture of the document, the inner architectonics of its sustained argument.

Of course, no one can hope to say everything there is to be said about an enduring construction such as Avot. So let me be clear about that single contribution I hope to make to your understanding and appreciation of this amazing Mishnah tractate. The goal of my explanation is to show you that the whole of Judaism speaks out of this small but perfect part of the Mishnah, the oral Torah of Judaism.

The
Mishnah

In context, the tractate of Avot finds its place in the Mishnah—the foundation of Judaism when joined with the Hebrew Bible, Tanakh. Avot is one of the sixty-three tractates (*massekhtot*) of the Mishnah. While we treat Avot as special, reading it by itself, to begin with, it serves a purpose in the larger document in which it is located. The Mishnah is a vast composition, in the form of laws or descriptions of how things are, in which an encompassing design for the life of Israel, the Jewish people, comes to full expression. The life of Israel, in the vision of the Mishnah, is lived in an orderly and stable world, in which the Temple stands at the center, and all things take up their proper positions in relationship to the Temple. That is why much of the Mishnah treats subjects important to the conduct of the life of service to God carried on by priests (*kohanim*) through the labor of the sacrifice of animals in the holy place in Jerusalem.

Of the Mishnah's six vast divisions (*sedarim*), no fewer than three treat subjects of principal interest to priests and deal with the sacrificial service to God. These are the first division, concerning the rations set aside from the yield of the Holy Land for the support of the priesthood; the fifth, concerning the everyday sacrificial service and the upkeep of the Temple; and the sixth, concerning the protection of the Temple and things pertaining to the cult from the dangers of uncleanliness described in Leviticus, chapters one through fifteen. In addition, the better part of the second division, concerning special seasons and appointed times, gives laws on what is done in the sacrificial service on extraordinary occasions, Yom Kippur and Passover, for example. (The remainder of that division concerns conduct in the home, analagous to what goes on in the cult, on those same days.) Only the third and fourth divisions—presenting laws pertaining to the family and women, on the one side, and to the conduct of civil life, institutions of government and justice and the laws for political, social, and commercial life, on the other—address that ordinary and practical world we know.

So the Mishnah as a whole covers the entire life of Israel, the Jewish people. But it is a strange picture. For the Mishnah portrays Judaism as if Israel were living in and around Jerusalem, or, if elsewhere, wholly in relationship to Jerusalem and the Temple. In fact, however, while materials or laws in the

Mishnah may derive from earlier times, the document was fashioned by people who flourished in the second century C.E., after Jerusalem and the Temple had been destroyed by the Romans—indeed, after the failure of the Bar Kokhba war led the Romans to prohibit Jews from even entering Jerusalem. So, from the viewpoint of the world to which the Mishnah's framers spoke, the document presents a fantasy. Perhaps the Jews hoped that the Temple-centered world once more would come into being. But when the Mishnah came forth as the constitution and by-laws of Israel, the Jewish people, most of it turned out to be as irrelevant to realities then as it is today.

The question facing the people who received the Mishnah therefore is clear: what is this vast, strange document? Why should we listen to its laws and obey those that we can, that is, those that prove relevant even now?

Now among the sixty-three tractates of the Mishnah there is one totally unlike all the others, and that tractate presents answers to the question of the standing and status of the document as a whole. The tractate Avot, the one we learn together here, does not present laws, so it is different from the other sixty-two. Rather, it presents wise sayings. Moreover, it is not organized topically, as are the legal tractates. Rather, it is organized around the names of particular authorities. These are presented in chains, or sequences, and the sequence of names is meant to tell the whole story. That is a fact you will see most tellingly in chapter one, which leads from Sinai to the founders of the Mishnah itself.

We further notice that the authorities who appear in this tractate and also in the other sixty-two tractates of the Mishnah, here present sayings (or, are given sayings) without any relationship at all to opinions or general principles ascribed to them elsewhere. It is as if you study with a teacher in physics, but one day the teacher writes you a poem or sings you an aria. Such a thing is entirely possible, but it still presents a surprise. So too here, the same great minds who speak of rather remote and impractical laws elsewhere now tell us how we should live our lives. They express great principles to guide us in small things. In this way, too, Avot is different from all the rest of the Mishnah. Perhaps framed last, it was meant to stand at the head and introduce the system of the Mishnah as a whole. That is what I think Avot's framers had in mind in making this remarkable tractate. It may be that they wanted to state in very general and accessible terms principles given elsewhere only in detail and therefore difficult to discern. You may think, then, that here are the generalizations, provided as particular exemplifications everywhere else. It is hard to know whether that is the fact. But it is a fact that the generalizations before us do exemplify attitudes and convictions that define Judaism as it comes to us.

It follows that some time after the Mishnah as a whole had reached pretty much the condition in which it now comes to us, the authorities of Judaism composed a further tractate for the Mishnah, one that would explain all the others. And that is the one at hand. Accordingly, in its context, in the Mishnah itself, Avot answers a set of enormously critical questions about the Mishnah. In our context, outside of the framework of the Mishnah and of the issues of Judaism of the third century, Avot answers equally central concerns of ours. The fact that we can and want to confront the tractate in its own terms serves as our tribute to the power of the framers of Avot. They turned backward, to speak of where the Mishnah came from and to pass on important sayings of sages who play significant parts in the Mishnah. In so doing, they turned forward, to the centuries stretching beyond the horizon of their imagination. Not many authors of the third or any century so framed words to an unknown future as did our sages of Avot.

The Task at Hand

The plan and program of our work to begin with depend on the task at hand. That task is to learn how to listen to people who lived long ago, in a world we scarcely can imagine. If, as I said before, we are able to hear what they say to a world they surely could never have imagined, that is our tribute to the power of what they said and how they said it. That tribute suffices.

So the hard work begins: the work of opening up these sayings and teaching ourselves how to make sense of them. What "making sense" must mean itself will become clear only in doing the work. It surely means framing a program of questions to be systematically addressed to the sayings in their groups.

Before we turn to the text of Avot, there is one further issue to raise: Who am I? And who do I imagine you to be? I am a teacher who writes in America, for North American Jews and for other Jews who read our American language. I imagine that you are a Jew, and that your native language is English. Why does that matter?

The reason is, first, that together we are trying to discover how to learn from a text written in a language other than our own. So we are engaged in a labor of moving from one culture to another, one world to another. The Jewish world, repreented by Avot, speaks in Hebrew. As I have stressed, it addresses a long-ago time and place. Ours is a work of making this mode of address intelligible to ourselves.

Second, the fact that we are English-speaking matters in yet another way. We are used to reading a book in a given way, from beginning to end, for example, without moving from a text to a commentary and back to a text. We are used to smooth and uninterrupted discussion of a topic, start to finish, rather than episodic jumping back and forth. We expect sustained and reasoned discussion of things we can understand. We take for granted that our capacity for reasoning and critical judgment matters.

But the classical works of the Jewish religion take shape in quite a different world, in which people thought in other ways and expressed themselves in a manner different from our own. They would take an old text and study that—so indicating that they stood in a direct line with the past. At the same time, they took for granted that they too had something of worth to add to the tradition. They were no different from ourselves in thinking so. But they adopted a manner of discourse not familiar to us. It took the form of adding their ideas along the edges of the page, around the sides, at the bottom, in the manner of writing footnotes. Accordingly, the text, received of old, was the main thing, and whatever they had to say took the form of this secondary addition—new points here and there—called commentaries.

My discussion of Avot does not take the classical form of a commentary. The reason is that you are unused to learning through the bits and pieces in which commentaries to texts express ideas. That is to say, if you study a text first, and then the observations of the commentator, you have this brick and that stone. Then you are supposed, on your own, to build the whole thing into a single construction, a building. That is not the way in which you ordinarily learn, so it is not the approach I take in this book. Rather, as I have indicated, I provide what I call an explanation—hence, not a commentary. I provide it by presenting, in a sustained way, at the end of a passage, whatever I have to say about that passage. My discussion is meant to be continuous, coherent, and comprehensible on its own, and so a complete statement. It is supposed to be something you can simply read.

In other words, I choose to talk to you in a way as close as possible to that in which most other books you read and study speak to you. I want to translate the text not merely into our shared language, but also into our shared American—and Western, modern—manner of learning, mode of thinking, method of speaking with one another. Let there be no point of difference, at the beginning, between the way you study a great Judaic text and how you would study great writing of any other kind.

Later on you may choose to master the modes of thought and expression that characterize classical Judaic discourse. I hope you do. That is all to the good. If this book of mine works for you, you will decide to learn more about Avot. You will turn to the many other books, including a large number in Hebrew, in which Avot is approached in a different way and so is made to say other things. So mine will have been a stage in your education in the literature of Torah. That is all I could ever hope it to be.

So here we draw near, through familiar means of learning, to an old and alien Jewish text. Later, you may come closer still to learn the ancient text in the time-honored way. Here the conversation starts.

Let us then learn how to look at and listen to the text. You now will find three things: first, an introduction to a chapter or a major segment of a chapter, telling you what to expect; second, a translation of the chapter or component thereof; and, third, a further reflection on what the chapter has said and what its sayings mean when seen all together.

Let me conclude with a brief personal confession. Until I undertook this sustained encounter with Avot, I kept my distance from it. The reason was that it had always seemed strange. My tastes in rabbinic literature had been shaped by the Mishnah. While appearing in the Mishnah, tractate Avot is profoundly "unMishnaic." The Mishnah's statements are expressed with great care, so that there are groups of sayings on a given problem. The contents of sayings in Avot, by contrast, bear no obvious relationship to a single sustained topical program. The Mishnah's language is restrained and exquisitely balanced, so that what one authority says relates in form as much as in substance to what stands nearby in the name of another authority. Avot's language, for its part, pays no mind to considerations of coherence, balance, contrast, and comparison. Above all, as I pointed out, the Mishnah treats legal subjects. Avot does not. The Mishnah tells us what to *do;* Avot tells us what we should *be.*

So to me the Mishnah tractate at hand contradicted the rest of the Mishnah tractates both in the things it chose to discuss, and in the manner in which it chose to discuss them. To offer an analogy out of music, if the Mishnah in general may be compared to Mozart's *Jupiter Symphony,* Avot calls to mind Stravinsky's *Rites of Spring.*

When, therefore, Seymour Rossel called me to work on this tractate, I found myself amazed and astonished by the freshness, the vitality, the daring, and the extreme points of insistence of Avot. Serving as the head and preface to the Mishnah, Avot turns out to complement the Mishnah precisely because it is so different in spirit, in substance, and in style. That is why I found myself charmed and enticed by the tractate: its alienness, its radical freshness, its power to surprise and always amaze. If in this account of the matter I can help you to see the tractate as I do, as extraordinary, I shall have attained my goal.

CHAPTER ONE
HOW TORAH
COMES TO US

CHAPTER ONE
HOW TORAH COMES TO US

Before us is the most important, but also the most difficult chapter of Avot, covering many names and sayings. To make the chapter accessible, I offer first a rapid view of its principal parts, followed by a second look to review the chapter as a whole. By doing things this way, we can make the details familiar and see how the larger structure incorporates these details. What are the principal parts? The answer may be seen if we simply notice the three groups into which the names of the authorities fall: an opening set of three single names given three sayings apiece; then an intermediate set of five pairs of names, also given three sayings each; then a concluding group of three individual names, each again given three sayings.

א מֹשֶׁה קִבֵּל תּוֹרָה מִסִּינַי וּמְסָרָהּ לִיהוֹשֻׁעַ, וִיהוֹשֻׁעַ לִזְקֵנִים, וּזְקֵנִים לִנְבִיאִים. וּנְבִיאִים מְסָרוּהָ לְאַנְשֵׁי כְנֶסֶת הַגְּדוֹלָה. הֵם אָמְרוּ שְׁלֹשָׁה דְבָרִים:
הֱווּ מְתוּנִים בַּדִּין.
וְהַעֲמִידוּ תַלְמִידִים הַרְבֵּה.
וַעֲשׂוּ סְיָג לַתּוֹרָה.

ב שִׁמְעוֹן הַצַּדִּיק הָיָה מִשְּׁיָרֵי כְנֶסֶת הַגְּדוֹלָה. הוּא הָיָה אוֹמֵר:
עַל שְׁלֹשָׁה דְבָרִים הָעוֹלָם עוֹמֵד:

עַל הַתּוֹרָה,
וְעַל הָעֲבוֹדָה,
וְעַל גְּמִילוּת חֲסָדִים.

ג אַנְטִיגְנוֹס אִישׁ סוֹכוֹ קִבֵּל מִשִּׁמְעוֹן הַצַּדִּיק. הוּא
הָיָה אוֹמֵר:
אַל תִּהְיוּ כַעֲבָדִים, הַמְשַׁמְּשִׁין אֶת הָרַב עַל
מְנָת לְקַבֵּל פְּרָס,
אֶלָּא הֱווּ כַעֲבָדִים, הַמְשַׁמְּשִׁין אֶת הָרַב שֶׁלֹּא
עַל מְנָת לְקַבֵּל פְּרָס.
וִיהִי מוֹרָא שָׁמַיִם עֲלֵיכֶם.

1 Moses received Torah at Sinai and handed it on to Joshua,
Joshua to elders, and elders to prophets. And prophets
handed it on to the men of the great assembly. They said
three things:
> Be prudent in judgment.
> Raise up many disciples.
> Make a fence for the Torah.

2 Simeon the Righteous was one of the last survivors of the
great assembly. He would say:
On three things does the world stand:
> On the Torah,
> and on the Temple service,
> and on deeds of lovingkindness.

3 Antigonus of Sokho received [the Torah] from Simeon the
Righteous. He would say:
> Do not be like servants who serve the master on condi-
> tion of receiving a reward,
> but [be] like servants who serve the master not on
> condition of receiving a reward.
And let the fear of Heaven be upon you.

Judges and Disciples

The first question is, To whom are the sayings addressed?
Without establishing the context in the minds of the authorities
at hand, we surely cannot interpret what those authorities

עַל שְׁלֹשָׁה דְבָרִים הָעוֹלָם עוֹמֵד

ON THREE THINGS DOES THE WORLD STAND:
ON THE TORAH, AND ON THE TEMPLE SERVICE, AND ON DEEDS OF LOVINGKINDNESS.

wish to tell us. The answer, for the men of the great assembly, is clear. They speak to judges, telling them to be prudent. They speak to masters, telling them to work at raising up disciples. So the sayings address men who have responsibilities as judges and administrators over Israel, the Jewish people, and who also teach disciples. I should imagine the mode of teaching is apprenticeship; the disciples watch what the master does—they observe him in court or in his role as administrator.

Discipleship means following a great master, a model of what one is supposed to be and do, and learning from the master's words and actions. That is not the only mode of transmitting knowledge, and it is not the customary one today. In our own time we transmit learning through instruction, most of it in classrooms. The teacher is not so much a model as a source of information, and learning is not so much a process of forming great human beings as it is a work of handing on information to technically proficient experts. So when we speak of teaching through apprenticeship, we also address the deepest level of the culture under study. It is for the nurture of great men and women, not for the education of experts at some one thing. Education by discipleship, then, serves the purpose of forming whole and complete people, not merely informing students' minds.

Up to this point, we may suppose that Judaism is a religion for professors of law and public administrators and for their students. Nothing could be further from the truth. For the climax of the first saying refers to Torah, and Torah speaks to all Israel, not only to judges and apprentices. What the sage does, everyone should do—it is not merely an issue of knowledge. Making a fence around the Torah means making certain, through an additional point of strictness, that we do not violate the law. To take a commonplace example: you honor parents not only by refraining from physically abusing them, but, additionally, by not yelling at them. In all, the message of the men of the great assembly sets the stage for what follows. For it has two points of interest: *the life of doing,* hence, judging and teaching; and *the life of learning,* hence, Torah. Here, to be sure, the issue of learning, is secondary. But the themes are announced at the outset. Few sayings that follow fail to take up both themes.

The Foundations of the World

Simeon the Righteous emphasizes that we build the world through learning in Torah, through doing our duty to God, and through doing more than our duty. Another Simeon, later on (at saying 18), phrases matters in more abstract language (the world, he says, stands on justice, truth, and peace), rather than as referring to concrete things. The first Simeon speaks of the particular; the second of the general, and they say the same thing. The general, without the specific, is hard to grasp and means little. The specific, without the general, is bound to a particular place and time and cannot really speak to us so far away and so long afterward. Having the two sayings together, we gain a vision of the world.

It is not, of course, the "real" world. It is, rather, the world we must attain and build for ourselves. But we take that for granted. Wisdom speaks not about how things are, but to how things should be. Wisdom tells us what to do. It does not merely describe what people happen to do. So when Simeon the Righteous says the world stands on Torah, sacrifice, and acts of grace, he also explains why the world we now construct for ourselves is so shaky. It is because our world does not stand on Torah, sacrifice, and acts of grace, but on other things.

Torah means learning and reflection. But people fail to reflect, so they do things without thinking about them. Sacrifice means giving something up. But people tend to selfishness and think everything is coming to them and they take things for granted. Without acts of grace, people adhere to rules, rather than understanding them. People tend to do what they *must,* rather than what they *should.* So the language seems to describe how things are. But it describes the opposite: *why* things are as bad as they are.

Between Us and God

Antigonus's saying is in three clauses, but it says only two things, and they are really one. When we do our duty, *why* do we do it? He thinks that the answer is important. He sets up the contrast between acting in hope of a reward and doing things not for some further compensation. He advocates doing something for its own sake, out of a sense of inner obligation rather than for the sake of something else, that is, the hope of compensation. In the one case, we do our duty for the wrong reason; in the other, we do our duty for the right reason.

What is the right reason? It is the fear of Heaven, that is, reverence and awe of God. Fear here does not mean something negative, being afraid of what God will do to you if you do not do your duty. That would contradict the sense of doing things not on condition of receiving a reward. It would mean we did our duty solely in order to receive the reward of not being punished for shirking our duty—an absurdity. So Antigonus instructs us to do our duty because of our awe and reverence for Heaven, which stands for God. Our service then must be for the right reason, which is recognition of who we are and who God is.

Mitzvah and Kavvanah

Underlying the saying attributed to Antigonus are the two most fundamental concepts of living a Jewish life: mitzvah, *commandment, and* kavvanah, *right attitude and intention. When Antigonus speaks of service without hope of reward, he means to do one's duty because one is commanded to do it, not out of mere whim or desire or good will. So what we do as Jews, the duties we undertake in service to others and to God, we do because we are commanded. That means we do our duty whether or not we feel like it. When Antigonus, moreover, demands that we do our duty not in the expectation of gaining a reward, he addresses the issue of attitude. We are commanded, so the issue of reward does not enter. The right attitude, the correct* kavvanah, *therefore is required: awe, reverence, fear of Heaven. That means, as I said, we know who we are, and we know who God is. Later on, in chapters three and four, there is still more emphasis on this matter of doing the right thing because we know who we are and Whom we serve.*

If you give a birthday present because you want the recipient to like you, that is the right thing for the wrong reason.

Your gift is no gift at all. Your wrong intention lessens the kindness of your right action. If you say prayers to show people how pious you are, rather than to address your heart to God, you do a holy deed for a wordly reason. The deed is null. God surely will not "hear" what you do not direct to God. Antigonus wants you to do the right thing the right way, for the right purpose: God wants the heart.

ד יוֹסֵי בֶּן יוֹעֶזֶר אִישׁ צְרֵדָה וְיוֹסֵי בֶּן יוֹחָנָן אִישׁ
יְרוּשָׁלַיִם קִבְּלוּ מֵהֶם. יוֹסֵי בֶּן יוֹעֶזֶר אוֹמֵר:
יְהִי בֵיתְךָ בֵּית וַעַד לַחֲכָמִים.
וֶהֱוֵי מִתְאַבֵּק בַּעֲפַר רַגְלֵיהֶם.
וֶהֱוֵי שׁוֹתֶה בְצָמָא אֶת דִּבְרֵיהֶם.

ה יוֹסֵי בֶּן יוֹחָנָן אִישׁ יְרוּשָׁלַיִם אוֹמֵר:
יְהִי בֵיתְךָ פָּתוּחַ לָרְוָחָה.
וְיִהְיוּ עֲנִיִּים בְּנֵי בֵיתֶךָ.
וְאַל תַּרְבֶּה שִׂיחָה עִם הָאִשָּׁה.
בְּאִשְׁתּוֹ אָמְרוּ, קַל וָחֹמֶר בְּאֵשֶׁת חֲבֵרוֹ. מִכָּאן
אָמְרוּ חֲכָמִים: כָּל זְמַן שֶׁאָדָם מַרְבֶּה שִׂיחָה עִם
הָאִשָּׁה —
גּוֹרֵם רָעָה לְעַצְמוֹ,
וּבוֹטֵל מִדִּבְרֵי תוֹרָה,
וְסוֹפוֹ יוֹרֵשׁ גֵּיהִנָּם.

ו יְהוֹשֻׁעַ בֶּן פְּרַחְיָה וְנִתַּאי הָאַרְבֵּלִי קִבְּלוּ מֵהֶם.
יְהוֹשֻׁעַ בֶּן פְּרַחְיָה אוֹמֵר:
עֲשֵׂה לְךָ רַב,
וּקְנֵה לְךָ חָבֵר,
וֶהֱוֵי דָן אֶת כָּל הָאָדָם לְכַף זְכוּת.

ז נִתַּאי הָאַרְבֵּלִי אוֹמֵר:
הַרְחֵק מִשָּׁכֵן רַע.

וְאַל תִּתְחַבֵּר לָרָשָׁע.
וְאַל תִּתְיָאֵשׁ מִן הַפֻּרְעָנוּת.

ח יְהוּדָה בֶּן טַבַּאי וְשִׁמְעוֹן בֶּן שָׁטָח קִבְּלוּ מֵהֶם.
יְהוּדָה בֶּן טַבַּאי אוֹמֵר:
אַל תַּעַשׂ עַצְמְךָ כְּעוֹרְכֵי הַדַּיָּנִין.
וּכְשֶׁיִּהְיוּ בַּעֲלֵי הַדִּינִים עוֹמְדִים לְפָנֶיךָ, יִהְיוּ
בְּעֵינֶיךָ כִּרְשָׁעִים.
וּכְשֶׁנִּפְטָרִים מִלְפָנֶיךָ, יִהְיוּ בְּעֵינֶיךָ כְּזַכָּאִין,
כְּשֶׁקִּבְּלוּ עֲלֵיהֶם אֶת הַדִּין.

ט שִׁמְעוֹן בֶּן שָׁטָח אוֹמֵר:
הֱוֵי מַרְבֶּה לַחְקוֹר אֶת הָעֵדִים.
וֶהֱוֵי זָהִיר בִּדְבָרֶיךָ,
שֶׁמָּא מִתּוֹכָם יִלְמְדוּ לְשַׁקֵּר.

י שְׁמַעְיָה וְאַבְטַלְיוֹן קִבְּלוּ מֵהֶם. שְׁמַעְיָה אוֹמֵר:
אֱהֹב אֶת הַמְּלָאכָה.
וּשְׂנָא אֶת הָרַבָּנוּת.
וְאַל תִּתְוַדַּע לָרָשׁוּת.

יא אַבְטַלְיוֹן אוֹמֵר:
חֲכָמִים, הִזָּהֲרוּ בְדִבְרֵיכֶם,
שֶׁמָּא תָחוּבוּ חוֹבַת גָּלוּת וְתִגְלוּ לִמְקוֹם מַיִם
הָרָעִים, וְיִשְׁתּוּ הַתַּלְמִידִים הַבָּאִים אַחֲרֵיכֶם
וְיָמוּתוּ, וְנִמְצָא שֵׁם שָׁמַיִם מִתְחַלֵּל.

יב הִלֵּל וְשַׁמַּאי קִבְּלוּ מֵהֶם. הִלֵּל אוֹמֵר:
הֱוֵי מִתַּלְמִידָיו שֶׁלְּאַהֲרֹן,
אוֹהֵב שָׁלוֹם וְרוֹדֵף שָׁלוֹם,
אוֹהֵב אֶת הַבְּרִיּוֹת וּמְקָרְבָן לַתּוֹרָה.

יג הוּא הָיָה אוֹמֵר:
נְגַד שְׁמָא אֲבַד שְׁמֵהּ,

וּדְלָא מוֹסִיף יְסוּף.
וּדְלָא יָלֵיף קַטְלָא חַיָּב.
וְדִשְׁתַּמַּשׁ בְּתָגָא חֲלַף.

יד הוּא הָיָה אוֹמֵר:
אִם אֵין אֲנִי לִי, מִי לִי?
וּכְשֶׁאֲנִי לְעַצְמִי, מָה אֲנִי?
וְאִם לֹא עַכְשָׁיו, אֵימָתַי?

טו שַׁמַּאי אוֹמֵר:
עֲשֵׂה תוֹרָתְךָ קֶבַע.
אֱמֹר מְעַט וַעֲשֵׂה הַרְבֵּה.
וֶהֱוֵי מְקַבֵּל אֶת כָּל הָאָדָם בְּסֵבֶר פָּנִים יָפוֹת.

4 Yose ben Yoezer of Zeredah and Yose ben Yohanan of
Jerusalem received [the Torah] from them. Yose ben Yoezer
says:
> Let your house be a gathering place for sages.
> And wallow in the dust of their feet,
> And drink in their words with gusto.

5 Yose ben Yohanan of Jerusalem says:
> Let your house be open wide.
> And seat the poor at your table ["make the poor
> members of your household"].
> And don't talk too much with women.

(He referred to a man's wife, all the more so is the rule to
be applied to the wife of one's fellow. In this regard did
sages say: So long as a man talks too much with a woman,
> he brings trouble on himself,
> wastes time better spent on studying Torah,
> and ends up an heir of Gehenna.)

6 Joshua ben Perahyah and Nittai the Arbelite received [the
Torah] from them. Joshua ben Perahyah says:
> Set up a master for yourself.
> And get yourself a companion-disciple.
> And give everybody the benefit of the doubt.

7 Nittai the Arbelite says:

>Keep away from a bad neighbor.
>And don't get involved with a bad person.
>And don't give up hope of retribution.

8 Judah ben Tabbai and Simeon ben Shetah received [the Torah] from them. Judah ben Tabbai says:

>Don't make yourself like one of those who advocate before judges [while you yourself are judging a case].
>And when the litigants stand before you, regard them as guilty.
>But when they leave you, regard them as acquitted (when they have accepted your judgment).

9 Simeon ben Shetah says:

>Examine the witnesses with great care.
>And watch what you say,
>lest they learn from what you say how to lie.

10 Shemaiah and Avtalyon received [the Torah] from them. Shemaiah says:

>Love work.
>Hate authority.
>Don't get friendly with the government.

11 Avtalyon says:

>Sages, watch what you say,
>lest you become liable to the punishment of exile, and go into exile to a place of bad water, and disciples who follow you drink bad water and die, and the name of Heaven be thereby profaned.

12 Hillel and Shammai received [the Torah] from them. Hillel says:

>Be disciples of Aaron,
>loving peace and pursuing grace,
>loving people and drawing them near to the Torah.

13 He would say [in Aramaic]:

>A name made great is a name destroyed,
>And one who does not add, subtracts.
>And who does not learn is liable to death.
>And the one who uses the crown, passes away.

14 He would say:
   If I am not for myself, who is for me?
   And when I am for myself, what am I?
   And if not now, when?

15 Shammai says:
   Make your learning of Torah a fixed obligation.
   Say little and do much.
   Greet everybody cheerfully.

Between
One Person
and
Another

As we saw with the men of the great assembly, the sages in our chapter serve as either teachers or students, masters or disciples. They take for granted that their craft is the work of justice, truth, and peace—that is, the work of judges, teachers of truth, and peace-makers. So when they speak of how you relate to other people, it is in terms of their own setting. Because they are speaking in concrete terms what they say is both remote and immediate. It is remote from us. It was immediate to their lives. The very specificity of what they say demands that we translate their words into words of our own, specific to our setting. So let us go through these sayings about sages, disciples, judges, people who sort things out and exercise judgment and taste.

As we proceed, it is necessary to remember that we ourselves make judgments, teach people around us, learn from people nearby. True, how we regard and act toward others bears no official standing. If we make a negative judgment, the other party does not go to jail. But we do make an impact upon, and receive an impact from, others; we judge and are judged, teach and are taught. So as we work our way through the sayings, we realize that they speak in very concrete terms about the general problem of relationships between one person and another person: you and the other.

If we turn, then, to the two Yoses—sayings 4 and 5—we notice an emphasis on two things: first, being receptive to learning and seeking sages, attending on their presence and wisdom; second, making a place for the poor. We note, alas, an attitude we cannot wish away, namely, low regard for women. It is indefensible. It is not one of the ornaments of this otherwise blameless text. It is there, part of its day, not ours—a reminder that we too have a contribution to make to the tradition of Judaism. In our day we can and shall attain full equality for women in the life of the Jewish religion and of the Jewish people. You might want to translate the statement into the notion of not talking too much with idle folk, people without ideas in their heads. But it does not remove the sting. So let us sadly walk away.

The next group of pertinent sayings, Joshua ben Perahyah's and Nittai the Arbelite's, sayings 6 and 7, goes over pretty much the same ideas.

Joshua emphasizes that we must have teachers—people whom we respect—and companion-students. Learning always is social, never entirely private. For when we act as if everything depends upon our own judgment alone, we cut ourselves off from criticism. We lose the ideas and stimulation of others. We end up talking to ourselves. Joshua then tells us how we can live both with teachers we respect and companion-students. It is by giving other people the benefit of the doubt. This, in a practical way, is the counterpart of the emphasis on deeds of grace and lovingkindness in the theoretical framework.

Nittai's negative statements form an apt complement to Joshua's affirmative ones. Just as you have to seek out the right teachers and companion-students, so you have to avoid the wrong ones. Just as you have to preserve a generous spirit toward others—giving them the benefit of the doubt—so you must sustain the hope that the evil get their just desserts as well. You give the benefit of the doubt, yes. But in the end, retribution sometimes overtakes those who deserve it.

The sayings of the next two teachers, Judah and Simeon, sayings 8 and 9, concern real judges in actual courts. They take for granted that the document in hand, Pirke Avot, is a handbook for law teachers and students. And yet, even here, we outsiders to the world of the law may learn something. Judah tells us not to be both judge and jury. That is advice worth heeding as we form opinions on others. He says that we should learn to be skeptical about what other people say ("regard them as guilty"). The beginning of wisdom is to doubt, to ask tough questions. He emphasizes that once we determine to trust someone, we should let that trust stand unshaken. It is just as important to trust the trustworthy as to doubt the dubious. The problem is to discern the difference.

Simeon's saying is also particular to law teachers and

students. Yet if he tells us to examine witnesses carefully, we can well learn not to believe everything we hear. When he says we should watch what we say, lest the other person learn, from what we say, how to lie, that is subtle but excellent advice. It means that if you really want to learn from someone else, then do not, in advance, signal to the other party what you want to hear.

The Honest Relationship

Simeon's saying yields not only several specific points but one general principle, relevant to our own circumstances. We should not take advantage of a superior position to influence someone else's response, to prejudice someone else's opinion. The main point here is that we have to allow the other party full and honest expression, rather than teasing out of another person what we want to hear. We should not humor other people, pretending to opinions we do not hold in order to please and therefore influence them. That sort of dishonesty in human relationships unfortunately is commonplace. Perhaps under some circumstances people think it is necessary. But there is still room for truth in our relationships with other people, and truth is liberating, if painful. Accordingly, Simeon's message lays emphasis upon the opposite of how things are. We tend to twist and turn the ties we have with others; Simeon tells us how to keep our relationships open and honest. We tend to signal what we want to hear. Simeon warns us to listen acutely so as to gain access to truth. That, I think, is a general lesson to be found in a saying which is, on the surface, addressed to a particular profession.

I cannot think of a more difficult lesson to learn than this: how to keep your own counsel. But if you really want to learn from others, you have to teach yourself two things: (1) to listen, and (2) to avoid imposing your own opinion in advance. People generally like to please. If they know what will please you, under normal circumstances they will say it or do it. It costs them nothing. But it costs you truth: you know less than you need to know.

Shemaiah (saying 10) gives some good advice about how to live in an unredeemed world, that is, a world lacking perfection. He says to mind your own business—not bad advice, most of the time. He tells us to love work. If you love what you do, you live the best possible life. If you love your work, your work becomes your faith, your hope, your vocation and your avocation. Then your life is rich in satisfaction, empty of disappointment. Shemaiah further says we should hate authority. That does not mean we should break the rules. Rather, we should be as self-reliant as possible and not try to curry favor with people more powerful than ourselves. This he says yet a third time when he advises people not to get too friendly with the government. In the broad sense, you are not apt to have the chance. But what about the administrators of schools or colleges, towns or businesses—the government you see every day?

Shemaiah's advice is to keep your distance and do your work. This is the advice of a seasoned sage, an experienced observer of life. He is telling us not to expect too much from others—from "the establishment," for instance—but to rely upon ourselves and our own hard work.

Avtalyon's advice is equally educated in long life: watch what you say. The rest of his saying expands upon the notion of guarding your speech. But it is not so distinctive to Avtalyon's world that it is difficult to know how it can be translated into the framework of our world. He is talking about care in expressing ourselves.

Hillel's Torah

We now come to the famous sayings of Hillel. The first thing we notice is that while nearly everyone else in our well-crafted chapter says three things, Hillel says a great many. The pattern normally followed is to have sayings set up in triplets of clauses closely related but distinct in counsel. Later, we may recognize a different sort of triplet. Instead, Hillel is given a triplet of three full sayings.

Hillel's first saying (12) tells us to become disciples of Aaron, the brother of Moses and the first high priest, and then simply tells us what it means to be a disciple of Aaron. It means to love peace and pursue grace, and it means to love people and so bring them near to learning in the Torah. Now what is jarring here—and I think most important—is that Aaron in Hillel's time stood for the high priesthood. The high priests then were not renowned for being peaceful, gracious, learned in Torah. They were better known for their punctilious mastery of the Temple sacrificial rites, their pride in their own ancestry and position, and their arrogance and contentiousness toward one another. Accordingly, there is a sharp edge to a saying that associates Aaron, ancestor of the priests, with qualities not then characteristic of the priesthood at all. For us the polemic is dulled since we have no quarrel with the Jewish priests, the *kohanim,* of our own time (of which I am one). But the notion that the principal calling of the truly noble is to love peace and love people and make our own tradition of Torah attractive to them—that notion is remarkably relevant.

We grasp Hillel's statement in context when we recall that in Hillel's day there were several kinds of Jewish authorities and they were quite different from one another. One kind was the priest. He was holy because of his ancestry since he traced his family line back to Aaron, founder of the priesthood. His job was to offer sacrifices in the Temple. That is how the Book of Leviticus describes matters.

Another kind of Jewish authority was the prophet. He or she was qualified through receiving God's word and credibly teaching it to Israel. [Scripture knows several women who were prophets.] Prophets furthermore made sense of what happened and what was going to happen, hence their title (when the Hebrew word, *navi,* is translated into Greek and then into English) "prophet," in the commonplace sense of the word. So the prophet was interested in history and what it meant.

Yet a third kind of Jewish authority in Temple times was the scribe and, in later times, the rabbi. He was qualified by his knowledge, specifically by his mastery of Torah. His interest was in the proper arrangement of the life of Israel, the Jewish people, so that everything conformed in detail to God's will in general—that is, to the prescriptions of Torah, written and oral.

These, then, represent three different kinds of authorities in Judaism, based on different fields of operation: (1) service to God in the cult, (2) interpretation of the history and destiny of Israel, (3) proper and appropriate conduct of the everyday life of the Jewish people wherever they live. So Hillel speaks of priests. But he asks them to live up to the ideals of Torah, that is, wisdom and learning—Aaron, after all, is part of the Torah—and to be peace-makers, men of wisdom. That is, his message is that priests should be more like rabbis.

Hillel's second saying (13) is a Torah saying, so it is appropriately joined to the end of the one before. The saying, phrased in Aramaic instead of in Hebrew, tells us two things, each stated twice. (I do not know why a saying was preserved in one language rather than the other. Both Hebrew and Aramaic were current.)

First, the point of learning Torah is not to make ourselves famous and important.

Second, if you are going to learn Torah, you have to keep at it, you have to study and add to what you know from one day to the next. If you do not, you lose what you have gained.

Now these two ideas are expressed in the order A, B; B, A, that is, "a name made great" matches "not using the crown (of the Torah)"; and "not adding subtracts" matches "not learning and so dying." The point then is simpler than the rather subtle way in which it is made. You have to keep at your work of learning Torah. But you must not expect a this-worldly reward for doing so, which is pretty much what Antigonus (saying 3) states in a general way.

The final saying in Hillel's group (14) is famous. Most Jews know it by heart. It sets up a remarkable tension between selfishness and selflessness. You cannot neglect your own needs. Neither can you attend only to your own needs. And the tension is not resolved but heightened at the end: you have to decide right away. It would be difficult to imagine a more profound and complete account of the condition of the moral human being, trying to keep in balance the ultimately irreconcilable demands of life, the inescapable requirement to meet those demands every day.

Standing back, we can see that to Hillel, too, are given three sayings, but they are long and fully articulated rather than the brief clauses or sentences assigned to the others. He has a saying about (1) the righteous priest and the proper attitude to people and to Torah, then (2) a saying about Torah study, and finally (3) a saying about the true meaning of the moral and good life. What he does, then, is to reiterate the themes of Simeon the Righteous, pertaining as they do to (1) Temple service, (2) Torah, and (3) deeds of lovingkindnss. The same themes are before us, in somewhat revised order. Temple comes before Torah and leads to it, but the open-ended requirements of goodness remain at the end and climax of the whole.

If we had to declare a three-part scheme for any philosophy of Judaism, we could do worse than follow the categories taken by Simeon the Righteous and Hillel alike. Simeon's conception of Temple service is broadened by Hillel to stand for the sacrifice of love offered for the benefit of other people, aimed at bringing that peace and wholeness for which one of the principal ritual sacrifices in the cult had stood. Simeon's Torah turns, for Hillel, into a temptation. It is the hope for reward for learning, this-worldly recompense in fame. But for Hillel, Torah is not a reward but a demand and a challenge: keep adding, or you die. It is a never-ending responsibility. The last item in the trilogy of both masters (deeds of lovingkindness for Simeon) becomes the most complex in Hillel's counterpart. We are responsbile for our own welfare. But we have to surrender what is ours—the equivalent of an act of grace—for others. And Hillel imparts to the whole a clear sense of urgency: it must be now, all the time. He offers urgency to the life of work and love.

Shammai of course bears the burden of the contrast to Hillel, both here and in many stories told about Hillel's patience and Shammai's impatience, Hillel's kindliness and Shammai's petulance. Yet when you get close up, as we do in Shammai's triplet (saying 15), we see a message not much different from Hillel's. In many ways Shammai's is the more relevant of the two, since it talks to ordinary people about things they really can do. Shammai tells us to make a fixed obligation of learning. That is not different from Hillel's message. But it is phrased in a simpler way. He tells us to say little and do much—good advice which surely will lead to peace among people. And his final saying—to greet people with good cheer and good will—surely would make us into disciples of Aaron. If we imme-

diately jump down to Simeon (saying 17) we see precisely the
same sage advice: keep your own counsel, emphasize the right
deeds, don't bother other people too much.

טז   רַבָּן גַּמְלִיאֵל אוֹמֵר:
עֲשֵׂה לְךָ רַב.
וְהִסְתַּלֵּק מִן הַסָּפֵק.
וְאַל תַּרְבֶּה לְעַשֵּׂר אֻמָדוֹת.

יז   שִׁמְעוֹן בְּנוֹ אוֹמֵר:
כָּל יָמַי גָּדַלְתִּי בֵּין הַחֲכָמִים, וְלֹא מָצָאתִי לַגּוּף
טוֹב אֶלָּא שְׁתִיקָה.
וְלֹא הַמִּדְרָשׁ הוּא הָעִקָּר, אֶלָּא הַמַּעֲשֶׂה.
וְכָל הַמַּרְבֶּה דְבָרִים מֵבִיא חֵטְא.

יח   רַבָּן שִׁמְעוֹן בֶּן גַּמְלִיאֵל אוֹמֵר: עַל שְׁלֹשָׁה דְבָרִים
הָעוֹלָם עוֹמֵד:
עַל הַדִּין,
וְעַל הָאֱמֶת,
וְעַל הַשָּׁלוֹם.
שֶׁנֶּאֱמַר: "אֱמֶת וּמִשְׁפַּט שָׁלוֹם שִׁפְטוּ בְּשַׁעֲרֵיכֶם".

16 Rabban Gamaliel says:
Set up a master for yourself.
Avoid doubt.
Don't tithe by too much guesswork.

17 Simeon his son says:
All my life I grew up among the sages, and I found
nothing better for a person [the body] than silence.
And not the learning is the thing, but the doing.
And whoever talks too much causes sin.

18 Rabban Simeon ben Gamaliel says: On three things does
the world stand:

on justice,
on truth,
and on peace.

As it is said, *Execute the judgment of truth and peace in*
Zech. 8:16   *your gates.*

To make sense of Gamaliel's saying, we had best know what tithing was and is. Scripture requires farmers to give portions of their crop for various sacred purposes: support of the Temple priesthood, support of the Levites, the landless and the poor, and the like. These portions were God's share of the gifts of the Holy Land, which God owns. For our part, we give back a share of what is ours, knowing that, in the end, what we get comes with God's blessing. So we give up part of what is not ours and keep the other part as our own. Today we do this when we give money to *tzedakah,* to righteous purposes of philanthropy. It is also something we do when we give a portion of our life—our time, energy, ability—to other people. So Gamaliel focuses upon a deed familiar to us.

Gamaliel is the first of the final triplet of masters, and both he and his son, Simeon, go over mostly familiar ground. Gamaliel tells us (saying 16), in general, to get a master, that is, a teacher; that will help us avoid doubt—again, a general statement. He refers, third, to a very specific sort of doubt. Gamaliel says that, when by designating tithes you set aside what is owing to God as God's rent for the Holy Land you use, you should do so accurately, not guess too much. This is a more concrete way of saying you should avoid doubt.

What Gamaliel wants is repeated in three ways: get a reliable teacher, avoid doubt, don't guess. In other words, he tells us to seek certainty. It isn't such bad advice. The problem is, how to do it in so uncertain a world as ours? His solution—get a teacher, do not guess too much, avoid doubt—is hardly of the same dimension as the problem. Simeon, his son, gives a better answer: listen, rather than talk, and the main thing is what you do.

We recall that the sayings of the two Simeons (sayings 2 and 18) match: (1) Torah, (2) Temple service, (3) deeds of lovingkindness, against the triplet of (1) justice, (2) truth, (3) peace.

The Torah in this context must mean the entire revelation of God to Israel from Sinai, that is *torah,* including sayings of the sages.

The Temple service, in accord with the Books of Leviticus and Numbers, in that age meant the worship of God through giving to God the things God's Holy Land produced. This was done through casting into the flames of the altar the produce of the land, grain, meat, and the like. That form of sharing—of giving back part of God's gifts to God—was obligatory.

There is yet another form of service, the things we do that we do not have to do; the expression "deeds of lovingkindness" refers to these gratuitous acts of grace and love.

For its part, the other Simeon's saying (2) may be set into a logical sequence. The Torah teaches rules of justice which govern relationships among people. Without rules we cannot live together. It is a simple matter of truth that God gives us whatever we have, so we owe to God the return, through the sacrifice of what we think is ours, of some of what God gives us. And the only road to peace is through giving up what we think is coming to us, that is, giving not only what we must, but also what we need not give up.

Now that we have studied the sayings group by group, go back and read them as they were intended, as a complete construction—the first chapter of Avot.

1   Moses received Torah at Sinai and handed it on to Joshua, Joshua to elders, and elders to prophets. And prophets handed it on to the men of the great assembly.
They said three things:
    Be prudent in judgment.
    Raise up many disciples.
    Make a fence for the Torah.

2   Simeon the Righteous was one of the last survivors of the great assembly. He would say:
On three things does the world stand:
    On the Torah,
    and on the Temple service,
    and on deeds of lovingkindness.

3   Antigonus of Sokho received [the Torah] from Simeon the Righteous. He would say:

Do not be like servants who serve the master on condition of receiving a reward,
but [be] like servants who serve the master not on condition of receiving a reward.
And let the fear of Heaven be upon you.

4 Yose ben Yoezer of Zeredah and Yose ben Yohanan of Jerusalem received [the Torah] from them. Yose ben Yoezer says:

Let your house be a gathering place for sages.
And wallow in the dust of their feet,
And drink in their words with gusto.

5 Yose ben Yohanan of Jerusalem says:

Let your house be open wide.
And seat the poor at your table ["make the poor members of your household"].
And don't talk too much with women.

(He referred to a man's wife, all the more so is the rule to be applied to the wife of one's fellow. In this regard did sages say: So long as a man talks too much with a woman,

he brings trouble on himself,
wastes time better spent on studying Torah,
and ends up an heir of Gehenna.)

6 Joshua ben Perahyah and Nittai the Arbelite received [the Torah] from them. Joshua ben Perahyah says:

Set up a master for yourself.
And get yourself a companion-disciple.
And give everybody the benefit of the doubt.

7 Nittai the Arbelite says:

Keep away from a bad neighbor.
And don't get involved with a bad person.
And don't give up hope of retribution.

8 Judah ben Tabbai and Simeon ben Shetah received [the Torah] from them. Judah ben Tabbai says:

Don't make yourself like one of those who advocate before judges [while you yourself are judging a case].
And when the litigants stand before you, regard them as guilty.
But when they leave you, regard them as acquitted (when they have accepted your judgment).

9 Simeon ben Shetah says:
> Examine the witnesses with great care.
> And watch what you say,
> lest they learn from what you say how to lie.

10 Shemaiah and Avtalyon received [the Torah] from them. Shemaiah says:
> Love work.
> Hate authority.
> Don't get friendly with the government.

11 Avtalyon says:
> Sages, watch what you say,
> lest you become liable to the punishment of exile, and
> go into exile to a place of bad water, and disciples
> who follow you drink bad water and die, and the
> name of Heaven be thereby profaned.

12 Hillel and Shammai received [the Torah] from them. Hillel says:
> Be disciples of Aaron,
> loving peace and pursuing grace,
> loving people and drawing them near to the Torah.

13 He would say [in Aramaic]:
> A name made great is a name destroyed,
> And one who does not add, subtracts.
> And who does not learn is liable to death.
> And the one who uses the crown, passes away.

14 He would say:
> If I am not for myself, who is for me?
> And when I am for myself, what am I?
> And if not now, when?

15 Shammai says:
> Make your learning of Torah a fixed obligation.
> Say little and do much.
> Greet everybody cheerfully.

16 Rabban Gamaliel says:
> Set up a master for yourself.
> Avoid doubt.
> Don't tithe by too much guesswork.

17   Simeon his son says:

All my life I grew up among the sages, and I foun
nothing better for a person [the body] than silence.
And not the learning is the thing, but the doing.
And whoever talks too much causes sin.

18   Rabban Simeon ben Gamaliel says: On three things doe
the world stand:

on justice,

on truth,

and on peace.

As it is said, *Execute the judgment of truth and peace ir*
Zech. 8:16   *your gates.*

The Chain of Tradition

Reading the chapter as one document, we again notice
that it begins with a stunning statement: Moses received Torah
The purpose is to introduce the chain by which Torah passes
on from one generation to the next, down to the men of the
great assembly, Simeon the Righteous, and Antigonus. We
see that each one of those authorities stands alone and has
three sayings. Then come five pairs of names, each one also
given three sayings. These run from saying 4 through sayings
12–15. At the end there are three more individual names.
Gamaliel, Gamaliel's son, and Simeon ben Gamaliel. Assuming
that Gamaliel's son Simeon and Simeon "his son" were the
same person, we see that the person who made the construction
wanted to have three groups of three sayings, and that is why
the name of one of the authorities was repeated. In all, therefore, there are three individuals, five pairs, and three individuals, each one given three sayings (nine, fifteen, and nine).
Clearly someone thought the numbers of names and of sayings
were important. Obviously, if you have a number, and you
want to memorize, it is easy to do it if the number is fixed.
The numbers that make memorizing easy are three and five:
five because you count on your fingers; three because you
establish a fixed pattern only when you reach the third item in
a series. So when we see the construction of the chapter as a
whole, we notice how carefully and thoughtfully the person
who framed it has put it together.

There is no exceptional pattern, however, in what the

arious authorities—the links in the chain of tradition—say.
You can see much repetition. I see some recurring themes, for
nstance, good advice to judges or to disciples or to house-
holders. But I do not see in the sayings any sort of pattern of
deas or themes, to match the remarkably thoughtful pattern
in which the components of the chain as a whole are worked
out. So let us now see how the sayings are put together.

Seen as a sequence of names, chapters one and two make
a startling point. *Torah at Sinai* is passed on in an unbroken
chain through Moses to Joshua and onward . . . to the very
ages cited in the Mishnah itself. Now if you know that *Torah
at Sinai* to others of that age—to the Christians, for example—
meant only the written Torah, the Five Books of Moses, and
the other prophetic books and the writings we know as *Tanakh,*
what we call the Hebrew Scriptures and Christians know as
"the Old Testament," you see everything clearly. Torah comes
to Israel not only in the Scriptures. What our sages teach in
the Mishnah is Torah, too. Sages in the Mishnah stand in a
direct line to Sinai. The Mishnah, containing their teachings,
also forms part of Torah revealed by God to Moses at Sinai.
What sages say was handed on in a chain of transmission and
tradition from Moses through the prophets and down to the
named authorities who predominate in the Mishnah itself. So,
as I stated earlier, tractate Avot serves to explain the Mishnah
and to certify its authority by giving us its genealogy: how we
received the Mishnah, how the sages received the Torah.

Patriarchs and Sages

Neither is that the only thing we learn from this
sequence of names. There is yet a second point. The Mishnah
rests upon the authority of Judah the Patriarch who headed
the Jewish nation of the Land of Israel and enjoyed Roman
recognition of his standing and authority over Israel in its
Land. Judah claimed descent from Simeon ben Gamaliel,
Gamaliel, and Hillel, which is why he named his sons
Gamaliel and Hillel, respectively. So the chain of tradition
was seen to extend from Sinai through Hillel to the house
of the patriarch, the government of Israel in the Land of
Israel. Indeed, Hillel was alleged to come from the line of
David—hence, the household of the Messiah. At the same
time, the Mishnah contains sayings of named sages, and so

A Continuous Chain

The opening chapter of Avot forms a single extended composition, beginning to end. It furthermore is continued into the second chapter. What is most important to the framers of these chapters is the sequence of names. It presents itself in an inverted Y: λ

Avot 1:1

Torah at Sinai
Moses
Joshua
Elders
Prophets

1–3

Men of the great assembly
Simeon the Righteous
Antigonus of Sokho

4–15

Yose ben Yoezer & Yose ben Yohanan
Joshua ben Perahyah & Nittai the Arbelite
Judah ben Tabbai & Simeon ben Shetah
Shemaiah & Avtalyon
Hillel & Shammai

16–18

Gamaliel
Simeon, his son
Simeon ben Gamaliel

2:1–7 Rabbi [Judah the Patriarch]
Gamaliel, son of Judah the Patriarch
Hillel [son of Judah the Patriarch]

2:8–14 Yohanan ben Zakkai
Eliezer ben Hyrcanus
Joshua ben Hananiah
Yose the Priest
Simeon ben Nethanel
Eleazar ben Arakh

t rests upon the learning of the great sages. They, too, claim a genealogy, extending through the relationship of sage to disciple, a spiritual family in the world of the Torah. The other ide of the way leads to Sinai through the disciples of Yohanan ben Zakkai, backward from him to Simeon ben Gamaliel, and onward also through Hillel, to Sinai.

Starting from the bottom of the list on page 46, that is, the two prongs of the inverted Y, let's review the point.

First, there is a direct line from Judah the Patriarch and his sons, Gamaliel and Hillel, back to the figure of Simeon ben Gamaliel, Gamaliel, and Hillel of ancient times—two hundred and fifty years earlier. Accordingly, the authority who promulgated the Mishnah, Judah the Patriarch (and his succesors) stands in a direct line to Hillel—and back to Moses at Sinai.

Second, there also is a direct line extending from the five disciples of Yohanan ben Zakkai—two of them, Eliezer and Joshua, among the principal sages of the generation after the destruction of the Temple in 70 c.e.—back to Simeon ben Gamaliel, Gamaliel, Hillel (and Shammai). Since among the most commonly cited authorities in several of the divisions of the Mishnah are Hillel and Shammai's houses, or schools, the most important point is this: the sages of the Mishnah, known on every page, stand in that same chain of tradition as do the authorities behind the Mishnah, Judah the Patriarch and his administration.

The authority of the Mishnah derives from two paths both emanating from one source. The patriarchs' and the sages' document, the Mishnah, comes from Sinai. The chain of tradition is direct, specific, and in context genealogical. Just as priests validate their standing through their family records, so patriarchs and sages validate their standing—their Torah tradition—through the record of who received, and who handed on, that Torah tradition. That is the stunning declaration of the opening two chapters of Avot.

Linking the Generations

A striking and recurrent pattern in the language of the first chapter as a whole also commands our attention. We notice the use of the language, "receive," "hand on," and "say." Moses "received"; the several pairs "received." So the principal thing the sages of this chapter do is "receive Torah" on the one side, and "say" three things on the other. We are not told whether the things the sages say form part of the Torah they received or whether these things constitute their contribution *to* the Torah. That point is not clear. Accordingly, we also do not know the status, the standing, of the three sayings assigned to each authority.

But we do know the purpose of the chapter as a whole. It is to tell us how the Torah came from Sinai to the sages of Avot themselves. As I pointed out in the beginning, the figures mentioned, from Hillel onward, are well known. They are the masters and teachers of the authorities of Avot who will appear in the coming chapters. The one who formed the list is saying that what we learn from Hillel and Shammai, Gamaliel and Simeon ben Gamaliel, is part of the Torah received by Moses at Sinai. The chain links Jews of the time of Avot to the giving of the Torah at Sinai, the beginnings of the Jewish people.

The word *Avot* itself has several meanings. One is "fathers." But a more important meaning—which can apply to both male and female sexes—is "founders." The sayings before us are the heritage of the founders and teachers of the Mishnah. The Mishnah therefore is placed squarely and firmly into relationship with the Torah of Moses at Sinai. What the masters of the Mishnah say—so goes the message of our chapter—is part of Torah. So the Mishnah itself (not only tractate Avot, not only the sayings at hand) is linked to the Torah. The Mishnah is claimed to be part of the Torah. How is this so? It is because of the process, beginning with Moses at Sinai, of receiving and handing on: receiving Torah, handing on Torah.

But what is it that the named sages receive and hand on? Whatever they received (let us assume it is the Torah), Avot represents them actually handing on sayings *not* in the written Torah, three sayings each. Accordingly, the status and standing of these sayings are explained at the outset. What a sage receives and hands on is Torah. His teacher gave him Torah (including three of the teacher's sayings). Then what he received—the Torah, including all the additions of the ones who came before him—and what he hands on are not quite the same. Why not? Because he adds his three sayings too. Accordingly, what he adds, as a sage in the Mishnah, is joined

o the Torah, and each link extends the chain and becomes
part of the chain as a whole. The message is powerful: what
sages in the time of the Mishnah stated forms part of the
Torah beginning at Sinai and extending onward through all
time.

Discovering Torah

Consider how many meanings we attribute to the word
torah. First, we notice, we sometimes find it comfortable
to say torah in a generic sense, namely, God's revelation of
God's will. Then we speak of the Torah, meaning God's
revelation as it reaches us in a particular book, the Torah,
"the Five Books of Moses"; or, still more, the entire
Hebrew Scriptures we call Tanakh (from the initial letters
of its three sections, Torah, Nevi'im = Prophets, and
Ketuvim = Writings). Again, we may speak of the "one
whole Torah of Moses, our rabbi," encompassing the
written Torah and also the oral Torah represented by the
Mishnah, the two Talmuds (Babylonian and Palestinian)
that explain the meaning of the Mishnah, and the great
collections of midrashim, explanations of the meaning of
the Scripture.

But torah bears a deeper meaning still, the meaning of
discovering what God teaches, or how God has made the
world—torah as a process of discovering the truth that
God implanted in the world. There can, really, be a torah
to how you live life, in addition to a written or oral Torah
coming from Sinai about how you should live life. This
other torah—not the one from Sinai, but the one we
discover—is the living by the right norms and in the right
way that sages discover and embody in their own lives.
When we reach the notion of a living Torah—a sage, a
rabbi, a great Jewish woman who in her gesture and
speech, as much as in her message, embodies everything
we believe God wants us to be—we reach the here and the
now.

The framers of Avot want us to conclude that Torah is not a closed book. Torah forms an unending chain of revelation. All of the great sages of Israel, to our own time, form links in that chain. God did not conclude with the written Torah all of the teaching—the revelation—God proposed to give to Israel through Moses, the elders, the prophets, the great assembly, the pairs, the masters. The revelation—Torah—goes forward. So there is always new teaching, to find its rightful place within Torah. That means God speaks now, not just then. God speaks to us, not only to those who lived long ago. So Torah—that is, Judaism—is unending and ongoing, not a dead legacy from a distant past, but an enduring process of learning and discovery in the living present.

Vocation and Vision

Now let us again ask ourselves, to what world do the sayings speak? What do the sages take as their center of interest? If we list the principal topics at hand, we find these:

1. Teachings to sages and their disciples, to judges;
2. Large and encompassing visions of the important things in the world;
3. Advice on how to serve God;
4. Counsel on how to live the good life.

The chapter tells teachers, who are judges, and their disciples how to conduct their affairs. It also contains a fair amount of wisdom for other people. Only at the beginning and the end is there attention to matters we should call "religious" in a narrow sense. That is to say, we find only at those points a theory of what it means to be a human being created in the image of God, of how to see the world as the creation of God, and of how to love and serve God. Obviously, the people who composed this chapter did not make any distinction between the religious and the secular. Their assumption was that they spoke to a single, whole group. But to what group? Was it to all Jews of their day? Self-evidently not, because of their very particular vocational concern. Then was it only to people we might call judges who taught young lawyers? Certainly not, because of their broad vision of the life of the people to whom they spoke.

What we see, therefore, is a small group of people—we

ight call them a profession—trying to frame a vision that
ould encompass the entire world. The sages whose teach-
gs are before us know who they are and what they are,
at is, a small group of teachers of Torah. But they are
ying very hard to rise above the limits of their group and
s labor. They want to speak to all Israel. They aim at
ving a message relevant to the life of everybody. That is
hy so much of the chapter in hand—the concerns above
umbered 2, 3, and 4—goes beyond the narrow limits of
hat judges and law students in our day would be expected
) discuss.

Before us therefore are sages trying to become more
an themselves, thinking the long thoughts of greatness.
hey aim to speak to everyone in their time and place. They
ropose to teach important lessons they have learned in
eir small corner of the world.

In many ways the sages do represent the Jewish people
nd its tenuous life. On the one side, the Jews are a very
nall and weak people, some living scattered among many
ther peoples, and some in a besieged land they cherish.
ccordingly, it is easy for the Jews to center on their own
terests and to ignore the world at large. They may well be
empted to turn inward and become selfish—to see life as
omething private, a struggle to keep the world at bay. On
he other side, the Jews also are human beings. True, they
re a special kind of human being. But in their very sense of
eing special, they turn out to be common. For every person
special and unique, each group sees itself as uncommon—
nd everyone is right, by definition.

But we all have heads and arms and legs; we all are
orn and die; we all suffer, dream, work, love, endure. So
veryone is in the Jewish circumstance of wondering why
ve are special, and how we are special.

In their very distinctive way, the sages who composed
his remarkable chapter capture that mixture of voices: the
pecial, the general. They speak about their own world and
ddress lessons to their own students. So the framework is
rivate and small. Yet the lessons take up issues confronting
he entire Jewish nation. They prove relevant not only in
he few hundred years represented by these names, but in
he succeeding centuries, down to today. That is quite an

achievement. It means that the sages, in being distinctiv
and modest, discover in themselves details of the whol
They turn out to find in what is private something ver
public, accessible, and human. That is the first and mo
important lesson of the chapter as a whole: its content whe
we see it in its entirety. Let us now review the details, th
lessons as they unfold, and ask a fresh question.

Do the sayings speak to our world? My view already
before you. I hope that you concur. Yes, the sayings of th
founders do speak to us. That is the shared convictio
between you and me. But what can they say to us, after tw
thousand years? Do the sayings all speak equally and in th
same voice?

Some of the sayings speak more directly and imme
diately, and some have to be translated not only into ou
language but also into our condition and circumstanc
Some are worldly; some sublime. Some give mere goo
advice. Others tell us truths so deep that we can spend ou
lives exploring the things they mean in the here and now. I
would take a very long book—which I do not want to writ
and you would not want to read—to try to draw out everythin
relevant to our own day in these sayings. And even if w
should succeed, the day would turn, change so fast, tha
tomorrow I should have to write another book, and you rea
it. To come up with the new points of contact between toda
and the eternal wisdom of the founders, we forever should b
pointing out what is relevant. There has to be a better approac
than to try to say it all and inevitably to fail, by definition.

So the purpose of taking up the sayings is not to exhaus
their message, or even to say all the things we think they mea
to us. Rather, it is to give an example of *how* to take up thes
sayings and to reflect on their use and value any time w
confront them, questions that can be asked any day. Th
Torah from our sages will always be there for you to learn—i
you choose to teach them to yourself, to discover in them th
lessons you require. You enter a partnership, never to b
dissolved, between the lessons of the founders—and all th
other great collections of Israel's wisdom—and yourself a
sometimes-student, sometimes-teacher, and always-seeker o
wisdom. As the sages themselves say, turn it over and over
for everything is there.

Let us now summarize and conclude. Because chapter ne really is a unified composition on a number of themes, he themes appear and reappear as discourse unfolds. The hemes are (1) learning, that is, Torah; (2) relating to thers—in context, making judgments—that is, the way we hould conduct ourselves with our friends and neighbors; nd (3) right attitude, the way we should think about our-elves, our fellow human beings, and God. These, we know, re the themes announced by Simeon the Righteous, resolved •y Simeon ben Gamaliel, and brought to their climax in he extraordinary and (in context) elaborate sayings given o Hillel.

So the sages and disciples who stand behind this emarkable document rise above their narrow setting and imited interests. They do this by seeing the world at large vithin the small details of their own life. They do this by inderstanding that, in the life of their profession and calling, ill of life was lived through Torah, duty, grace—these are he three themes that play themselves out in the varied ways xplored by the individual sayings.

If we were to generalize and speak of Torah as repre-enting right knowledge and attitude, duty as right deed, grace as going beyond the limits of the law, we should not rr. But being Jews, we do not have to generalize so far, ince today just as two thousand years ago, we understand hese same things in much the same way: study of Torah, oractice of the religious deeds taught through that study, and above all, doing more than the law specifies. The Torah comes to us through these sages, and it teaches us these three things. That is the foundation of Avot. Everything else stands upon that foundation.

CHAPTER TWO
WHAT TORAH TEACHES US
From Sinai to Patriarch and Sage

IT IS NOT YOUR JOB TO FINISH THE WORK, BUT YOU ARE NOT FREE TO WALK AWAY FROM IT.

CHAPTER TWO
WHAT TORAH TEACHES US
From Sinai to
Patriarch and Sage

Chapter two is in two parts. Each presents a continuation of the chain of tradition begun at Sinai. The first continuation gives the names of the genealogical heirs of Hillel, Gamaliel, Simeon ben Gamaliel, Judah the Patriarch and his sons, Hillel and Gamaliel. Judah the Patriarch, ruler of Israel in its Land, thus assumes his place in the line of tradition begun with God's revelation to Moses at Sinai.

The second continuation moves from Hillel, Gamaliel, and Simeon, to a different sort of authority over Israel, namely, the great sages, teachers of the Torah. The central name on this continuum is Yohanan ben Zakkai, who flourished at the time of the destruction of the Temple in 70 C.E. He formed a circle of disciples who emerged after the destruction of the Temple to be the great teachers and authorities of Israel, the Jewish nation.

Before we take up the substance of the chapter, let us turn aside for a moment and ask about the patriarch and his office. For it is clear that the document at hand, this tractate of the Mishnah, emerges under the sponsorship of an important Jewish authority. Having asked *to whom* sayings speak, we also have to ask *for whom*—at least in part. The answer is simple. The Patriarch was the Roman-appointed and recognized ruler of the Jewish nation in the Land of Israel. The Romans controlled the Land of Israel and decided who should take charge of the government and administration of the life of various groups. Their policy was to make the important decisions themselves. But they left in local hands decisions on

matters bearing no consequence to the Roman empire. Ther
were diverse communities, different religious and ethnic groups
Other groups had their own names for what Jews knew, an
still today know, as the Land of Israel. In this speckled map o
peoples, the Jewish spots fell within the rule of the Jewis
authority, called in Hebrew *nasi,* and in Greek (and henc
English) *patriarch.* The family that held the office on a heredi
tary basis (one of whom was Judah, the patriarch who issue
the Mishnah and was called "our rabbi," "our holy rabbi," or
simply, "Rabbi,") claimed descent from Hillel. They furthe
maintained that Hillel was descended from King David. Tha
explains who the patriarch was, what he did, and why th
chain of tradition served a critical purpose in the politics o
the Jewish nation in its land.

The patriarchate—that is, the Jewish government of th
Jewish nation in the Land of Israel (as distinct from the Roma
government of Palestine)—employed scribes, men learned i
the laws and traditions of the Jewish nation. They bore a titl
that signified respect, "my lord," or "rabbi." That title serve
not their group alone, but various groups as ways of honorin
their learned men. *Rabban,* a variation of the title, is wha
Christians who spoke Aramaic called some of their grea
teachers. Jesus was called "rabbi" and he in no way matche
the description of rabbis known to us in the Mishnah and th
Talmud. So we are dealing with an honorific title, not a classi
fication of social role or office or profession. But in Judaism
the title of honor came to be identified with a particular kin
of man. A person who was called "rabbi" also enjoye
appointment to the administration or bureaucracy of the patri
archal government; the Talmud of the Land of Israel make
that fact clear. Accordingly, in that context, at least, it was
title of honor which also signified possession of a given offic
and authority. When we refer to a physician as "doctor," w
take a title meaning "teacher," signifying people possessin
certain educational credentials, and apply that title to on
form of authority or teacher only. Such, too, was the cas
here.

The rabbis of the Mishnah were men who had learne
Torah through discipleship, and who then taught Torah t
their own disciples, hence—and this is the heart of th
matter—a rabbi was a link in the chain of tradition extendin

ack to Sinai. At the same time, as we now understand, a abbi also held public office in the Jewish nation's government. Accordingly, he stood in an ambiguous position. On the one ide, he was a disciple and a master, not a bureaucrat. On the ther side, he could tell people what to do because of his osition and standing in the Jewish administration. Significantly, the chapter at hand resolves that tension. True, the abbi claims an independent stand in relationship to Sinai. rue as well, the rabbi serves as subordinate to a separate and n some ways different kind of Jewish authority, the patriarch. hat is why the inverted Y (see chart, page 46) takes the two irections it does. Both patriarch and sage claim a single escent, from Sinai. There is no ambiguity about that. The ensions in theory prove to be resolved in practice in our emarkable tractate.

Does that mean Avot is a rabbinical tractate or a patriarhal tractate? Has one party the upper hand? My view is that he power of the tractate lies in its joining the two sorts of eader into a single, common doctrine. Both the patriarch and he sage stand for the same thing. Two kinds of leaders, each vith its specific task, join together in a single cause. That is vhy we have to read closely to uncover the partisan roots f a composition that rises above parties and factions. True, ve see clearly that there are different kinds of authorities epresented here. But the message is one and the same. I annot distinguish, for one thing, the truths enunciated by ages such as Yohanan ben Zakkai and Akiba from truths ronounced by Hillel's descendants, the patriarchal figures uch as Gamaliel, Judah the Patriarch, or Judah's sons. Peraps the framers of Avot wanted us to see that underneath the iffering institutional forms of Jewish leadership of the day— ages with their schools, patriarchs with their courts and dministration—lay a single message coming from both sides. ʾor the message of Avot is one and seamless.

Accordingly, both the patriarchal and the rabbinical continuators of the great masters of the period before the destruction of the Temple in 70 C.E. are represented in this chapter. Γo each group are assigned sayings of the two sorts paramount ιp to now—about study of Torah, including application of Γorah teachings to everyday life; and about the good life and ιow it is to be lived. So the tradition goes forward beyond the

catastrophe represented by the destruction of the Temple
Whether Israel is ruled by the patriarch, as was the case from
the second century to the beginning of the fifth, or by the
great sages, as was the case throughout the latter history of
the Jewish nation, does not matter. For the content of the life
of Israel, the Jewish nation, remains the same: service to God
through Torah; and living a good and moral life. That is the
message of this chapter.

א רַבִּי אוֹמֵר: אֵיזוֹהִי דֶרֶךְ יְשָׁרָה שֶׁיָּבֹר לוֹ הָאָדָם? כָּל
שֶׁהִיא תִפְאֶרֶת לְעוֹשָׂהּ, וְתִפְאֶרֶת לוֹ מִן הָאָדָם.
וֶהֱוֵי זָהִיר בְּמִצְוָה קַלָּה כְּבַחֲמוּרָה, שֶׁאֵין אַתָּה
יוֹדֵעַ מַתַּן שְׂכָרָן שֶׁלַּמִּצְוֹת.
וֶהֱוֵי מְחַשֵּׁב הֶפְסֵד מִצְוָה כְּנֶגֶד שְׂכָרָהּ, וּשְׂכַר עֲבֵרָה
כְּנֶגֶד הֶפְסֵדָהּ.
וְהִסְתַּכֵּל בִּשְׁלֹשָׁה דְבָרִים, וְאִי אַתָּה בָא לִידֵי
עֲבֵרָה. דַּע מַה לְמַעְלָה מִמָּךְ:
עַיִן רוֹאָה,
וְאֹזֶן שׁוֹמַעַת,
וְכָל מַעֲשֶׂיךָ בַּסֵּפֶר נִכְתָּבִין.

1 Rabbi says: What is the straight path which a person should
choose for himself? Whatever is an ornament to the one
who follows it, and an ornament in the view of others.
Be meticulous in a small religious duty as in a large one, for
you do not know what sort of reward is coming for any of
the various religious duties.
And reckon with the loss [required] in carrying out a religious duty against the reward for doing it; and the reward
for committing a transgression against the loss for doing it.
And keep your eye on three things, so you will not come
into the clutches of transgression. Know what is above you:
An eye which sees,
and an ear which hears,
and all your actions are written down in a book.

When we see the title "Rabbi" all by itself, the reference is **Rabbi**
to Judah the Patriarch, the authority behind the Mishnah. As
I said earlier, he flourished toward the end of the second
century. My guess is 170–220 C.E. Since Gamaliel and his son,
Simeon (chapter one, sayings 16–18), lived before the destruction of the Temple, we realize that the person who put Rabbi's
saying after the sayings of Gamaliel and Simeon wanted to
make a point. In fact, it was so important a point that the
framer was willing to skip over authorities—great sages—who
lived from the time of Gamaliel and Simeon, before 70, over
the next century, to about 170.

The point is that Rabbi stands in a direct line to Moses at
Sinai. What does this mean? The Mishnah that Rabbi had
published thus also stood on a straight line with the Torah of
Moses at Sinai. Then it was part of that Torah, revealed by
God to Moses.

So by placing Rabbi at the outset of this unit of materials,
the framer did precisely what was done in the first verse of
chapter one. That is to say, the entire account of the Torah
was begun by declaring the chain that linked Moses to the last
of the great sages before the destruction of the Temple. Then,
having done that work, the framer did it all over again, this
time by announcing the chain that linked the last of the great
sages before the destruction of the Temple, Hillel's family, to
the great authority of the Mishnah, Rabbi himself. In fact, as
we shall see in just a moment, the arranger of it all took yet
another step forward by inserting the names of Rabbi's sons,
Gamaliel and Hillel, and their sayings. So the link runs from
Sinai through sages and prophets and men of the great
assembly to the authorities before 70, and then, in a great
leap, to the masters and sponsors of the Mishnah itself, Rabbi
and his heirs and successors to ca. 250 C.E.

When we look at what Rabbi actually says, as distinct
from the place in which his saying is located within the document, we do not see anything meant to provoke argument. On
the contrary, Rabbi's point of emphasis is the same as the
emphasis of Simeon the Righteous, on the one side, and Hillel,
on the other. Rabbi stresses pleasing other people. He thinks
the straight path is to do what is an ornament to you, what

makes you look honorable and wins respect for you, and is something other people will approve. That is his first point. It is an ironic, conciliatory philosophy of life—and politics!

His second point, as is clear, is that everything counts. We have to remember that there is divine reward and punishment to be taken into account.

The third point carries forward the second. If we remember where we are, we shall not make mistakes. We are here on earth, with a God who cares what we say and do and who keeps track of it all. This is phrased in vivid images: an eye, an ear, a pen recording what the eye sees and the ear hears. The point, it is clear, is that there is a reward for doing one's religious duty and a penalty for not doing it or for committing a transgression.

Now when we think of living life within such a vision of our place, it is easy enough to conclude life is threatening and unfriendly. After all, who wants to live in such a way as to imagine someone on high watching and listening all the time? And who wants to be subject to constant surveillance? In our century, it is not a happy vision. Yet in his own context, Rabbi has something else in mind. It is that because God loves and cares for us, God watches over us and takes an interest in what we say and do. God is not indifferent and uncaring. The mark of God's caring is the constant attention. True, concern may spill over into meddling; and love may be used to justify surveillance. But the main point should not be missed. We want our deeds to speak well of what we are. That is why we care what others think.

It is only a short step to Heaven when we affirm the further point in Rabbi's triplet. Just as we want to do what is an ornament to ourselves and in the sight of others, so we want the good that we do to be noticed, appreciated, understood, in the eyes of Heaven and in the ears of Heaven. The three sayings then form a single statement, ascending from this world to the world above, speaking—as we expect—in very human terms about what is beyond humanity. What Rabbi attempts to do is to bring down to earth and to phrase in ordinary language a conception of how God loves us, here and now, in small and particular ways.

ב רַבָּן גַּמְלִיאֵל בְּנוֹ שֶׁלְרַבִּי יְהוּדָה הַנָּשִׂיא אוֹמֵר: יָפֶה
תַלְמוּד תּוֹרָה עִם דֶּרֶךְ אֶרֶץ, שֶׁיְּגִיעַת שְׁנֵיהֶם מְשַׁכַּחַת
עָוֹן. וְכָל תּוֹרָה שֶׁאֵין עִמָּהּ מְלָאכָה, סוֹפָהּ בְּטֵלָה
וְגוֹרֶרֶת עָוֹן.
וְכָל הָעֲמֵלִים עִם הַצִּבּוּר — יִהְיוּ עֲמֵלִים עִמָּהֶם לְשֵׁם
שָׁמַיִם, שֶׁזְּכוּת אֲבוֹתָם מְסַיְּעָתַן וְצִדְקָתָם עוֹמֶדֶת לָעַד.
וְאַתֶּם, מַעֲלֶה אֲנִי עֲלֵיכֶם שָׂכָר הַרְבֵּה כְּאִלּוּ עֲשִׂיתֶם

ג הֱווּ זְהִירִין בָּרְשׁוּת, שֶׁאֵין מְקָרְבִין לוֹ לָאָדָם אֶלָּא
לְצֹרֶךְ עַצְמָן. נִרְאִין כְּאוֹהֲבִין בִּשְׁעַת הֲנָאָתָן, וְאֵין
עוֹמְדִין לוֹ לָאָדָם בִּשְׁעַת דָּחְקוֹ.

ד הוּא הָיָה אוֹמֵר: עֲשֵׂה רְצוֹנוֹ כִּרְצוֹנֶךָ, כְּדֵי שֶׁיַּעֲשֶׂה
רְצוֹנְךָ כִּרְצוֹנוֹ. בַּטֵּל רְצוֹנְךָ מִפְּנֵי רְצוֹנוֹ, כְּדֵי שֶׁיְּבַטֵּל
רְצוֹן אֲחֵרִים מִפְּנֵי רְצוֹנֶךָ.
הִלֵּל אוֹמֵר:
אַל תִּפְרֹשׁ מִן הַצִּבּוּר.
וְאַל תַּאֲמֵן בְּעַצְמָךְ עַד יוֹם מוֹתָךְ.
וְאַל תָּדִין אֶת חֲבֵרָךְ עַד שֶׁתַּגִּיעַ לִמְקוֹמוֹ.
וְאַל תֹּאמַר דָּבָר שֶׁאִי אֶפְשָׁר לִשְׁמוֹעַ, שֶׁסּוֹפוֹ
לְהִשָּׁמַע.
וְאַל תֹּאמַר: לִכְשֶׁאֶפָּנֶה אֶשְׁנֶה, שֶׁמָּא לֹא תִּפָּנֶה.

ה הוּא הָיָה אוֹמֵר:
אֵין בּוּר יְרֵא חֵטְא,
וְלֹא עַם הָאָרֶץ חָסִיד,
וְלֹא הַבַּיְשָׁן לָמֵד,
וְלֹא הַקַּפְּדָן מְלַמֵּד,
וְלֹא כָל הַמַּרְבֶּה בִסְחוֹרָה מַחְכִּים.
וּבְמָקוֹם שֶׁאֵין אֲנָשִׁים הִשְׁתַּדֵּל לִהְיוֹת אִישׁ.

אַף הוּא רָאָה גֻלְגֹּלֶת אַחַת שֶׁצָּפָה עַל פְּנֵי הַמַּיִם.
אָמַר לָהּ:
עַל דַּאֲטֵפְתְּ אֲטִיפוּךְ,
וְסוֹף מְטִיפַיִךְ יְטוּפוּן.

הוּא הָיָה אוֹמֵר:
מַרְבֶּה בָשָׂר, מַרְבֶּה רִמָּה;
מַרְבֶּה נְכָסִים, מַרְבֶּה דְאָגָה;
מַרְבֶּה נָשִׁים, מַרְבֶּה כְשָׁפִים;
מַרְבֶּה שְׁפָחוֹת, מַרְבֶּה זִמָּה;
מַרְבֶּה עֲבָדִים, מַרְבֶּה גָזֵל.

מַרְבֶּה תוֹרָה, מַרְבֶּה חַיִּים;
מַרְבֶּה יְשִׁיבָה, מַרְבֶּה חָכְמָה;
מַרְבֶּה עֵצָה, מַרְבֶּה תְבוּנָה;
מַרְבֶּה צְדָקָה, מַרְבֶּה שָׁלוֹם.
קָנָה שֵׁם טוֹב, קָנָה לְעַצְמוֹ.
קָנָה לוֹ דִבְרֵי תוֹרָה, קָנָה לוֹ חַיֵּי הָעוֹלָם הַבָּא.

2 Rabban Gamaliel, a son of Rabbi Judah the Patriarch says
Fitting is learning in Torah along with a craft, for the labor
put into the two of them makes one forget sin. And all
learning of Torah which is not joined with labor is destined
to be null and causes sin.
And all who work with the community—let them work with
them [the community] for the sake of Heaven. For the merit
of the fathers strengthens them, and the righteousness which
they do stands forever. And, as for you, I credit you with a
great reward, as if you had done [all the work required by
the community].

3 Be wary of the government, for they get friendly with a
person only for their own convenience. They look like
friends when it is to their benefit, but they do not stand by a
person when he is in need.

He would say: Make His wishes into your own wishes, so that He will make your wishes into His wishes. Put aside your wishes on account of His wishes, so that He will put aside the wishes of other people in favor of your wishes. Hillel says:

>Do not walk out on the community.
>
>And do not have confidence in yourself until the day you die.
>
>And do not judge your companion until you are in his place.
>
>And do not say anything which cannot be heard, for in the end it will be heard.
>
>And do not say: When I have time, I shall study, for you may never have time.

He would say:

>A coarse person will never fear sin,
>nor will an *am ha-Aretz* ever be pious,
>nor will a shy person learn,
>nor will an ignorant person teach,
>nor will anyone too occupied in business get wise.

In a place where there are no individuals, try to be an individual.

Also, he saw a skull floating on the water and said to it [in Aramaic]:

>Because you drowned others, they drowned you,
>and in the end those who drowned you will be drowned.

He would say:

>Lots of meat, lots of worms;
>lots of property, lots of worries;
>lots of women, lots of witchcraft;
>lots of slave girls, lots of lust;
>lots of slave boys, lots of robbery.
>
>Lots of Torah, lots of life;
>lots of discipleship, lots of wisdom;
>lots of counsel, lots of understanding;
>lots of righteousness, lots of peace.

[If] one has gotten a good name, he has gotten it for himself. [If] he has gotten teachings of Torah, he has gotten himself life eternal.

The two sons of Judah the Patriarch, named for their ancestors Gamaliel and Hillel, complete one great chain of tradition beginning at Sinai. Gamaliel's sayings turn on rather practical matters. He knows that sages devote their lives to study of the Torah, that is, the written Torah revealed at Sinai and the oral Torah represented by the Mishnah his own father had issued. He offers remarkably relevant advice, therefore when he tells people that learning in Torah is fine, but you have to make a living too. A person who only learns—who only studies Torah—but does not earn a living, does not fully carry out the good life. The obverse need not be stated. Obviously, all sages of the Mishnah know, one who earns a living but does not study Torah does not live the good life either.

Living in the public eye and engaged in governing the Jewish nation in the Land of Israel, Gamaliel also offers solid advice on how to deal with power. If you exercise power, you learn one thing from him. If you do not exercise power, you learn another. The two go together. If you are in power and work for the community, do it in order to serve Heaven. If you do it for the right motive, you turn out to enjoy the reward, even if the work is not wholly done. If you are not in power, then watch out for people in power. They have their motives and their needs, and what they do may serve their responsibilities, not your needs. Power itself is neutral in Torah—it can be holy and it can be evil.

Gamaliel's fourth statement regarding our wishes and God's wishes is separate from the others. God responds to our own attitudes and feelings. So God shares the emotional life of human beings. This reminds us of how Rabbi, Gamaliel's father, tried to express the same notion that God cares for and loves us. What Gamaliel says is profound. Try to *want* the things God wants. Try not to want the things God does not want. It is one thing to do what God says to do. It is another to turn mere obedience into something more. Doing the right thing is good, but doing the right thing for the right reason is still better. And the only way you can do the right thing for the right reason is to reshape your own heart, your wishes and your motives, into the model of Heaven: to make God's wishes into your own wishes. Then you may hope that God will respond to you by entering into your heart and understanding your wishes too.

I do not imagine that Gamaliel thinks we can *make* God want what we want by a mere exchange of good will. His idea seems to me far deeper. For if we make God's wishes into our wishes, then quite naturally the two will become one and the same, that is, our wishes will become God's wishes. In fact, Gamaliel says the same thing twice. If you do the one, then the other follows. If you make God's wishes into your wishes, God will certainly and assuredly make your wishes into God's wishes—because they *already* are God's wishes. It would be easy to reduce all this into a mere exchange of gifts: I give, so now You give. But it seems to me clear that Gamaliel's saying is directed to the human heart and soul.

Hillel, Judah's other son, has a substantial number of sayings, but they fall into clear and easily grasped patterns. There is a set of five sayings, grouped for easy memorization but essentially distinct from one another. Then there is a set of contrasts which establish a sequence of self-evident paradoxes. The first group presents five absolutely fundamental truths. Hillel insists on these virtues.

First, we cannot walk out on the community. We are social creatures. We truly live by living with other people.

Second, he says, we have to avoid arrogance or pride, taking full confidence in ourselves only at the moment of death. That means that, living with others, we have to preserve a measure of humility.

The third saying makes concrete what it means not to be over-confident. When you judge others, try to imagine yourself in their place. That is surely a good cure for overconfidence. Seeing another person's circumstance, we also judge matters sensitively.

The fourth piece of advice for a healthy life in society is not to assume anything you say will be confidential. The best advice is to assume that every time you open your mouth everyone in the world is going to hear you.

Finally, this second Hillel advises, establish a regular time for studying.

The next sets of sayings contrast one quality with some other. We see how the passage works in any of the sayings, but the third, that a shy person will not learn, shows the picture best. The third-century Hillel wants to say that you must participate in your own education. You learn actively, by engagement, by trial and error, by doing. You do not learn when you hang back and wait for something to happen to you. The other side of the same saying comes next. Just as a shy person cannot learn, so an intolerant person cannot teach. Such a person drives away the student, instead of drawing the student out. The impatient teacher makes a person shy. The shy student makes the teacher impatient. If you move backward, you see the same equations. A person who fears sin cannot be a coarse person and a coarse person does not know the meaning of the word sin.

Hillel's statement at saying 6, preserved in Aramaic, about the skull floating in the water, presents another kind of reasoning, namely, one in which just measure is emphasized in a very homely and specific way. The principle that God metes out justice, that God responds to what people feel and do, is reiterated in this saying.

The final group of sayings simply joins together things that relate to one another, just as the first group contrasts things that are the opposite of one another. (That is to say, just as the intolerant teacher makes the student shy, and the shy student makes the teacher impatient, so one quality calls into being its very opposite.) In the final group, one thing leads to the next: possessions, worries; Torah, life; discipleship, wisdom; counsel, understanding; and so on. We could construct further sayings on the same model. Obviously, we need not accept each of the items the later Hillel's saying takes in, and we again scurry away from the things he says about women and slaves. They reflect his class and his age. But the mode of thought endures as a model of how to organize observations into meaningful patterns.

The final element comes at the end of saying 7, the contrast of a mere good name with the acquisition of Torah. If people think well of you, that is fine but it is essentially a private gain. If you master Torah, by contrast, you take part in that chain of learning which provides gain to all.

So, in sum, the third-century Hillel's large collection of sayings falls into fairly clear groups of three components: first, a set of five pieces of very good advice; second, a sequence of opposites; third, a set of items that relate to one another and stand as cause and effect for one another. What Hillel II says, as distinct from the *way* he says it, presents us with no surprises. The values at hand, the things he wants us to feel, do, and believe—these carry forward the themes of the opening chapter.

The Hope for Justice

Hillel's conviction that God corrects the imbalances of life—pays back the evil and rewards the good—must capture our attention. For while we hope this is how things come out, no one has good reason to think so. That is to say, we hope that there is justice. But we fear that there is nothing but accident. We look for design; we perceive chaos. Good things happen to bad people; bad things happen to good people. Moreover, in Hillel's time, things were the same as in our own. So when Hillel says that those who drowned you will be drowned, he expresses a hope and a conviction. But he does not describe the way things really are.

We, for our part, must preserve that same hope for justice, even in the face of despair. We have to believe, despite the world, that God cares. We have to affirm that there is a design, and a plan governs. We do not see it, and we hardly understand what we do see. But part of the meaning of having faith in God is believing there is justice when we see injustice, believing there is meaning when we face what seems an empty accident. Ours is not a time for complex explanation. We cannot appeal to how things come out right in the end. We have been through too much. We remember too much. Ours is an age that demands simple faith—or no faith at all. All the standard explanations have proved empty. But Hillel's, also, was an age that required simple faith in God's just rule. The world in his day gave no more evidence than it does now that God rules, and rules with justice. Yet Hillel said it, and so must we: against it all, despite it all. There is no alternative.

ח רַבָּן יוֹחָנָן בֶּן זַכַּאי קִבֵּל מֵהִלֵּל וּמִשַּׁמַּאי. הוּא הָיָה
אוֹמֵר:

אִם לָמַדְתָּ תּוֹרָה הַרְבֵּה,

אַל תַּחֲזִיק טוֹבָה לְעַצְמָךְ,

כִּי לְכָךְ נוֹצַרְתָּ.

חֲמִשָּׁה תַלְמִידִים הָיוּ לְרַבָּן יוֹחָנָן בֶּן זַכַּאי, וְאֵלּוּ
הֵן: רַבִּי אֱלִיעֶזֶר בֶּן הֻרְקָנוֹס, וְרַבִּי יְהוֹשֻׁעַ בֶּן חֲנַנְיָה,
וְרַבִּי יוֹסֵי הַכֹּהֵן, וְרַבִּי שִׁמְעוֹן בֶּן נְתַנְאֵל, וְרַבִּי אֶלְעָזָר
בֶּן עֲרָךְ. הוּא הָיָה מוֹנֶה שְׁבָחָן:

רַבִּי אֱלִיעֶזֶר בֶּן הֻרְקָנוֹס — בּוֹר סִיד, שֶׁאֵינוֹ מְאַבֵּד
טִפָּה.

רַבִּי יְהוֹשֻׁעַ — אַשְׁרֵי יוֹלַדְתּוֹ.

רַבִּי יוֹסֵי — חָסִיד.

רַבִּי שִׁמְעוֹן בֶּן נְתַנְאֵל — יְרֵא חֵטְא;

וְרַבִּי אֶלְעָזָר בֶּן עֲרָךְ — מַעְיָן הַמִּתְגַּבֵּר.

הוּא הָיָה אוֹמֵר: אִם יִהְיוּ כָל חַכְמֵי יִשְׂרָאֵל בְּכַף
מֹאזְנַיִם, וֶאֱלִיעֶזֶר בֶּן הֻרְקָנוֹס בְּכַף שְׁנִיָּה — מַכְרִיעַ
אֶת כֻּלָּם.

אַבָּא שָׁאוּל אוֹמֵר מִשְּׁמוֹ: אִם יִהְיוּ כָל חַכְמֵי יִשְׂרָאֵל
בְּכַף מֹאזְנַיִם וְרַבִּי אֱלִיעֶזֶר בֶּן הֻרְקָנוֹס אַף עִמָּהֶם,
וְרַבִּי אֶלְעָזָר בְּכַף שְׁנִיָּה — מַכְרִיעַ אֶת כֻּלָּם.

ט אָמַר לָהֶם: צְאוּ וּרְאוּ אֵיזוֹהִי דֶרֶךְ יְשָׁרָה שֶׁיִּדְבַּק בָּהּ
הָאָדָם.

רַבִּי אֱלִיעֶזֶר אוֹמֵר: עַיִן טוֹבָה.

רַבִּי יְהוֹשֻׁעַ אוֹמֵר: חָבֵר טוֹב.

רַבִּי יוֹסֵי אוֹמֵר: שָׁכֵן טוֹב.

רַבִּי שִׁמְעוֹן אוֹמֵר: הָרוֹאֶה אֶת הַנּוֹלָד.

רַבִּי אֶלְעָזָר אוֹמֵר: לֵב טוֹב.

אָמַר לָהֶם: רוֹאֶה אֲנִי אֶת דִּבְרֵי אֶלְעָזָר בֶּן עֲרָךְ
שֶׁבִּכְלָל דְּבָרָיו דִּבְרֵיכֶם.
אָמַר לָהֶם: צְאוּ וּרְאוּ אֵיזוֹהִי דֶּרֶךְ רָעָה שֶׁיִּתְרַחֵ
מִמֶּנָּה הָאָדָם.
רַבִּי אֱלִיעֶזֶר אוֹמֵר: עַיִן רָעָה.
רַבִּי יְהוֹשֻׁעַ אוֹמֵר: חָבֵר רַע.
רַבִּי יוֹסֵי אוֹמֵר: שָׁכֵן רַע.
רַבִּי שִׁמְעוֹן אוֹמֵר: הַלֹּוֶה וְאֵינוֹ מְשַׁלֵּם.
אֶחָד הַלֹּוֶה מִן הָאָדָם כְּלֹוֶה מִן הַמָּקוֹם בָּרוּךְ הוּא
שֶׁנֶּאֱמַר: "לֹוֶה רָשָׁע וְלֹא יְשַׁלֵּם, וְצַדִּיק חוֹנֵן וְנוֹתֵן"
רַבִּי אֶלְעָזָר אוֹמֵר: לֵב רַע.
אָמַר לָהֶם: רוֹאֶה אֲנִי אֶת דִּבְרֵי אֶלְעָזָר בֶּן עֲרָךְ
שֶׁבִּכְלָל דְּבָרָיו דִּבְרֵיכֶם.

י הֵם אָמְרוּ שְׁלֹשָׁה שְׁלֹשָׁה דְּבָרִים. רַבִּי אֱלִיעֶזֶר אוֹמֵר
יְהִי כְּבוֹד חֲבֵרְךָ חָבִיב עָלֶיךָ כְּשֶׁלָּךְ.
וְאַל תְּהִי נוֹחַ לִכְעוֹס.
וְשׁוּב יוֹם אֶחָד לִפְנֵי מִיתָתָךְ.

וֶהֱוֵי מִתְחַמֵּם כְּנֶגֶד אוּרָן שֶׁלַּחֲכָמִים, וֶהֱוֵי זָהִיר
בְּגַחַלְתָּן שֶׁלֹּא תִכָּוֶה —
שֶׁנְּשִׁיכָתָן נְשִׁיכַת שׁוּעָל, וַעֲקִיצָתָן עֲקִיצַת עַקְרָב
וּלְחִישָׁתָן לְחִישַׁת שָׂרָף.
וְכָל דִּבְרֵיהֶם כְּגַחֲלֵי אֵשׁ.

יא רַבִּי יְהוֹשֻׁעַ אוֹמֵר:
עַיִן הָרַע,
וְיֵצֶר הָרַע,
וְשִׂנְאַת הַבְּרִיּוֹת מוֹצִיאִין אֶת הָאָדָם מִן הָעוֹלָם.

ב רַבִּי יוֹסֵי אוֹמֵר:
יְהִי מָמוֹן חֲבֵרְךָ חָבִיב עָלֶיךָ כְּשֶׁלָּךְ.
וְהַתְקֵן עַצְמְךָ לִלְמוֹד תּוֹרָה, שֶׁאֵינָהּ יְרֻשָּׁה לָךְ.
וְכָל מַעֲשֶׂיךָ יִהְיוּ לְשֵׁם שָׁמָיִם.

ג רַבִּי שִׁמְעוֹן אוֹמֵר:
הֱוֵי זָהִיר בִּקְרִיַת שְׁמַע וּבִתְפִלָּה.
וּכְשֶׁאַתָּה מִתְפַּלֵּל, אַל תַּעַשׂ תְּפִלָּתְךָ קֶבַע, אֶלָּא
רַחֲמִים וְתַחֲנוּנִים לִפְנֵי הַמָּקוֹם בָּרוּךְ הוּא,
שֶׁנֶּאֱמַר: "כִּי-(אֵל) חַנּוּן וְרַחוּם הוּא אֶרֶךְ
אַפַּיִם וְרַב-חֶסֶד וְנִחָם עַל-הָרָעָה".
וְאַל תְּהִי רָשָׁע בִּפְנֵי עַצְמָךְ.

ד רַבִּי אֶלְעָזָר אוֹמֵר:
הֱוֵי שָׁקוּד לִלְמוֹד תּוֹרָה;
וְדַע מַה שֶׁתָּשִׁיב לָאַפִּיקוֹרוֹס;
וְדַע לִפְנֵי מִי אַתָּה עָמֵל; וְנֶאֱמָן הוּא בַּעַל
מְלַאכְתָּךְ, שֶׁיְשַׁלֶּם לָךְ שְׂכַר פְּעֻלָּתָךְ.

8 Rabban Yohanan ben Zakkai received [the Torah] from
Hillel and Shammai. He would say:
   If you have learned much Torah,
   do not puff yourself up on that account,
   for it was for that purpose that you were created.
He had five disciples, and these are they: Rabbi Eliezer ben
Hyrcanus, Rabbi Joshua ben Hananiah, Rabbi Yose the
Priest, Rabbi Simeon ben Nethanel, and Rabbi Eleazar ben
Arakh. He would list their good qualities:
   Rabbi Eliezer ben Hyrcanus—a plastered well, which
      does not lose a drop of water.
   Rabbi Joshua—happy is the one who gave birth to him.
   Rabbi Yose—a pious man.
   Rabbi Simeon ben Nethanel—a man who fears sin,
   and Rabbi Eleazar ben Arakh—a surging spring.
He would say: If all the sages of Israel were on one side of

the scale, and Rabbi Eliezer ben Hyrcanus were on the other, he would outweigh all of them.
Abba Saul says in his name: If all of the sages of Israel were on one side of the scale, and Rabbi Eliezer ben Hyrcanus was also with them, and Rabbi Eleazar [ben Arakh] were on the other side, he would outweigh all of them.

He said to them: Go and see what is the straight path to which someone should stick.
> Rabbi Eliezer says: A generous spirit.
> Rabbi Joshua says: A good friend.
> Rabbi Yose says: A good neighbor.
> Rabbi Simeon says: Foresight.
> Rabbi Eleazar says: Good will.
He said to them: I prefer the opinion of Rabbi Eleazar ben Arakh, because in what he says is included everything you say.
He said to them: Go out and see what is the bad road, which someone should avoid.
> Rabbi Eliezer says: Envy.
> Rabbi Joshua says: A bad friend.
> Rabbi Yose says: A bad neighbor.
> Rabbi Simeon says: A loan.
> (All the same is a loan owed to a human being and a loan owed to the Omnipresent, the blessed, as it is said, *The wicked borrows and does not pay back, but the righteous person deals graciously and hands over [what is owed]*.)   Ps. 37:21
> Rabbi Eleazar says: Ill will.
He said to them: I prefer the opinion of Rabbi Eleazar ben Arakh, because in what he says is included everything you say.

10 They [each] said three things. Rabbi Eliezer says:
> Let the respect owing to your companion be as precious to you as the respect owing to yourself.
> And don't be easy to anger.
> And repent one day before you die.
And
> Warm yourself by the fire of the sages, but be careful of their coals, so you don't get burned—
> for their bite is the bite of a fox, and their sting is the sting of a scorpion, and their hiss is like the hiss of a snake,
> and everything they say is like fiery coals.

11 Rabbi Joshua says:

Envy,

desire of bad things,

and hatred for people push a person out of the world.

12 Rabbi Yose says:

Let your companion's money be as precious to you as your own.

And get yourself ready to learn Torah, for it does not come as an inheritance to you.

And may everything you do be for the sake of Heaven.

13 Rabbi Simeon says:

Be meticulous about the recitation of the *Shema* and the Prayer.

And when you pray, don't treat your praying as a matter of routine; but let it be a [plea for] mercy and supplication before the Omnipresent, the blessed, as it is said, *For He is gracious and full of compassion, slow*

Joel 2:13 *to anger and full of mercy, and repents of the evil.*

And never be evil in your own eyes.

14 Rabbi Eleazar says:

Be constant in learning of Torah;

And know what to reply to an Epicurean;

And know before whom you work, for your employer can be depended upon to pay your wages for what you do.

A Spiritual Family

In the beginning of chapter two, we heard from the line of tradition extending from Sinai through Gamaliel and Hillel, the two sons of the patriarch Judah, in the first half of the third century, down to 250 C.E. Now, we take up a new line emanating from Sinai, the second prong of our inverted Y. This is the line beginning at the destruction of the Temple in 70 and running through the great sages, masters and disciples. They too reach back to Sinai through the same chain of tradition given in chapter one. But the chain, for them, is not the family of the patriarch. Rather, it is a spiritual family.

This family is created by people who learn Torah together. It is the family in which the master takes the role of father, the disciple becomes child and heir. Yohanan ben Zakkai, leader of the Jewish nation after the destruction of the Temple in 70, represents such a master; and his five disciples, such a family.

As you have come to expect, the construction of sayings around Yohanan ben Zakkai and his disciples is exceedingly meticulous, and its formal traits are easy to analyze. We discern three components, all of them pointing toward the excellence of one of the disciples over the others. In the first composition, Yohanan begins with the expected three-part saying. Then the main event—the account of the five disciples—begins. The first set, at saying 8, lists and identifies the men. The second set, at saying 9, presents a closely matched group of sayings, very much like the one that Rabbi gives us at the beginning of this chapter in saying 1. The five good qualities are matched against the five bad qualities, and the whole construction repeats the original point about Eleazar ben Arakh's superiority. The third and final component of the whole matches the first in that, just as the master has three sayings, so do the disciples. Here there is no effort to match the disciples' sayings against one another. Nor do we see the intent to take up and spell out the five sets of good and bad qualities in the triplets of sayings. It is constructed with close attention to balance and order. And, relative to what we have seen up to now, the construction is huge. We see a fine example of the kind of beauty achieved in Avot through the orderly exposition of diverse ideas.

When we turn to these ideas, we see that the overall theme, predictably, is (1) study of Torah joined to (2) sound advice about good conduct, that is, wisdom about the ways of the world. So the paramount concerns of chapter one define the recurrent themes of the rest of the collection of lessons.

Yohanan's saying is the simplest part of the whole. But it makes a very telling point. Yohanan wishes to explain by reference to study of Torah the very purpose of human life, the reason we are born. He states this idea in its purest form by simply declaring that if we learn a lot, we should not take pride on that account—it was for that purpose that we were created.

Yet, if you take that simple declaration a step further, you recognize his deeper intent. Each human being was created to learn, that is, to use mind and heart and soul as they are supposed to be used, in the mastery of Torah. Does Yohanan understand the word *torah* to mean a few books of the Tanakh? I am inclined to think not. To his mind *torah* has a far wider framework: revelation of God's will and truth in the whole of the tradition of Israel. That, in context, surely is his meaning. Torah encompasses all of being: how to live with people, how to serve God, what it means to love and work. When we reach this level of meaning, then, Yohanan turns out to be saying that we were created to understand our being, to make sense of why we were created—*torah.*

The qualities of the disciples are not symmetrical one to another. Some descriptions refer to the powers of intellect of the students—not forgetting, for instance, or being full of new ideas (a "surging spring"). Other descriptions speak of personal qualities—piety, fearing sin. Joshua has no equivalent to what the others enjoy since the saying simply praises him by referring to his mother's joy in his achievements. Perhaps the intent was to give the five in three sets: Eliezer and Eleazar, Yose and Simeon, Joshua. It hardly matters. The sequence taken whole tells us that good properties of mind must be joined to good traits of the soul: a good head, fearing sin. These are equally important virtues.

The good-way bad-way set at saying 9 presents us with yet another group of virtues and their matched vices. Eliezer's and Eleazar's advice speak of attitudes and emotions: generosity of spirit, good will; against envy and ill will. They are saying that your attitude toward other people is what counts the most. You have to be glad at another person's good fortune or achievement. You must not envy. You may not rejoice at another's bad fortune or failure. Perhaps these standards will make you either a good friend and neighbor or a bad friend and neighbor (the difference between the Hebrew words for friend and neighbor is not entirely clear). Simeon's sayings in this group stand by themselves. You should see what is coming—hence, avoid borrowing money you can not repay. These sayings of wisdom bear no relationship to the overall theme of Torah study. But that is not surprising since, we now know, two equally important concerns generate the sayings at hand.

The three things assigned to each of the disciples turn out to be quite unoriginal. What they say is independent of the

PIRKE AVOT ב 77

arlier opinions they express. Joshua, for example, at saying 1, says the same thing as Eliezer at saying 9. That does not matter to anyone. Eliezer's advice about repentance is congruent with what Hillel has stated earlier. If there were a Talmudic commentary to this tractate, someone would point out how one saying goes over the ground of another, and would then show the distinctions between the one and the other. In a collection such as this one, by contrast, no one thinks wisdom needs to be original. What is important is that is truth. Later on, we shall see a sage's contribution consisting simply of a verse of Scripture!

Eliezer has two triplets, one on right conduct and the other on Torah study. The first set emphasizes relationships between one person and the next; the second, relationships between disciple and master. You have to care as much for someone else's self-respect as for your own. Perhaps this is another way of saying you should not judge someone until you stand where that person stands. Eliezer advises against quick anger. He counsels a life of repentance every day, because you never know when you are going to die. Here, too, it may be that, if you live a life aware of death, you will find it natural to respect others and to avoid losing your temper with others. The relationships with sages, by contrast, present another kind of experience entirely. Like Simeon ben Gamaliel, Eliezer is wary of sages: treat them with great respect, but avoid getting burned. Don't come too close. You can imagine the awe and reverence—the fear—associated with sages, for people to frame sayings such as these. It is the fear of the sacred—awe, reverence; but also, fright.

Joshua's saying, as we noticed just now, goes over familiar ground—the five negative qualities you should avoid. These center on relationships to others. You should not envy. If you hate someone, you may turn out to be hated. That "removes you from the world."

In his interest in proper relationships both among people and in study of Torah, Yose's saying is similar in intent to Eliezer's. Eliezer spoke of honor, Yose refers to property or money. The point is the same. Care as much for the other as you do for yourself. There is nothing new here, since Leviticus 9:18 says the same thing: *Love your neighbor as yourself.* Eliezer and Yose simply make that general statement specific, applying it to familiar and homely things like self-respect a▮ property.

The Value of Property

Yose's saying carries with it a surprising affirmation. He thinks that what people have is worth having. He says we owe people respect not only for their persons, but also for their material possessions. It is conventional for some religions to negate the importance of property or money. Even though the leaders of these religions may live very handsomely, they pretend to a kind of holy poverty, and, symbolically, once in a while, walk barefooted or give some other demonstration of stunning humility.

Judaism, represented by Yose, understands that people have rights to possess what they have made and done. People naturally want to live a decent life. It is normal to want to eat a satisfying meal, sleep in a comfortable bed, live under a solid roof, wear nice clothes, reside in a pleasant neighborhood. Yose does not deny that these things matter. He says we owe one another respect for the things that, in the natural course of life, do matter. Is that to say we must spend our lives seeking material wealth? Every line of our tractate declares the opposite. We live our life to study and carry out and embody the teachings of the Torah. We live to seek a holy life, to become ourselves in the image of God. To that quest for a holy way of life, material possessions hardly are important.

But holiness does not reside in poverty, nor in wealth: it is in our hearts and in how we dispose of what we have and what we are. In the ancient Temple, people gave up part of their wealth—animals were capital in those days—to serve God in the holy way the Torah instructed them to follow. Today, when we treat possessions as a trust and share our wealth through support of tzedakah, "the charity that is righteousness," we do the same. So material possessions, as much as our minds and our hearts, present an opportunity for sanctification. Just as we respect all the other gifts we enjoy from God, so we respect also the material possessions that are ours.

Yose's second point brings us back to Yohanan's. Yohanan ben Zakkai holds it is natural to learn Torah. That is the reason we were created. Does that then mean it is easy to acquire learning? Yose says that it is hard to do the work. You have to get ready to do it, make yourself worthy. It is not an inheritance, but something you yourself earn.

The third part of his saying matches the third part of Eliezer's. It turns from this world to the next. Just as Eliezer speaks of death, which comes to us all, Yose reminds people to do what they do for the right motive. He refers us back to the idea of Antigonus (see chapter one, saying 3): doing things for the sake of Heaven, that is, not to receive a reward but out of fear or awe of Heaven, God.

Beyond Death

Since in later sayings we shall hear a good bit about this world and the world to come, we had better pause for a moment and go over this idea. There are two separate, but intertwined themes concerning our present existence and a coming one—that is, life and death, or this age and some better age, or this world and the next world.

One theme focuses upon the individual and divides life at the grave. We live, we die. These are the two "worlds" or "ages" we know as human beings. From this angle of vision, our sages ask about the contrast between life and what happens after death. The answer addresses everyone who ever lived. The deepest convictions of all forms of Judaism from the first century onward begin in the simple affirmation that we do not die at the grave. There is a life after death, the soul lives on, or the being, or the personhood—however it is phrased. Since that is taken as fact, it follows that this life prepares us for another one, a different one, in which everything changes, but each individual person persists. All of the sayings in Avot about living now in preparation for life then refer to this article of faith.

Lest you think that I am describing the strange fantasies of some far-off tribe, I state my deepest conviction that all

*of us are possessed of an immortal soul from God, and
that all of us hope for life in the world to come. Death is
not the end for any human being. The grave receives only
our tired bodies.*

*Another theme about now and then, this world and the
next, this age and the age to come, frames a social and a
national picture. It addresses the condition not of individuals but of the Jewish people. It takes up not the private
story of each one of us, but the public and collective story
of all of us together, our history.*

*This body of belief holds that, in the end of time, a Mes-
siah will restore Israel, the Jewish nation, to the Land of
Israel, and bring peace and harmony to all of the nations
of the world. So this second set of convictions centers
upon history and destiny, the meaning and end of Israel in
the life of nations and peoples. This dimension of beliefs
about the end of history and the purpose of life is not
found in Avot; it rarely makes an appearance in the
Mishnah as a whole. Our tractate speaks to a smaller and
more accessible world: the one we live in, individually.
That is why our tractate has won the hearts of the Jews,
individually and in all times and places. It takes seriously
who we are in the here and now, not only what we are
part of in the world out there.*

Simeon's three sayings take up a completely different
aspect of the good life: prayer. His main point is that when
you pray, you have two separate and essential tasks. First,
you have to be careful about it. You must remember before
whom you stand, and whom you address. At the same time,
you must not treat prayer as a matter of routine. Merely being
meticulous, you can turn prayer into little more than a habit,
a set of conventions. Knowing before whom you stand means
that you will plead for mercy before the All-Merciful. You
can only do that if you respect yourself. For that purpose, you
have to preserve your own dignity. Accordingly, Simeon
advises us not to become weighed down by guilt. We must
never be evil in our own eyes. We must preserve self-respect:
"If I am not for myself, who will be for me?"

Eleazar's triplet is equally well formed and cogent. The three sayings focus upon the theme of Torah-study. Eleazar advises that you keep at it, and, at the third clause, he points out before whom you do the work. This matches the general intent of Simeon's reminder about the One before whom we pray. The "Epicurean" of his second clause stands for someone who denies there is any sense in the world and claims that there is no justice, no ruling Judge. By the placement of this clause, it seems that one of the reasons to study Torah is to know what to reply to an unbeliever.

Confronting Others

The "Epicurean" represents the unbelief of the Greek-speaking world in which the rabbis of the Mishnah lived. Our sages clearly recognized that, within Israel and beyond, people denied the fundamental convictions of the Torah as the sages taught it. They therefore urged their disciples to know what to say to such people. That meant, in practice, that the disciples had to come to know and understand the unbelief of the world at large. They could not pretend there were no "Epicureans," or deliberately avoid encounters with unbelievers. The healthy counsel of the sages was to accept reality and learn to cope with it.

Knowing "what to answer" meant taking an affirmative— even an aggressive—position. The task of the disciple of Torah was to learn not only Torah but also other peoples' "torah" (so to speak), to engage in the philosophical thinking of the age and to come to an accurate assessment of what was true and what was false. Now, in antiquity, given the prestige and power of the ruling Greek culture, the sages demanded remarkable courage. The easier path would have been to counsel isolation from the prestigious philosophies of the day. The more difficult and honest path brought the disciples to a confrontation with the self-evident facts, the established convictions, the universally accepted truths of their age. But that has always been the condition of Israel, the Jewish people. Small and weak,

*Israel has always asserted its right to live. At the fringes of
history, often the object of events, Israel has always seen
itself at the center of history and the cause and subject of
what happens. To be a Jew, to be Israel, always has
demanded conviction despite, not on account of, the condition of the world—and of Israel itself. So it was then,
and so it is today.*

*To be a Jew is an act of affirmation, an act of faith, an act
of hope. It is not a ratification of how things really are. To
know what to answer the unbeliever is to know how to
live in the world as it is. To maintain the faith of Israel is
to know how to live in the world as it should be; and, we
believe, as in God's own time, it will be.*

The sayings of Yohanan and his disciples form a counter
part to those collected in the great chain of tradition in chapter
one. When we recall the paramount themes of the opening
chapter, we realize that before us is a reprise. The triplet of
interests at the outset are learning in Torah, relating to others
and right attitude. Within these three categories we find ample
room for everything attributed to Yohanan and his disciples.
So the sayings deal with our minds (Torah), our everyday
lives (relationships between individuals), and our hearts and
emotions (attitude). What we think, do and feel—all these
matter. They form, all together, our being, and impart meaning
to our breath and life.

Our minds must be shaped to understand Torah, to
understand the mind and plan of the Creator of the world and
to make sense of creation, the world we know. We live not by
ourselves, but always and only with others. So we have to use
our minds to think carefully how to live a reliable and con-
structive life in society. These two by themselves leave a great
gap, to be filled by ourselves: the inner world we make. For
knowing the world is not the same thing as knowing ourselves.
Relating to others is not the same as discovering who we are
beyond all relationships to others. The one who knows, the
one who relates—that is you. And you are important not only
in what you think about the outside world and how you behave
toward the outside world, but in how you feel and what you
are.

These three count—learning and deed and inner being.
ıt the inner being governs everything else. That is Eleazar's
sson, and, we now recognize, it is the fundamental point of
e several themes of the sages of Avot.

טו רַבִּי טַרְפוֹן אוֹמֵר:
הַיּוֹם קָצָר,
וְהַמְּלָאכָה מְרֻבָּה,
וְהַפּוֹעֲלִים עֲצֵלִים,
וְהַשָּׂכָר הַרְבֵּה,
וּבַעַל הַבַּיִת דּוֹחֵק.

טז הוּא הָיָה אוֹמֵר:
לֹא עָלֶיךָ הַמְּלָאכָה לִגְמוֹר, וְלֹא אַתָּה בֶן חֹר
לְבָטֵל מִמֶּנָּה.
אִם לָמַדְתָּ תּוֹרָה הַרְבֵּה, נוֹתְנִים לָךְ שָׂכָ
הַרְבֵּה.
וְנֶאֱמָן הוּא בַּעַל מְלַאכְתָּךְ, שֶׁיְּשַׁלֶּם לָךְ שְׂכַ
פְּעֻלָּתָךְ.
וְדַע מַתַּן שְׂכָרָן שֶׁלַּצַּדִּיקִים לֶעָתִיד לָבֹא.

5 Rabbi Tarfon says:
The day is short,
the work formidable,
the workers lazy,
the wages high,
the employer impatient.

6 He would say:
It's not your job to finish the work, but you are not free
to walk away from it.
If you have learned much Torah, they will give you a
good reward.
And your employer can be depended upon to pay your
wages for what you do.
And know what sort of reward is going to be given to
the righteous in the coming time.

The Human Condition

Tarfon lived at the same time as the disciples of Yohanan ben Zakkai, so the framers of the tractate included his sayings together with theirs. The first one is rather piquant. Tarfon captures the human condition. There is plenty of work, but not much time in which to accomplish it. The workers are paid well and work little. The employer—and that is God!—is pressing. And you are in the middle. You do not have to be a contractor, coordinating the construction of a building, to understand what Tarfon is saying. But if you missed the point in saying 15, saying 16 goes over it. You may not be able to finish the project, but you have to do your best at it. You cannot master the whole of the Torah, but you get a reward for what you accomplish. The employer may be impatient but the employer is reliable. Here, then, is the human condition: never adequate, always urgent.

Perhaps the sages' constant reminder that life is short, that we must live every day as if it were our last, and that there is much to do but little time in which to do—perhaps that lesson is the most important thing the sages have to tell us. When we ask why their words have spoken with such immediacy to the heart of Jews living far from and long after the sages' place and time, here is another part of the answer. The sages of Israel, the founders and teachers, take up our condition and explain it. Through time and through change, these are the things that endure: our living, our dying, our caring, our labor. Do they mean anything? We were created for a purpose. There is work to be done, and you must do your best. "And your employer can be depended upon to pay your wages for what you do. And know what sort of reward is going to be given . . ."

Avot's chapter two has broadened the range of discourse. After reading the sayings in chapter one, we had a sense that we were looking in on other peoples' lives. For we are neither masters nor disciples. What began as a manual for disciples and apprentice judges grows in this chapter into something more encompassing, more interesting: Torah for us all, now as much as then. How so? Analyzing the messages emerging from the two wings of the inverted Y, we discover one question phrased in two ways: What is the straight path (Rabbi)? and What is the way a person should choose (Yohanan ben Zakkai)?

Again, while in chapter one of our tractate there was little about making a living, chapter two inquires about the relationship of time spent in study of Torah to time spent earning a living. The whole range of discourse thus broadens to treat issues of everyday life and ordinary people.

At the same time, a powerful theme of the chapter at hand directs our attention to the afterlife: the world to come, the coming of the Messiah, life after death, retribution, divine justice—the entire complex of ideas that, all together, confront the deepest perplexities of history. So we consider not only the practical needs of the here and now, but also the more profound questions of society as it endures, of history as it unfolds, of meaning in a world of chaos and disorder. Avot's chapter one starts with Sinai. Chapter two carries us into the turmoil of the streets and marketplaces of our own day—but also beyond.

CHAPTER THREE
SAGE COUNSEL
BETWEEN WARS

כֹּל שֶׁרוּחַ
הַבְּרִיּוֹת נוֹחָה
הֵימֶנּוּ—

רוּחַ הַמָּקוֹם
נוֹחָה הֵימֶנּוּ.

ANYONE FROM WHOM PEOPLE
TAKE PLEASURE—
THE OMNIPRESENT TAKES PLEASURE.

CHAPTER THREE
SAGE COUNSEL
BETWEEN WARS

The authorities of chapter three in the main succeeded those of chapter two and inherited their task. They lived between the war of 66–73 C.E.—with its climax at the destruction of the Temple of Jerusalem in 70—and the war of 132–35 C.E., known by the name of its principal Jewish general, Bar Kokhba. Accordingly, before us are the sages of the interval between one rebellion and the next. (Chapter four will present sages who flourished after the Bar Kokhba Revolt, from 135 to 250 C.E.).

Before approaching the text, let us stand aside and ask about the age to which the text refers. That age—from 70 to about 250—falls into two divisions: 70–135, the age of waiting; and 135–250, the age of restoration and reconstruction. In between comes the vast Jewish revolt against Rome and for the freedom of Israel, the war from 132 to 135.

That war marks the decisive shift from the ancient world of a Judaism centered on a Temple and worship of God (in part, through offering up animal sacrifices), and the world of a Judaism centered on the life of the Jewish people. This new Judaism, based on the old, called for the service of God through worship, study of Torah, practice of the commandments, and the building of a holy life for Israel, the Jewish people. What brought about the turning was a massive military defeat, and the defeat brought on an extraordinary crisis in the heart and soul of Israel.

From 70 to 132, people looked back. This was true because what happened in 70—the destruction of the Temple, the burning of Jerusalem—had happened before. People therefore could confidently expect to witness a repetition of the familiar pattern of old. Just as the Temple had been destroyed in 586 B.C.E., but miraculously the Jews had been restored to their land and the Temple rebuilt three generations later, so, many hoped, the ancient pattern would be repeated. Moreover, many firmly believed that the second time would be the last. We may surmise that the hope for the coming of the Messiah, in his guise as national leader and liberator, proved very strong. Many historians think that Bar Kokhba was greeted as the Messiah. What must follow for our argument is simple.

While 70 marked a catastrophic event, the old order endured in the minds of the people. If they waited patiently, the people reasoned, they would see what it all meant. God would intervene, as God had done before. So the sayings attributed to sages in the present chapter are assigned to people who have suffered an enormous calamity, but who retained hope. The world they knew yet lasted. All that they had to give was faith, and the great sin of the age was the sin of despair. The old rules governed: the old age, with all its logic and its sense and order, remained.

The story of Bar Kokhba's heroic leadership, of how the Jewish people fought the strongest empire the world had ever known, in the very hour of its greatest might, is well known. The damages brought on by the war remain, alas, all too familiar. In the history of the Jewish people from Bar Kokhba to the renewal of the Jewish nation in the Land of Israel in our own day, the psychological and national costs of defeat are decisively portrayed. The Jews lost. In their own minds, they might have become a people of losers. In the destruction of the Temple what was gone was not a building but a way of serving God. In the devastation of Jerusalem what was lost was not a holy city but even the right to return to the place where the city had stood. Along with the blood of the martyrs what flowed out was the surging stream of hope that had brought Israel to do battle against Rome. What was left? Disorder, destruction, despair.

That is the world that the sages named in chapter four had to address—a world of devastation, a world that had lost its moorings. The sages who stand behind the Mishnah, led by the irenic and conciliatory patriarch, Judah, undertook a labor of renewal and reconstruction. They cast lines backward to

e old world that had been set adrift. In memory and in
ope, they created the Mishnah as a picture of that world, to
hich, they remained certain, Israel once more would gain
ccess. Jerusalem now was a Roman possession, a forbidden
ity. Jews were forbidden to set foot there. the Temple lay in
uins. The old means of service, the sacrifices, were no more.
Vhat the sages did in part, was done in the Mishnah: the
ecord of the past, the design and plan for the future. But a
ore important part of what they did is not in the Mishnah
ut only indicated by their making of the Mishnah. Their
reatest achievement was that they did anything at all.

Let us put it negatively. They did not give up. They did
ot despair. They did not abandon the world to the chaos that
verwhelmed Israel. They sought order despite disorder, a
table and reliable world despite the breaking of all the old
ules, a life of hope and promise despite the death that lay
ound about them. Millions (so the sources tell us) had died.
ome lived on. They were the survivors. We are Jews today
ecause of what they did. In chapter three we hear from their
eachers. In chapter four we hear from them. So the other half
f the Mishnah tractate at hand—the half beyond the genea-
ogical history of the Torah of which the Mishnah forms a
rincipal part, given in chapters one and two—lies before us.
Ve know where the Torah came from and we know what it
tands for. Now we have to learn what the Torah, as the sages
f Israel taught it in their day, had to say at the most difficult
noment in the history of Israel, to the Jewish nation then,
nd from then to our own critical time of Holocaust and
ebirth.

Chapters three and four of Pirke Avot differ from the
irst two. We have come to expect truly sizable constructions
f coherent sayings, or, more accurately, sayings of coherent
roups. Now we come to singletons. These are sayings assigned
o individuals who bear no relationship to one another. The
urpose of the sayings remains the same: they are teachings
bout the right attitude we need for the good life we must live.
As I said, the sayings as a whole come from great sages of the
econd and early third centuries.

I read chapter three in four parts: sayings 1–10, sayings
1–12, sayings 13–16, and sayings 17–18. The first part on the
urface gives a collection of diverse statements. But when we

reflect on the sequence of ideas, from stunning start to pro
found conclusion, we see a cogent progression of closely relate
principles. The entire construction presents an encompassin
philosophy of what it means to be a human being, and of hov
the Torah transforms our everyday reality. In order to presen
this philosophy, the framers of the passage juxtapose opposite:
setting up powerful contrasts and providing a picture of jarrin
extremes. The message with little interruption flows forth fron
the generative tension inaugurated at the outset to the complet
resolution of that tension, accomplished at the conclusior
Read whole, and not singly, the sayings convey a stunnin
message.

The next unit, sayings 11 and 12, consists of two single
tons. But if we remember that the two sayings refer to master
who lived shortly after the destruction of the Temple, we ma
propose a link between the two. Together they present a mes
sage of hope and endurance in the difficult age. They speal
both to sages, to whom our document is addressed, and to th
nation at large. The message remains apt, even now.

The third unit, sayings 13–16, presents a huge compositior
in the name of Akiba, with a brief closing word in the name o
one of his contemporaries. How all of Akiba's materials coher
will become clear in due course. The fourth group consists o
sayings of two Eleazars.

א עֲקַבְיָא בֶּן מַהֲלַלְאֵל אוֹמֵר: הִסְתַּכֵּל בִּשְׁלֹשָׁה
דְּבָרִים וְאִי אַתָּה בָא לִידֵי עֲבֵרָה:
דַּע מֵאַיִן בָּאתָ,
וּלְאָן אַתָּה הוֹלֵךְ,
וְלִפְנֵי מִי אַתָּה עָתִיד לִתֵּן דִּין וְחֶשְׁבּוֹן.
מֵאַיִן בָּאתָ? — מִטִּפָּה סְרוּחָה.
וּלְאָן אַתָּה הוֹלֵךְ? — לִמְקוֹם עָפָר, רִמָּה וְתוֹלֵעָה.
וְלִפְנֵי מִי אַתָּה עָתִיד לִתֵּן דִּין וְחֶשְׁבּוֹן? — לִפְנֵי מֶלֶךְ
מַלְכֵי הַמְּלָכִים הַקָּדוֹשׁ בָּרוּךְ הוּא.

ב רַבִּי חֲנַנְיָה סְגַן הַכֹּהֲנִים אוֹמֵר: הֱוֵי מִתְפַּלֵּל
בִּשְׁלוֹמָה שֶׁלַּמַּלְכוּת, שֶׁאִלְמָלֵא מוֹרָאָה אִישׁ אֶת
רֵעֵהוּ חַיִּים בָּלָעוּ.

1 Akavyah ben Mahalalel says: Reflect upon three things and you will not fall into the clutches of transgression:
Know from whence you came,
whither you are going,
and before whom you are going to have to give a full account of yourself.
From whence do you come?—from a putrid drop.
Whither are you going?—to a place of dust, worms, and maggots.
And before whom are you going to give a full account of yourself?—before the King of king of kings, the Holy One, the blessed.

2 Rabbi Hananiah, Prefect of the Priests, says: Pray for the welfare of the government; for if it were not for fear of it, one person would swallow another alive.

Akavyah's saying is given its own explanation, phrase by phrase. His sentiment is familiar. If you know who you are, before whom you stand, for whom you labor—in other words, if you have right knowledge—then you will do the right thing. You will not sin. Right knowledge means that you know you came from nothing and are going to nothing, but have to give a full account of yourself to God. If we are humble and not arrogant, aware and not unthinking, we shall have a good statement to make for ourselves.

Like Akavyah, Hananiah lived both before and after the destruction of the Temple. Like him, Hananiah had seen enough of suffering and evil to want to emphasize a simple truth. Human beings are capable of much evil, of not much good. His saying forms a counterpart to Akavyah's, since the emphasis of both is on the darker side to things. We come from nowhere and are worth nothing. Now, Hananiah adds, people's natural impulse is to do evil. Therefore authority is needed to keep people from one another's throats. You can be sure that both sages endured much. Hananiah, in particular, had witnessed how, under extreme conditions, people fended for themselves and threw off all the normal obligations of civilized society.

Akavyah's and Hananiah's sayings are jarring. They hardly link up with the ones we considered in chapters one

and two. Nor does what follows relate to what they say. In a
collection of sage counsel about studying Torah and living the
good life, it is good to be reminded of the essential character
of the people to whom the Torah is given, of whom the good
life is asked: people who come from nothing and go nowhere
who would eat each other up alive if they could.

We cannot then imagine that our sages knew only the
sweet, but not the true, nature of humanity. We cannot suppose
they addressed an unreal world of people able to do good and
learn benign wisdom, unlike the world of total destruction
which we endure. Whether or not what they said proved relevant to their contemporaries, we do not know. But we cannot
doubt they speak directly to our time and place. And yet, God
lives among us, and we serve God. Torah teaches truth about
us—about what we are and may become—even though, we
know, we come from nothing and end up nothing. Formed of
dust from the ground, we live through the breath of God.

The government restrains us from swallowing each other
up alive—yet, as we shall now see, when we eat our meals
together, we may bring God to our table. The contrast between
this saying and the next is astonishing: in one, we are cannibals;
in the next, we sup with God.

רַבִּי חֲנַנְיָה בֶּן תְּרַדְיוֹן אוֹמֵר: שְׁנַיִם שֶׁיּוֹשְׁבִין וְאֵין
בֵּינֵיהֶן דִּבְרֵי תוֹרָה, הֲרֵי זֶה מוֹשַׁב לֵצִין, שֶׁנֶּאֱמַר:
"וּבְמוֹשַׁב לֵצִים לֹא יָשָׁב".
אֲבָל שְׁנַיִם שֶׁיּוֹשְׁבִין וְיֵשׁ בֵּינֵיהֶם דִּבְרֵי תוֹרָה, שְׁכִינָה
בֵּינֵיהֶם, שֶׁנֶּאֱמַר: "אָז נִדְבְּרוּ יִרְאֵי ה' אִישׁ אֶל־רֵעֵהוּ,
וַיַּקְשֵׁב ה' וַיִּשְׁמָע וַיִּכָּתֵב סֵפֶר זִכָּרוֹן לְפָנָיו לְיִרְאֵי ה'
וּלְחֹשְׁבֵי שְׁמוֹ".
אֵין לִי אֶלָּא שְׁנַיִם.
מִנַּיִן שֶׁאֲפִלּוּ אֶחָד שֶׁיּוֹשֵׁב וְעוֹסֵק בַּתּוֹרָה, שֶׁהַקָּדוֹשׁ
בָּרוּךְ הוּא קוֹבֵעַ לוֹ שָׂכָר? שֶׁנֶּאֱמַר: "יֵשֵׁב בָּדָד וְיִדֹּם
כִּי נָטַל עָלָיו".

ג רַבִּי שִׁמְעוֹן אוֹמֵר: שְׁלשָׁה שֶׁאָכְלוּ עַל שֻׁלְחָן אֶחָ
וְלֹא אָמְרוּ עָלָיו דִּבְרֵי תוֹרָה, כְּאִלּוּ אָכְלוּ מִזְבְ
מֵתִים, שֶׁנֶּאֱמַר: "כִּי כָּל־שֻׁלְחָנוֹת מָלְאוּ קִיא צֹא
בְּלִי מָקוֹם".
אֲבָל שְׁלשָׁה שֶׁאָכְלוּ עַל שֻׁלְחָן אֶחָד וְאָמְרוּ עָל
דִּבְרֵי תוֹרָה, כְּאִלּוּ אָכְלוּ מִשֻּׁלְחָנוּ שֶׁלַּמָּקוֹם בָּרוּ
הוּא, שֶׁנֶּאֱמַר: "וַיְדַבֵּר אֵלַי זֶה הַשֻּׁלְחָן אֲשֶׁר לִפְ
ה'".

Rabbi Hananiah ben Teradyon says: If two sit together and between them do not pass teachings of Torah, lo, this is a *seat of the scornful,* as it is said, *Nor sits in the seat of the scornful.*

Ps. 1:1

But two who are sitting, and words of Torah do pass between them—the Presence is with them, as it is said, *Then they that feared the Lord spoke with one another, and the Lord hearkened and heard, and a book of remembrance was written before Him, for them that feared and gave thought to His name.*

Mal. 3:16

I know that this applies to two.
How do I know that even if a single person sits and works on Torah, the Holy One, the blessed, sets aside a reward for him? As it is said, *Let him sit alone and keep silent, because he has laid it upon him.*

Lam. 3:28

Rabbi Simeon says: Three who ate at a single table and did not talk about the teachings of Torah while at that table are as though they ate from *dead sacrifices,* as it is said, *For all tables are full of vomit and filthiness [if they are] without God.*

Ps. 106:28

But three who ate at a single table and did talk about teachings of Torah while at that table are as if they ate at the table of the Onmipresent, the blessed, as it is said, *And He said to me, This is the table that is before the Lord.*

Ezek. 41:22

The two sayings, the second section of saying 2 and all of saying 3, belong together because they clearly move from two sitting together to three eating together. They are phrased in negative way, then in a positive way, so they match.

The Continuity of Torah

You will have noticed something new in this passage: the reference to biblical statements (the references are given in the column). Why quote Scripture?

In asking this question, we raise the critical issue of Judaism: the relationship of one holy book to another. For Judaism begins, as we saw at the very first line of Avot, with the claim that God revealed Torah at Sinai; moreover, it is clear that within the rubric of Torah, that is, revelation, is the Mishnah, including tractate Avot, the very book in our hands. Accordingly, if this is Torah too, then we quote the written Torah in some unusual way. What is that way?

Let us see first of all the simple and decisive fact: the quotation is not solely a proof-text. That is to say, the purpose of citing a verse of the written Torah, of Scripture, is not only to prove that an opinion formed later really is true. Why not? Because the opinion at hand also comes from Sinai, as much as what is found in Psalms, Malachi, Lamentations, or Ezekiel. Torah is Torah, whether it turns up in a book of the Hebrew Bible, a tractate of the Mishnah, a law of the Talmud, a chapter of Maimonides, a story of a Hasidic rabbi, or a teaching of a learned woman or man of our own day. Hence Judaism is not a religion that stopped the day it started, so to speak, with one authoritative Torah, the written one.

The very existence of the Mishnah, with Avot its head and heart, testifies to the opposite. God speaks to Israel, the Jewish people, in Torah; and Torah is in the Mishnah as much as in Scripture. Whatever is continuous with the written Torah and the oral Torah of the Mishnah, whether the Talmud or the compilations of biblical explanations we call midrash, whether in later times the teachings of the

arned man and woman or the informed and thoughtful
esture of the informed Jew—God speaks Torah through
hem all.

What, then, is the purpose of citing a particular Scriptural
erse? If you take a second look, you find the language,
"as it is said." What follows then is a verse of Scripture
that serves to illustrate what Hananiah says. Or, if you
wish, what Hananiah says refers to and illustrates what
the verse of Scripture says. The direction of the exchange
is not important. Hananiah adds to Torah by citing verses
of the written Torah in his effort to extend and expand the
boundaries of Torah. He sees himself as a student of the
Torah and not equivalent to Moses. At the same time, he
does what Moses originally did, so he acts like Moses. He
tells truth to Israel. Moses received Torah at Sinai.
Whoever receives and hands on Torah is as if he or she
also is at Sinai.

So, while the written Torah quite naturally provides
proofs of important facts, matters do not end there. On
the contrary, Hananiah, like any other great master of the
Mishnah and the two Talmuds and the compositions of
Midrash, learns Torah and he also teaches Torah. He is
part of the process of receiving and handing on. In citing a
proof for what he says, he therefore claims to stand in the
same relationship to Sinai as does the text he cites. What
he has seen for himself he tests against and squares with
the already available revelation, the Torah of Sinai. And
then, he shows, he too teaches Torah. The passage of the
written Torah is cited to do two things: first, to prove that
we teach Torah; and, so, second, to demonstrate that
Torah reaches Israel, also, through us. God speaks to each
generation. Judaism is the religion of the ongoing revelation, the religious experience of Torah.

To the thought of the sage is added a proof-text of Scripture. Here is an instance in which the status of the teaching of
the sage is worked out. What the sage says enjoys the standing

of what we find in the written Torah revealed by God to Moses at Mount Sinai.

The message is repeated twice—once for Hananiah, once for Simeon. The point is that when Jews speak of Torah, God is with them. Even if you work all by yourself in studying Torah, God is with you. At a meal, when you talk about Torah, it is as if you are eating at the table of the Lord. Now there are two points to bear in mind in reflecting on these sayings.

First, as I just said, Hananiah, Prefect of the Priests, had just spoken about peoples' eating one another up alive. Now in a breathtaking shift, the framer of the sayings introduces a statement on eating a meal, a rather daring way of continuing a difficult theme. The point is precisely a counterpoint. Torah makes the difference. When you eat at a table and speak about Torah, God is with you. When Torah is not in the world, we need strong government to keep us from swallowing each other up alive. So we go from one extreme to the other. Torah makes the difference.

The second point to note is that Simeon flourished after the destruction of the Temple. In the time of the Temple, the Temple's altar was regarded as God's table. On the altar sacrifices of meat, grain, oil, and wine were offered up to God. These sacrifices Scripture knows as God's bread, God's food. Accordingly, Simeon's saying does not surprise us by its reference to sacrifices—*dead sacrifices*. Then the reverse is all the more daring: if Torah is present on the table, it is God's table. We will come back to this amazing transformation.

Thus you have the power to recreate the table of the Lord. This you do through talking about Torah at your own table. Torah transforms an ordinary meal into a holy meal. Torah succeeds in reconstituting the table of the Lord smashed in the ruined Temple. Simeon contrasts dead sacrifices with the living Torah, teaching that, when words of Torah come out of our mouths, it is as if we eat at the table of God, in the holy city, in the holy place, in the age that is no more.

I think this is an effort to make public life and private life correspond: both dimensions of life are to be made holy. The public life was lived in the Temple. The private life is lived at home. Private life must conform to, exhibit the virtues of public life. What we are, we must be wherever we are. So the able at home is to be modeled (in the mind of our sages) upon the table of God in the Temple. The way we eat is to be the way (priestly writers had long maintained, the Torah had always held) God received the nourishment offered by Israel at the altar in the Temple. We try to emulate the priests, to be holy in some way as they were holy. They served at the table of the Lord, we serve at our own table at home. These things matter because they are paths to holiness.

ד רַבִּי חֲנַנְיָה בֶּן חֲכִינַאי אוֹמֵר:
הַנֵּעוֹר בַּלַּיְלָה,
וְהַמְהַלֵּךְ בַּדֶּרֶךְ יְחִידִי,
וְהַמְפַנֶּה לִבּוֹ לְבַטָּלָה —
הֲרֵי זֶה מִתְחַיֵּב בְּנַפְשׁוֹ.

4 Rabbi Hananiah ben Hakhinai says:
He who gets up at night,
and he who walks around by himself,
and he who turns his desire to emptiness—
lo, this person is liable for his life.

When Hananiah says you are "liable for" your life, he means you endanger your life. Getting up at night and walking around by yourself, in his day, were thought dangerous. Many believed that the world was peopled by shades or demons who preferred to attack at night or when a person was alone. But while we do not believe in shades or demons, we do know that if you spend a lot of time talking to yourself, in the end you start believing that what you *think* is true and what *really* is true are one and the same thing. You tend to construct a world that is only private and totally personal. You separate your life from the lives of others. What, then, is left of your life but empty things, fantasies, wishes in place of facts, pretense instead of solid achievement?

Accordingly, we recognize, there may be more dangerous demons than the ones people in Hananiah's time believed lurking in dark corners of the night. More dangerous are the demons that lurk in the dark places of the soul, especially the soul unillumined by the souls of others. The demons we create for ourselves when we walk too much alone, when we wake at night and fear—these demons are no less real to us than Hananiah's demons were to him.

Hananiah speaks of more than mere demons. Darkness is empty, to love to be alone is to love darkness and not light. To be with people is to be in the light, to be in life: life is with people. You become "liable for" your life when you want to be empty, lonely. A holy man in the Talmud cries out, "Give me friends, or give me death." That is the way of Judaism: to draw together with others, to gain life in the living with others. Ours is not a faith meant to yield solitary holy men and women living in caves in the wilderness, in deserts or on mountain tops, despising the love of humanity and seeking only the love of God. To us, to love humanity is to love God in whose image human beings are made, to serve God is to serve other people, and to seek God is to seek God's face in the faces of human beings. The opposite is emptiness; the penalty is the forfeiture of life itself.

ה רַבִּי נְחוּנְיָא בֶּן הַקָּנָה אוֹמֵר:
כָּל הַמְקַבֵּל עָלָיו עֹל תּוֹרָה, מַעֲבִירִין מִמֶּנּוּ עֹל
מַלְכוּת וְעֹל דֶּרֶךְ אֶרֶץ.
וְכָל הַפּוֹרֵק מִמֶּנּוּ עֹל תּוֹרָה, נוֹתְנִין עָלָיו עֹל
מַלְכוּת וְעֹל דֶּרֶךְ אֶרֶץ.

5 Rabbi Nehunya ben Hakkanah says:
From whomever accepts upon himself the yoke of Torah do they remove the yoke of the state and the yoke of hard labor.
And upon whoever removes from himself the yoke of Torah do they lay the yoke of the state and the yoke of hard labor.

Nehunya hardly describes the world we daily experience. In his own day, you can be sure, the great sages of the Torah

ill had to pay their taxes and do the physical labor the state
emanded of everyone who lived within the empire. If, there-
re, Nehunya means to tell us that by accepting the disciplines
the Torah—faith, deeds, learning—we remove from our-
lves the yoke of the state and of hard work, he seems to be
rong for his own day, and irrelevant to ours.

But there is a second possibility in this matter of "the
ke of Torah." How do we accept "the yoke of Torah?"
/hat do we accept? Those who say the *Shema* morning and
ight know the answer. In reciting the *Shema* prayer, we
:cept the yoke of the kingdom of Heaven. We take on our-
lves the yoke—the discipline of the commandments. So when
ehunya contrasts the yoke of the Torah and the yoke of the
ate, he is saying that there are two domains. We accept the
ne or the other. If you live in the realm of the Torah, you are
o longer imprisoned as a slave to the state. If you accept the
oke of doing the deeds required by the Torah, you no longer
o hard labor.

So there is the state within, the realm we govern in our
earts; and there is the empire without, the domain of the
orld. There is the labor of the Torah; and there is mere hard
ork. Torah and works of Torah—study, commandments,
eeds of lovingkindness—these form one reality. There is the
ther reality as well: mere laws, mere labor. When we do the
ne, we create for ourselves a holy framework, to which the
ther is not truly relevant. When we do not do the one, we
ave ourselves wholly within the framework of the other. So
nce more, Torah transforms us from a putrid drop, living a
iserable life in a mean world, into citizens of another world,
nother age. The stunning contrast drawn before, between
ead sacrifices and eating at God's table, now returns in full
orce: Torah turns us from one thing into something else
ntirely.

ו רַבִּי חֲלַפְתָּא אִישׁ כְּפַר חֲנַנְיָה אוֹמֵר: עֲשָׂרָה
שֶׁיּוֹשְׁבִין וְעוֹסְקִין בַּתּוֹרָה, שְׁכִינָה שְׁרוּיָה בֵּינֵיהֶם
שֶׁנֶּאֱמַר: "אֱלֹהִים נִצָּב בַּעֲדַת־אֵל".
וּמִנַּיִן אֲפִלּוּ חֲמִשָּׁה? שֶׁנֶּאֱמַר: "וַאֲגֻדָּתוֹ עַל
אֶרֶץ יְסָדָהּ".

וּמִנַּיִן אֲפִלּוּ שְׁלֹשָׁה? שֶׁנֶּאֱמַר: "בְּקֶרֶב אֱלֹהִים יִשְׁפֹּט".

וּמִנַּיִן אֲפִלּוּ שְׁנַיִם? שֶׁנֶּאֱמַר: "אָז נִדְבְּרוּ יִרְאֵי ה' אִישׁ אֶל־רֵעֵהוּ וַיַּקְשֵׁב ה' וַיִּשְׁמָע" וְגוּ'.

וּמִנַּיִן אֲפִלּוּ אֶחָד? שֶׁנֶּאֱמַר: "בְּכָל הַמָּקוֹם אֲשֶׁר אַזְכִּיר אֶת־שְׁמִי אָבוֹא אֵלֶיךָ וּבֵרַכְתִּיךָ".

6 Rabbi Halafta of Kefar Hananiah says: Among ten who s
and work hard on Torah the Presence comes to rest, as it i

Ps. 82:1   said, *God stands in the congregation of God.*

And how do we know that the same is so even of five? For i

Amos 9:6   is said, *And He has founded his group upon the earth.*

And how do we know that this is so even of three? Since i

Ps. 82:1   is said, *And He judges among the judges.*

And how do we know that this is so even of two? Because i
is said, *Then they that feared the Lord spoke with on*

Mal. 3:16   *another, and the Lord hearkened and heard.*

And how do we know that this is so even of one? Since it i
said, *In every place where I record My name I will come t*

Ex. 20:24   *you and I will bless you.*

Let us begin with the proof-texts, each one of which i
meant to prove that the number in the preceding statement i
valid. Since, at first, Halafta speaks of ten people, with th
Presence of God among them, next it is proved that Go
comes to ten people. The verse refers to a "congregation," an
congregation, in the understanding of Judaism, requires ten
"Group" in the next clause is understood to mean five. Clea
is the proof that follows, since the smallest plural beyond th
dual of two is three. The verse refers to judges, in the plural
So God will come among three. Likewise, it is shown tha
God will come to two ("one another") and then that God wi
come even to "you," that is, to a single person. Here, again
Scripture reflects facts important to the proposition now adde
to Torah.

In the light of saying 5, we should not be surprised to fin
another reference to hard work on Torah. What we have i
saying 6 completes Nehunya's thought. Once we contras

avery to service to God, and misery to dignity, we proceed to
mphasize that God is with those who work on Torah. Why is
ais important? It is because of the use of the word "work" in
ae very context of the yoke of the Torah, on the one side, and
ard labor, on the other. So our chapter of sages' sayings
roceeds within a topical logic of its own. We go from the
aatter of sustaining our life through eating to sustaining our-
lves through working.

In each instance we draw the contrast between what
appens when Torah informs life and what it means when
"orah is absent. When there is no Torah, eating is consuming
ead sacrifices, and work is slavery. When there is Torah,
ating is to participate in the meal of the Lord, work is service
ɔ God. Halafta's saying then concludes this sequence of
houghts with the observation that Torah changes us, whether
s a community or as a single individual.

ז רַבִּי אֶלְעָזָר אִישׁ בַּרְתּוֹתָא אוֹמֵר: תֶּן לוֹ מִשֶּׁלּוֹ
שֶׁאַתָּה וְשֶׁלָּךְ שֶׁלּוֹ.
וְכֵן בְּדָוִד הוּא אוֹמֵר: "כִּי־מִמְּךָ הַכֹּל וּמִיָּדְךָ נָתַנּ
לָךְ."

Rabbi Eleazar of Bartota says: Give Him what is His, for you
and yours are His.
For so does it say about David, *For all things come of
You, and of Your own have we given You.*   I Chron. 29:14

Eleazar's saying contrasts with Akavyah's. How can both
ɔe right? Do we come from a mere putrid drop and go to a
ɔlace of dust and worms? Yes, we do. But what we are, and
vhatever we have, belong to God. Would Akavyah concur?
Df course, he would: "Before whom you are going to give a
ull account . . ." We are nothing, except that we belong to
Ɉod; and, for that reason, we are precious. What we again see
s the same balancing of opposites we noticed when we looked
ut the difference Torah makes in our life of work.

רַבִּי שִׁמְעוֹן אוֹמֵר: הַמְהַלֵּךְ בַּדֶּרֶךְ וְשׁוֹנֶה וּמַפְסִיק
מִמִּשְׁנָתוֹ, וְאוֹמֵר: מַה נָּאֶה אִילָן זֶה! וּמַה נָּאֶה נִיר
זֶה! — מַעֲלֶה עָלָיו הַכָּתוּב כְּאִלּוּ מִתְחַיֵּב בְּנַפְשׁוֹ.

ר רַבִּי דוֹסְתַּאי בַּר יַנַּאי מִשּׁוּם רַבִּי מֵאִיר אוֹמֵר: כָּל
הַשּׁוֹכֵחַ דָּבָר אֶחָד מִמִּשְׁנָתוֹ, מַעֲלֶה עָלָיו הַכָּתוּב
כְּאִלּוּ מִתְחַיֵּב בְּנַפְשׁוֹ, שֶׁנֶּאֱמַר: "רַק הִשָּׁמֶר לְךָ וּשְׁמֹר
נַפְשְׁךָ מְאֹד פֶּן־תִּשְׁכַּח אֶת־הַדְּבָרִים אֲשֶׁר־רָאוּ עֵינֶיךָ".
יָכוֹל אֲפִלּוּ תָקְפָה עָלָיו מִשְׁנָתוֹ? תַּלְמוּד לוֹמַר:
"וּפֶן־יָסוּרוּ מִלְּבָבְךָ כֹּל יְמֵי חַיֶּיךָ".
הָא אֵינוֹ מִתְחַיֵּב בְּנַפְשׁוֹ עַד שֶׁיֵּשֵׁב וִיסִירֵם מִלִּבּוֹ.

Rabbi Simeon says: He who is going along the way an(
repeating [his Torah tradition] but interrupts his repetitior
and says: How beautiful is that plowed field—Scriptur(
reckons it to him as if he has become liable for his life.

8 Rabbi Dosetai ben Rabbi Yannai, in the name of Rabb(
Meir, says: Whoever forgets a single thing from what h(
has learned—Scripture reckons it to him as if he ha
become liable for his life, as it is said, *Only take heed t(*
yourself and keep your soul diligently, lest you forget th(

Deut. 4:9 *words which your eyes saw.*
Is it possible that this is so even if his learning became to(
much for him? Scripture says, *Lest they depart from you*

Deut. 4:9 *heart all the days of your life.*
Thus he becomes liable for his life only when he will si'
down and actually remove [his learning] from his owr
heart.

Standing by itself, Simeon's saying means one thing. But
in the context of the statement of Dosetai ben Rabbi Yannai in
Meir's name, which follows, it means yet another. By itself,
Simeon tells us that repeating the words of Torah must go on
uninterrupted. We cannot allow our admiration even for the
greatness of God's creation to take our minds off the learning
of God's Torah. There can be no competition between creation

d revelation. Each has its place and its hour. "Give God
hat is God's" must mean give thanks for creation in its time,
ut give all due honor to Torah in its time. If the time is
evoted to Torah, then we must not take away from that time
nd speak of things other than Torah.

This is a stern message. It emphasizes that the beauty of
he tree, the beauty of a field one has worked to plow—the
creation of God, the creation of humanity—must not take our
minds away from the labor of Torah, which belongs both to
od and humanity. God created the tree, humanity plowed
he field, we as earnest students of Torah take God's creation
nd make it humanity's.

The use of the shared predicate, "reckons it to him as if
e has become liable for his life," links Dosetai's saying in
Meir's name to what is given to Simeon in the just-preceding
statement. There are two important sides to the saying.

We must work hard not to forget what we have learned,
s Hillel says, for in not adding, we lose what we have.

But the danger comes only when you make the effort to
orget what you know—and that is a very different thing.
How so? If, for example, you interrupt your study of Torah to
dmire something else, you deliberately remove yourself from
hat you are learning and give your heart to something else.

Accordingly, the rather ominous threat—if you ever
orget anything, you are lost—takes on a somewhat different
character. You yourself may cause forgetfulness. You may
deliberately remove from your mind the teachings of Torah
ou have mastered. That is when you become liable for your
ife.

What Simeon says therefore has to be read in light of
Meir's qualification of the adjoined saying. For Simeon tells
ou what you do to sit down and actually remove what you
know from your heart, deliberately and knowingly. In fact, of
course, there is no such thing as deliberate forgetfulness. By
definition, forgetting happens to us. If you remember to forget,
ou do so deliberately.

Obviously, beneath the surface is a set of ironies, phrased
n rather stark images. If, while studying Torah, you admire a
tree, you are worthy of death! It is an extreme statement. If,
by chance, you forget what you knew, you might as well drop

dead! This is an amazing sentence of death. So what comes a
the end is the key to everything that precedes. The sayings o
Simeon and Meir belong together and deliver a profoun
message about what it means to create ourselves, to form ou
own consciousness.

רַבִּי חֲנִינָא בֶּן דּוֹסָא אוֹמֵר:
כָּל שֶׁיִּרְאַת חֶטְאוֹ קוֹדֶמֶת לְחָכְמָתוֹ, חָכְמָתוֹ
מִתְקַיֶּמֶת.
וְכָל שֶׁחָכְמָתוֹ קוֹדֶמֶת לְיִרְאַת חֶטְאוֹ, אֵין חָכְמָתוֹ
מִתְקַיֶּמֶת.
הוּא הָיָה אוֹמֵר:
כָּל שֶׁמַּעֲשָׂיו מְרֻבִּין מֵחָכְמָתוֹ – חָכְמָתוֹ
מִתְקַיֶּמֶת.
וְכָל שֶׁחָכְמָתוֹ מְרֻבָּה מִמַּעֲשָׂיו – אֵין חָכְמָתוֹ
מִתְקַיֶּמֶת.

הוּא הָיָה אוֹמֵר:
כָּל שֶׁרוּחַ הַבְּרִיּוֹת נוֹחָה הֵימֶנּוּ – רוּחַ הַמָּקוֹם
נוֹחָה הֵימֶנּוּ.
וְכָל שֶׁאֵין רוּחַ הַבְּרִיּוֹת נוֹחָה הֵימֶנּוּ – אֵין רוּחַ
הַמָּקוֹם נוֹחָה הֵימֶנּוּ.
רַבִּי דוֹסָא בֶּן הַרְכִּינָס אוֹמֵר:
שֵׁנָה שֶׁלְשַׁחֲרִית,
וְיַיִן שֶׁלְצָהֳרַיִם,
וְשִׂיחַת הַיְלָדִים,
וִישִׁיבַת בָּתֵּי כְנֵסִיּוֹת שֶׁלְעַמֵּי הָאָרֶץ
מוֹצִיאִין אֶת הָאָדָם מִן הָעוֹלָם.

9 Rabbi Hanina ben Dosa says:
For anyone whose fear of sin takes precedence over his
wisdom, his wisdom will endure.
And for anyone whose wisdom takes precedence ove
his fear of sin, his wisdom will not endure.

He would say:
> Anyone whose deeds are more than his wisdom—his wisdom will endure.
> And anyone whose wisdom is more than his deeds—his wisdom will not endure.

0 He would say:
> Anyone from whom people take pleasure—the Omnipresent takes pleasure.
> And anyone from whom people do not take pleasure—the Omnipresent does not take pleasure.

Rabbi Dosa ben Harkinas says:
> Sleeping late in the morning,
> drinking wine at noon,
> chatting with children,
> and attending the synagogues of the ignorant
> drive a man out of the world.

Hanina introduces a new set of issues: the balance between learning and doing. Given the savage hyperbole of the preceding allegations (if you merely admire a tree, you are worthy of death), we should be glad for the relief of Hanina's irenic qualification of learning with wisdom, and of doing with wisdom. While Hanina in fact discussed fear of sin, deeds, and wisdom, the two contrasts lead to a third stage: giving people pleasure. Wisdom by itself is sufficient. There must be fear of sin (right attitude) and also practical deeds. These, moreover, must be so formed as to give pleasure to other people. So you cannot separate your learning of Torah from the life you lead. The one is the foundation of the other. The other gives meaning and purpose to the one. You learn in order to do, not merely in order to know. And what you do matters when it is for the benefit of other people.

We can now examine the full tension that the sages' stress on Torah imposes. On the one side, Torah learning represents the highest calling. If you learn Torah, you transform the world in which you live. You leave this world of suffering and deceit and enter a world in which hard work is labor in Torah, and in which authority is exercised by God. It would be easy to conclude that the sages propose to construct a fantasy world, a realm of their own making. Then we might imagine

that the sages speak of a private and special place for them
selves, dismissing the great plaza of Israel's common life
Hanina places limits on the matter when he says that the poin
of it all is to give pleasure to others. God loves us, if we brin
love to the people among whom we live. God responds to th
feelings of humanity.

In context, Dosa's saying is a valuable corrective. True
we give pleasure to others, but not this-worldly pleasure. Peopl
take pleasure in sleeping late, drinking wine, playing witl
children, attending synagogue worship in which no difficul
demands are made. It is a life of relaxation. We are not askec
to become more than we are—lazy, amiable, people who g
through motions without much understanding.

When we speak of pleasure, as Hanina does, this is no
what we mean. Apathy and laziness drive you out of th
world of Torah, the world of the balance among fear of sin
wisdom, deeds, the world in which God responds to our heart
and loves those who give pleasure. When we speak of pleasure
and joy, what we mean is not what others may mean: sloth
self-indulgence, the easy life. Placing Dosa's saying aftei
Hanina's serves as a powerful corrective.

Creation and Torah

We now have completed examination of the first full
segment of chapter three, the essay on the deep considerations
of life: who we are, what we can become, how Torah makes
the difference. The tensions inaugurated by Akavyah's terrible
vision of who we are, of Hananiah's awful notion of what we
are—these are resolved in the Torah-sayings that follow.
Accordingly, when we sustain our life through eating, when
we maintain ourselves and our families through hard labor,
we are able to transform what we are and do—eating into
sacrifice to God, hard work into labor in Torah. Then we
belong to God. Whatever we have is God's. Then we celebrate
what God has made—creation—and what God has given—
Torah—recognizing that what we owe to Torah is no less than
what we naturally owe as part of creation.

We cannot allow ourselves deliberately to desert study of
Torah, to forget what has been mastered. It is living by the
teaching of Torah that matters, not merely knowing what is in
it. That requires not wisdom alone, but fear of sin, deeds,

ing joy to others. But the joy of Torah is not indulgence.
at is the whole, cogent message of the ten sayings we have
countered. The first picture of chapter three is complete.

יא רַבִּי אֶלְעָזָר הַמּוֹדָעִי אוֹמֵר:
הַמְחַלֵּל אֶת הַקֳּדָשִׁים,
וְהַמְבַזֶּה אֶת הַמּוֹעֲדוֹת,
וְהַמַּלְבִּין פְּנֵי חֲבֵרוֹ בָּרַבִּים,
וְהַמֵּפֵר בְּרִיתוֹ שֶׁלְּאַבְרָהָם אָבִינוּ עָלָיו הַשָּׁלוֹ
וְהַמְגַלֶּה פָנִים בַּתּוֹרָה שֶׁלֹּא כַהֲלָכָה —
אַף עַל פִּי שֶׁיֵּשׁ בְּיָדוֹ תּוֹרָה וּמַעֲשִׂים טוֹבִים —
לוֹ חֵלֶק לָעוֹלָם הַבָּא.

Rabbi Eleazar the Modite says:
He who treats Holy Things as secular,
and he who despises the Appointed Times,
he who humiliates his companion in public,
he who removes the signs of the covenant of
   Abraham, our father (may he rest in peace),
and he who exposes aspects of the Torah not in
   accord with the law—
even though he has in hand learning in Torah and good
deeds, will have no share in the world to come.

Coming on the heels of Hanina ben Dosa's reminder that
ere are more important things than wisdom alone, Eleazar
e Modite's saying presents no surprises. Mere knowledge
ot only does not suffice, it also may lead people to think they
ay do things they should not do. Eleazar lists bad attitudes
d actions of several types.

First comes an attitude of disdain for religious require-
ents. We are supposed to preserve the status of Holy Things
d not to treat them as secular. "Holy Things" at the time
ferred to things consecrated for use in the Temple cult. If, as
highly likely, Eleazar lived after the destruction of the
emple, he means that if people declare an animal to be in the

Dimensions of Responsibility

status of Holy Things, that declaration must be honored. Ev
though, in fact, the animal will not be offered up (the alt
having been destroyed), still the person's pious deed (of sy
bolic consecration) demands respect.

Conforming

*Removing the mark of the covenant of Abraham refers to
an operation performed to make the male organ appear
uncircumcised. When and why did Jews in ancient times
do such a thing?*

*First, in the time of the Maccabees, around 175 B.C.E.,
some Jews exercised in the gymnasium, in the nude, like
other athletes. But the mark of circumcision set them
apart from the other athletes, while they wanted to look
like them: to be received as people of culture and standing,
which meant to be accepted as Greeks. Second, in the time
of Hadrian's repression of the Jewish revolt led by Bar
Kokhba, in the third and fourth decades of the second
century—the very time in which the sages at hand lived—
circumcision was forbidden. The Romans (for a time)
regarded circumcision as a mark of rebellion; someone
who circumcised a son also was likely to join the revolt or
start a new revolt. So as a measure of self-protection,
some Jews went so far as to undergo a painful operation
to remove the mark of circumcision. In Maccabean times,
it was an effort to conform and to assimilate. In Roman
times, it was a gesture of self-preservation.*

*Eleazar's stand in saying 11 is implacable. Nothing justi-
fies a Jew's attempt to be other than what he or she is. A
Jew may not conform to the ways of the world, if doing so
removes the marks of sanctification. A Jew may not deny
the fundamentals of the faith, pretend to be other than a
Jew, even in times of oppression and persecution. The lessons for our own day and age derive more from the time
of the Maccabees than from the age of Bar Kokhba and
Hadrian. But the lessons apply equally, whatever the circumstance: no surrender, no dissimulation, no compromise where compromise is degrading.*

Appointed Times, likewise, were the great festivals and
abbaths, observed in part in the Temple, in part at home.
Perhaps here too the context supplies the meaning. People
may have supposed that with the end of the Temple celebration
of such profoundly cultic festivals as Sukkot and Passover,
both observed through acts of sacrifice—killing an animal,
giving part to the altar-fires and roasting or boiling and eating
the other part—there was no need to observe the pilgrim
festivals, or any Appointed Times, any longer. Hanina says
that is just not so.

When Eleazar speaks of mistreating Holy Things, despising Appointed Times, and removing the marks of circumcision,
what sin does he describe? It is the sin of despair brought on
by the destruction of the Temple and its meaning for the
Jewish nation. The hope for the rebuilding must be kept fresh,
so if a beast is designated for the altar, that status must be
honored. Perhaps the Temple may be rebuilt today. Surely
the pilgrim festivals, involving cultic rites, and other holy
times and seasons, demand respect and observance. Israel, the
Jewish nation, endures, so the mark that a male is a Jew must
not be removed.

The second category of sins is not national but social. It
bears no relationship to the historical context, but rather to
the setting in the mind and imagination of the wise person.
The wise person knows more than others, has a more informed
mind. That gives him or her no right to lord it over others, or
to make those with lesser gifts of mind feel they are smaller in
any other way. It is, of course, a two-way street, since people
with limited abilities feel jealous of those with greater ones
and claim they have been slighted where the other party has
done no wrong. Still, the wise person must avoid any sort of
public deed to humiliate others.

The third category of sins is intellectual. The wise person
may not teach the Torah in ways that cause doubt or provoke
dissension.

So these sins—historical and national, social, and intellectual—must register, lest a sage think that mere knowledge,
mere good deeds, suffice. The wise person bears responsibilities
beyond wisdom and its requirements. These are national and
social as much as individual. The wise person is part of a
community and must use wisdom in the service of the nation.

Having reached that dimension of Eleazar's saying, we realiz
that he speaks about all of us.

ב רַבִּי יִשְׁמָעֵאל אוֹמֵר:
הֱוֵי קַל לָרֹאשׁ,
וְנוֹחַ לַתִּשְׁחֹרֶת,
וֶהֱוֵי מְקַבֵּל אֶת כָּל הָאָדָם בְּשִׂמְחָה.

12 Rabbi Ishmael says:
Be quick [in service] to a superior,
efficient in service [to the state],
and receive everybody with joy.

Ishmael's advice about duty to the state presents th
necessary complement to Eleazar's emphasis on remainin
ready for the Temple's restoration. Just as Eleazar tells peopl
not to despair, so Ishmael warns them not to expect too much
There has to be a balance between hope and endurance. So
together, the two sayings form a complete message for grievin
Israel. The Temple is no more. Do not take this to be the las
word of history. But do not try, yourself, to write the nex
word. Serve the state, if need be. But keep the faith. Accord
ingly, receive everybody with joy, not with sorrow and a lon
face. Under the circumstances of the age, such optimism wa
the highest form of heroism, the most courageous act of all
To defy the day, to keep up hope and encourage others throug
good cheer despite it all and against it all—that was Israel
task. It still is.

ג רַבִּי עֲקִיבָא אוֹמֵר: שְׂחוֹק וְקַלּוּת רֹאשׁ מַרְגִּילִין
לְעֶרְוָה.
מָסוֹרֶת סְיָג לַתּוֹרָה.
מַעְשְׂרוֹת סְיָג לָעֹשֶׁר.
נְדָרִים סְיָג לַפְּרִישׁוּת.
סְיָג לַחָכְמָה שְׁתִיקָה.

יד הוּא הָיָה אוֹמֵר:
חָבִיב אָדָם שֶׁנִּבְרָא בְצֶלֶם.
חִבָּה יְתֵרָה נוֹדַעַת לוֹ שֶׁנִּבְרָא בְצֶלֶם, שֶׁנֶּאֱמַר
"בְּצֶלֶם אֱלֹהִים עָשָׂה אֶת־הָאָדָם".
חֲבִיבִין יִשְׂרָאֵל, שֶׁנִּקְרְאוּ בָנִים לַמָּקוֹם.
חִבָּה יְתֵרָה נוֹדַעַת לָהֶם, שֶׁנִּקְרְאוּ בָנִים לַמָּקוֹם
שֶׁנֶּאֱמַר: "בָּנִים אַתֶּם לַה׳ אֱלֹהֵיכֶם".
חֲבִיבִין יִשְׂרָאֵל, שֶׁנִּתַּן לָהֶם כְּלִי חֶמְדָּה.
חִבָּה יְתֵרָה נוֹדַעַת לָהֶם, שֶׁנִּתַּן לָהֶם כְּלִי חֶמְדָּ
שֶׁבּוֹ נִבְרָא הָעוֹלָם, שֶׁנֶּאֱמַר: "כִּי לֶקַח טו
נָתַתִּי לָכֶם תּוֹרָתִי אַל־תַּעֲזֹבוּ".

טו הַכֹּל צָפוּי, וְהָרְשׁוּת נְתוּנָה.
וּבְטוֹב הָעוֹלָם נִדוֹן.
וְהַכֹּל לְפִי רֹב הַמַּעֲשֶׂה.

טז הוּא הָיָה אוֹמֵר: הַכֹּל נָתוּן בָּעֵרָבוֹן, וּמְצוּדָה פְרוּשָׂ
עַל כָּל הַחַיִּים.
הַחֲנוּת פְּתוּחָה,
וְהַחֶנְוָנִי מַקִּיף;
וְהַפִּנְקָס פָּתוּחַ,
וְהַיָּד כּוֹתֶבֶת.
וְכָל הָרוֹצֶה לִלְוֹת יָבֹא וְיִלְוֶה.
וְהַגַּבָּאִים מַחֲזִירִים תָּדִיר בְּכָל יוֹם, וְנִפְרָעִין מ
הָאָדָם מִדַּעְתּוֹ וְשֶׁלֹּא מִדַּעְתּוֹ.
וְיֵשׁ לָהֶם עַל מַה שֶׁיִּסְמֹכוּ.
וְהַדִּין דִּין אֱמֶת.
וְהַכֹּל מְתֻקָּן לַסְּעוּדָה.

13 Rabbi Akiba says: Laughter and lightheadedness turn lewd-
ness into a habit.
   Tradition is a fence for the Torah.

Tithes are a fence for wealth.
Vows are a fence for abstinence.
A fence for wisdom is silence.

14 He would say:
Precious is the human being, who was created in the
image [of God].
It was an act of still greater love that it was made known
to him that he was created in the image [of God], a
Gen. 9:6   it is said, *For in the image of God He made man.*
Precious are Israelites, who are called children to the
Omnipresent.
It was an act of still greater love that it was made known
to them that they were called children to the Omni
resent, as it is said, *You are the children of the Lord*
Deut. 14:1   *your God.*
Precious are Israelites, to whom was given the preciou
thing.
It was an act of still greater love that it was made known
to them that to them was given that precious thing
with which the world was made, as it is said, *For*
Prov. 4:2   *give you a good doctrine. Do not forsake My Torah*

15 Everything is foreseen; and free choice is given.
In goodness the world is judged.
And all is in accord with the abundance of deed[s].

16 He would say: All is handed over as a pledge, and a net i
cast over all the living.
The store is open,
the storekeeper gives credit;
the account book is open,
and the hand is writing.
Whoever wants to borrow may come and borrow.
The charity collectors go around every day and collec
from man whether he knows it or not.
And they have grounds for what they do.
And the judgment is a true judgment.
And everything is ready for the meal.

Akiba's collection breaks up into three main parts, each
making a single important point. The first set, at saying 13

esses that specific religious requirements underwrite our
ndamental principles. Nothing is unimportant when per-
ived in context. The second point, at saying 14, is that Israel
it only enjoys God's love but also enjoys knowledge of that
ct. The third point, at sayings 15–16, is that what we do
atters.

Taken all together the three points emphasize the impor-
nce on earth and in the sight of Heaven of everything we say
d do. Concerning these and the next several sayings, keep
mind their original context. It would be easy to forget it,
r they speak as much to us as they did to the ones who first
ard them so long ago. When you consider the impact of the
struction of the Temple, ending a mode of service nearly a
ousand years old, taking away one mark of God's enduring
lationship to Israel, you realize how important is Akiba's
atement. He emphasizes that Israel still matters. Moreover,
e know Israel matters because all about us are marks of
od's love for Israel, God's concern for each Jew under all
rcumstances. The setting, in the aftermath of the calamity of
e Temple destruction, imparts to these sayings a measure of
gency.

Akiba warns that the things you love require protection,
e doing of lesser things for the sake of other, more important
ings. He starts with a negative point. Lightheadedness, rid-
ule, disregard—these tend to turn bad behavior into a habit.
hen he speaks in positive terms. The Torah is protected
y tradition. Wealth is protected by separating tithes. Absti-
nce is protected by vows. These three statements constitute
aradoxes.

How so? Let us start with the middle one. When you
parate a tithe—a tenth of your wealth—and give it away,
e you richer or poorer? You give away wealth, so on the
irface you are poorer. But that is not really the case. Similarly,
oes tradition—the teachings of sages over the centuries—
reserve the written Torah, as is? No, that is not the case.
radition amplifies and augments the Torah. But by preserving
adition along with the written word, the sages protect the
orah. The tradition is a fence around the Torah. Finally, you
ke a vow not to drink wine or eat a certain food or to
ostain from some other desirable thing. (This is on the model
f the Nazirites of Numbers 6:1 ff.) The vow focuses your

attention on the thing you want, by making you unable to [
it. Paying attention to that from which you abstain by taki
a vow, you both miss what you will not have, while maki
sure you will not have it. In this setting the concluding sayi
indeed is apt. You think wisdom consists in saying wise thing
It is the very opposite: it consists in saying nothing. Silence
a protection, a fence around wisdom. These are piqua
observations.

The next set makes the same point three times. T
emphasis is not on how precious and beloved is humanit
and—within humanity—Israel. It is on something else: t
fact that we know it, that we have been made aware. It is o
thing to love, it is another to openly profess love. It is o
thing to be loved from afar. It is another thing to be lov
intimately, up close. The mark of caring is not merely th
you care, but that you show it.

The climax of the saying—the final statement—holds y
a deeper significance. The Torah imposes upon Israel a gre
many obligations and concerns. Let us take a simple a
obvious one: laws about what Jews eat and do not eat.
Akiba's hands, those laws, which look to be mere tribal cu
toms and ceremonies, become transformed into testimonies
God's love for Israel. God loves us so much that God ev
cares what we eat for breakfast. We know it, because G
told us so in the Torah. Once again, in the aftermath of t
Temple's loss, the sayings that underline how God's love st
manifests itself for Israel—in the Torah and its way of life
take on heightened meaning.

It seems to me the fifteenth and sixteenth sayings revol
around a single issue: how we are judged. God cares for us,
God pays heed to what we do. God foresees all, but we ma
choices. God judges the world in goodness but pays attenti
to the good we ourselves do. These principles, expressed
general terms in saying 15, are rephrased in very concrete on
in saying 16. Again, the delicate balance is between love a
judgment. The judgment expresses love. The love is uncon
tional. It is better, in Akiba's mind, for us to know that we a
loved and taken seriously, than for us to believe that what
do does not matter anyhow.

What a contrast to Akavyah's opening statement! For
issue, in this day, was not whether or not there was justice

e world, but whether or not what Israel could do made any
fference any longer. Atheism, in ancient times, was not to
:ny God's existence, but to deny that God cared—that there
justice. Given the calamity of the recent past, Israel needed
know that God yet cared. Akiba emphasizes the exquisitely
:licate balance maintained by each Jew—enjoying free choice
:fore a God who knows what will be; experiencing God's
:ep love for Israel in full awareness that God rewards good
nd punishes evil. Akiba therefore laid open the condition of
rael, the Jewish people, then and now.

יז רַבִּי אֶלְעָזָר בֶּן עֲזַרְיָה אוֹמֵר:

אִם אֵין תּוֹרָה, אֵין דֶּרֶךְ אֶרֶץ.

אִם אֵין דֶּרֶךְ אֶרֶץ, אֵין תּוֹרָה.

אִם אֵין חָכְמָה, אֵין יִרְאָה.

אִם אֵין יִרְאָה, אֵין חָכְמָה.

אִם אֵין בִּינָה, אֵין דַּעַת.

אִם אֵין דַּעַת, אֵין בִּינָה.

אִם אֵין קֶמַח, אֵין תּוֹרָה.

אִם אֵין תּוֹרָה, אֵין קֶמַח.

הוּא הָיָה אוֹמֵר: כָּל שֶׁחָכְמָתוֹ מְרֻבָּה מִמַּעֲשָׂיו –
לְמָה הוּא דוֹמֶה? לְאִילָן שֶׁעֲנָפָיו מְרֻבִּין וְשָׁרָשָׁיו
מוּעָטִין.

וְהָרוּחַ בָּאָה וְעוֹקַרְתּוּ וְהוֹפַכְתּוּ עַל פָּנָיו, שֶׁנֶּאֱמַר
"וְהָיָה כְּעַרְעָר בָּעֲרָבָה וְלֹא יִרְאֶה כִּי־יָבוֹא טוֹ
וְשָׁכַן חֲרֵרִים בַּמִּדְבָּר אֶרֶץ מְלֵחָה וְלֹא תֵשֵׁב".

אֲבָל כָּל שֶׁמַּעֲשָׂיו מְרֻבִּין מֵחָכְמָתוֹ – לְמָה הוּ
דוֹמֶה? לְאִילָן שֶׁעֲנָפָיו מוּעָטִין וְשָׁרָשָׁיו מְרֻבִּי
שֶׁאֲפִלּוּ כָּל הָרוּחוֹת שֶׁבָּעוֹלָם בָּאוֹת וְנוֹשְׁבוֹת בּ
אֵין מְזִיזוֹת אוֹתוֹ מִמְּקוֹמוֹ, שֶׁנֶּאֱמַר: "וְהָיָה כְּעֵ׳
שָׁתוּל עַל־מַיִם וְעַל־יוּבַל יְשַׁלַּח שָׁרָשָׁיו, וְלֹא יִרְאֶ
כִּי־יָבֹא חֹם, וְהָיָה עָלֵהוּ רַעֲנָן וּבִשְׁנַת בַּצֹּרֶת לֹ
יִדְאָג, וְלֹא יָמִישׁ מֵעֲשׂוֹת פֶּרִי".

17 Rabbi Eleazar ben Azariah says:
If there is no learning of Torah, there is no prope
conduct.
If there is no proper conduct, there is no learning i
Torah.
If there is no wisdom, there is no reverence.
If there is no reverence, there is no wisdom.
If there is no understanding, there is no knowledge.
If there is no knowledge, there is no understanding.
If there is no sustenance, there is no Torah learning.
If there is no Torah learning, there is no sustenance.
He would say: Anyone whose wisdom is greater than h
deeds—to what is he to be likened? To a tree with abundar
foliage but few roots.
When the winds come, they will uproot it and blow it dowr
as it is said, *He shall be like a tamarisk in the desert and sha*
not see when good comes, but shall inhabit the parche
Jer. 17:6 *places in the wilderness.*
But anyone whose deeds are greater than his wisdom—t
what is he likened? To a tree with little foliage but abundar
roots.
For even if all the winds in the world were to come an
blast at it, they will not move it from its place, as it is saic
He shall be as a tree planted by the waters, and that spread
out its roots by the river, and shall not fear when hea
comes, and his leaf shall be green, and shall not be carefu
in the year of drought, neither shall cease from yieldin,
Jer. 17:8 *fruit.*

Eleazar's sayings remind us of Hillel's, since they ar
constructed on the same principle. We relate one thing t
something else, so as to present the contrast. We might thin!
you have to choose one over the other. But no, Eleazar says
the one is the necessary condition that makes the other possible
Learning and proper conduct go together, wisdom and rever
ence, understanding with knowledge. Knowing facts is no
enough. Getting the hang of things is not sufficient. You hav
to know, but you have also to understand. You cannot lear
on an empty belly. You cannot find nourishment in foo
alone.

In all, Eleazar's mode of thought speaks first and foremost
ancient sages. So he contrasts the opposites of wisdom and
'oper conduct, wisdom and deeds. But what he says obviously
»plies now. We all know smart people who behave like asses,
ch people with nothing in their minds, learned fools. Follow-
g his mode of thought, moreover, we may add many exam-
es to his list: things people think contradict one another
hich, in fact, complete and so are necessary to one another.

Vhat We Are

*he Mishnah's masters clearly have a theory of the human
*rsonality in mind, what you might call a philosophy of
;ychology. They recognize the complexity of the human
*art, the contrasting urges that exist within each of us—
* "impulse" to do good, an "impulse" to do evil. Recog-
'zing that we are complex creatures, they ask us to
*nctify all of ourselves, not just the good part. That is,
*ey think that we can make good use even of the impulse
* do evil, "sanctify the evil impulse" by turning it into a
*otive to do good. It is natural to want to achieve fame,
* let that base motive lead you to study Torah, which can
've you distinction. It is normal to want to enter sexual
*lations. Let that motive lead you to love and devote
*urself to another person, thus creating a holy relation-
*ip. It is part of our nature to be hungry, but we can
*nctify the act of eating. In our hearts we want to be the
*nter of attention. We can gain attention for ourselves in
*od ways, through service and learning and setting a
*od public example. In all, we can sanctify the "impulse"
* do evil—because it turns out to be, also, the thing that
*pels us to act in positive and important ways in the
'orld.*

יח רַבִּי אֶלְעָזָר (בֶּן) חִסְמָא אוֹמֵר: קִנִּין וּפִתְחֵי נִדָּה – הֵ
הֵן גּוּפֵי הֲלָכוֹת.
תְּקוּפוֹת וְגִמַטְרִיָאוֹת – פַּרְפְּרָאוֹת לַחָכְמָה.

18 Rabbi Eleazar Hisma says: The laws of bird offerings and th absolution of vows—they are indeed the essentials of th Torah.
Calculations of the equinoxes and reckoning of the nume ical value of letters are the savories of wisdom.

Since Eleazar refers to two tractates of the Mishnah, l me briefly describe them. The first, on the laws of bird offe ings, is tractate Kinnim. The problem of this tractate is rath odd, and the tractate as we have it is practically incompr hensible. The subject is bird offerings brought by women i the aftermath of certain experiences of cultic uncleannes That is to say, if a woman undergoes a certain form of bodi excretion, she is not permitted to come to the Temple unt she has undergone a rite of purification. That is the rule Leviticus 12, for example, for the woman who has given birt
Two birds are involved. Each serves a different purpos One is a sin offering or purification offering (the Hebre word means both). The other is a whole offering. The form is killed and its blood is tossed on the altar. Some of the me of the bird goes to the priest, and some to the woman herse The latter is killed and its blood tossed on the altar, to be sur But the carcass of the bird itself then is burned up on the alta Neither the priest nor the woman receives any part of it. Th woman thus purchases two birds. She designates one for or purpose, the other for the second. Once the bird is designate for its particular purpose, it is subject to the rules governir sacrifices of that classification. Now comes the problem tractate Kinnim.
Catastrophe! The birds are confused. The woman do not know which is which. Such a thing can happen, with th Temple courtyard filled with women carrying doves. Or, wors catastrophe! Birds belonging to two women are confuse Now there are—as any mathematician can tell you—solutior to the problem. The tractate attempts to tell what these are. is, as I said, murderously difficult, and even if we had a clear and more credible text than we do, it would still be hard t figure out. So, it follows, Eleazar refers here to exceedingl complicated laws. The laws of bird offerings take up nearl

finite possibilities of doubt and confusion and show us how
ᵒ sort things out.

The laws for the absolution of vows (in tractate Nedarim)
ᵉly upon a sage's good judgment. You take a vow referring to
ᵒne set of conditions, which you think prevails. You suppose
ᵗhat facts are one way, on account of which—in anger,
ᵉrhaps—you take a vow. But you discover that the facts
ᵉere not at that time as you supposed them to be. So your
ᵒw to begin with was never valid, having been based upon
ᵗlse perception of the facts. If, on the other hand, things later
ᵗhange and turn out not as you expected, your original vow is
ᵗnaffected. A sage and only a sage can distinguish the one
ᵗtuation from the other.

So too with the rather recondite matters referred to as
ᵗhe savories of wisdom." Eleazar groups these things to say
ᵗhat the essentials of the Torah devolve upon your own judg-
ᵗent. What you read in the book is vital. How you reckon
ᵗith what you learn is what makes all the difference. So you
ᵗust be more than a mere master of the literal text. You have
ᵗ make sense of things. That means you must rely on your
ᵗbility to determine matters which, in the end, never can be
ᵗholly and finally settled. The essentials of the Torah some-
ᵗmes present us with doubts and confusion. Everything then
ᵉpends on our own judgment. That is the ultimate irony.
ᵗkavyah would have been amazed.

I said at the outset of this chapter that these sayings are
ᵗtributed to authorities who we think flourished in the period
ᵗom 70 to 130, that is, after the destruction of the Temple,
ᵗut before the war led by Bar Kokhba. But on the basis of the
ᵗyings themselves, could we have come to that conclusion? I
ᵗm inclined to think not.

The sayings speak to us, in particular, because they
ᵈddress the issues of *any* time of trouble and turbulence. The
ᵒwer of the chapter is that the sayings transcend the age,
ᵖeak to what is specific and concrete in the experience of any
ᵍe and any time in the aftermath of disaster. Indeed, all of
ᵗe Mishnah—therefore all of Judaism as we know it—comes
ᵒ full expression in the age beyond the calamities of the later

Enduring Despite Disaster

first and early second centuries, the end of the old Temple, tl decisive destruction of Jerusalem.

What then do people have to say to one another when thousand-year-old civilization, such as rested upon the Temp of Jerusalem, reaches utter destruction? What do you say you survive? The answer is before us in this poignant chapt and the one that follows. People recognize the transience ar uncertainty of life—but they live. They speak of the need maintain government—but are not taken in by it and do n sell out to it. They seek and find the lasting things, they re upon what endures: Torah, the study of Torah, the practice the teachings of Torah.

The sanctity of Israel, the Jewish people, once flow from the altar of the Lord in the Temple. But Israel, tl Jewish people, itself is holy and lives a holy life in the Ho Land of Israel. So the sages speak of how, despite it all ar against it all, Israel may continue to live that holy lif through Torah.

What more? Israel beyond disaster seeks the company Israel, the Jewish people. The survivors help one another endure. The people survived, the people goes forward: huma life is in community. God comes to ten, to five, to three— Israel assembled for God's name, for learning in Torah. Co stant devotion to Torah, even when the natural world beckon is the condition of Israel's life together—and life is with peopl

CHAPTER FOUR
WISDOM IN
THE AGE OF
RECONSTRUCTION

CHAPTER FOUR
WISDOM IN THE AGE OF RECONSTRUCTION

The intent of the framers of our tractate as a whole becomes clear in chapter four. Here are assembled sayings in the names of sages who flourished from about the middle of the second century to about the middle of the third (we cannot reckon the exact dates too closely). Since we discern very little effort to link what is assigned to groups of sages, we realize that what was important to the framers was to present a continuing chain of tradition, laid out in accord with the epochs of the Torah, from Sinai onward. Chapter two gives us two such epochs: first, from the masters before the destruction of the Temple to the great household of the patriarch, Judah; second, from the masters before the destruction to the sages afterward, via the spiritual household of Yohanan ben Zakkai. Chapter three presents sayings of authorities who flourished, in the main, from the time of Yohanan ben Zakkai's disciples to the earlier part of the second century, the time of the war of Bar Kokhba fought from 132 to 135. Chapter four is continuous with chapter three, in that the framers simply string together sayings of authorities who evidently lived at pretty much the same time. Thus, chapter three treats the later first and earlier second century; then chapter four takes up the later second and earlier third century.

If this view is sound, then the tractate as a whole was brought into being toward the middle of the third century. Avot took shape after the completion and adoption of the Mishnah as the constitution of the Jewish people in the Land of Israel (and in Babylonia). The purpose of the tractate then is to tell us the authority and standing of the sages of the Mishnah, and therefore of the Mishnah as a whole. Just as any good writer prepares the introduction of a book only after the book is written, so the framers of Avot introduced the Mishnah once the Mishnah had come into being. That is the implication of the arrangement of the sages in chronological groups. The important point of the group as a whole lie simply in the names cited and given sayings. I see no effort to formulate large compositions in this chapter, such as we have in chapters one and two, and also to some extent in chapter three. Rather, we review sayings of authorities, one by one.

Sayings Ancient and Recent

The chronology of this chapter presents an interesting fact. If the whole of chapter four was composed, as we believe, in the middle of the third century and includes sages from the early third century, then the proximity of the last authorities to the formulation of Avot itself is surprising. There is no large interval of time in which these sayings became "famous" or "venerated." Instead, the prestige of these teachers was so well established that within fifteen and certainly within fifty years of their speaking, the words already had gained currency.

This circumstance may also account for the fact that there are no large constructions or arrangements of sayings, since the selections were made from what might be considered "current" materials, as opposed to historical materials. And while the framers were practiced at arranging materials at a distance, it is always more difficult to arrange contemporary materials into elaborate or methodical constructions.

א בֶּן זוֹמָא אוֹמֵר:
אֵיזֶהוּ חָכָם? הַלוֹמֵד מִכָּל אָדָם, שֶׁנֶּאֱמַר: "מִכָּל-
מְלַמְּדַי הִשְׂכַּלְתִּי".

אֵיזֶהוּ גִבּוֹר? הַכּוֹבֵשׁ אֶת יִצְרוֹ, שֶׁנֶּאֱמַר: "ט
אֶרֶךְ אַפַּיִם מִגִּבּוֹר וּמֹשֵׁל בְּרוּחוֹ מִלֹּכֵד עִיר
אֵיזֶהוּ עָשִׁיר? הַשָּׂמֵחַ בְּחֶלְקוֹ, שֶׁנֶּאֱמַר: "יג
כַּפֶּיךָ כִּי תֹאכֵל אַשְׁרֶיךָ וְטוֹב לָךְ". אַשְׁרֶיךָ-
בָּעוֹלָם הַזֶּה, וְטוֹב לָךְ – לָעוֹלָם הַבָּא.
אֵיזֶהוּ מְכֻבָּד? הַמְכַבֵּד אֶת הַבְּרִיּוֹת, שֶׁנֶּאֱמַרו
"כִּי־מְכַבְּדַי אֲכַבֵּד וּבֹזַי יֵקָלּוּ".

Ben Zoma says:

Who is a sage? He who learns from everybody, as it is said, *From all my teachers I have gotten understanding.* Ps. 119:99

Who is strong? He who overcomes his desire, as it is said, *He who is slow to anger is better than the mighty, and he who rules his spirit than he who takes a city.* Prov. 16:32

Who is rich? He who is happy in what he has, as it is said, *When you eat the labor of your hands, happy will you be, and it will go well with you.* (Happy will Ps. 128:2
you be—in this world; *and it will go well with you*—in the world to come.)

Who is honored? He who honors everybody, as it is said, *For those who honor Me I shall honor, and they who despise Me will be treated as of no account.* I Sam. 2:30

As we have noticed, sages love to pair opposites and ow them belonging together. They speak through paradox. ιeir favored mode of seeking truth is through contrast and mparison. Accordingly, Ben Zoma says that everything is e opposite of what it seems. Most people think a wise person someone who knows everything. But, no, it is one who ιows that there is something to be learned from everybody.) a wise person knows his or her ignorance. The strong rson is not physically strong but self-controlled. The rich rson is not materially rich but satisfied with what is now in nd. The honored person is not someone who gets honor but meone who gives honor to others. Once more, these are

lessons worthy of the founders. Reading them, you know how
they saw the world and learned its truths.

בֶּן עַזַּאי אוֹמֵר: הֱוֵי רָץ לְמִצְוָה קַלָּה כְּבַחֲמוּרָה,
וּבוֹרֵחַ מִן הָעֲבֵרָה, שֶׁמִּצְוָה גוֹרֶרֶת מִצְוָה וַעֲבֵרָה
גוֹרֶרֶת עֲבֵרָה, שֶׁשְּׂכַר מִצְוָה מִצְוָה וּשְׂכַר עֲבֵרָה
עֲבֵרָה.

הוּא הָיָה אוֹמֵר: אַל תְּהִי בָז לְכָל אָדָם, וְאַל תְּהִי
מַפְלִיג לְכָל דָּבָר, שֶׁאֵין לָךְ אָדָם שֶׁאֵין לוֹ שָׁעָה וְאֵין
לָךְ דָּבָר שֶׁאֵין לוֹ מָקוֹם.

2 Ben Azzai says: Run after the most minor religious duty as
after the most important, and flee from transgression. For
doing one religious duty draws in its wake doing yet another,
and doing one transgression draws in its wake doing yet
another.
For the reward of doing a religious duty is a religious duty,
and the reward of doing a transgression is a transgression.

3 He would say: Do not despise anybody and do not treat
anything as unlikely. For you have no one who does not
have his time, and you have nothing which does not have
its place.

Ben Azzai emphasizes that everything matters. What you
do governs what you are going to do. If you get into the habit
of doing religious deeds, you are apt to do more of them; so
too, with doing what you should not do. We *are* what we do.
Then, it must follow, the rewards and punishments are clear.
His other point is that everybody matters. You must see yourself in someone else's place. You cannot treat anybody as of
no account. For somewhere, somehow, everybody does matter.
God made us all: we all have our moment of glory.

רַבִּי לְוִיטָס אִישׁ יַבְנֶה אוֹמֵר: מְאֹד מְאֹד הֱוֵי שְׁפַל
רוּחַ, שֶׁתִּקְוַת אֱנוֹשׁ רִמָּה.

Rabbi Levitas of Yavneh says: Be exceedingly humble, for the hope of humanity is the worm.

Life Eternal

Life does not end at the grave. There is life after death. Once in being, we do not cease to be. In a worldly sense, we live on in our distinctive contribution. What we give to others goes on with them, passes from them to others— just as we, for our part, receive the heritage of generations before us. And, in a transcendent sense, there is a certain logic that carries our life beyond the limits of this world. God whom we love, who gives us life in this world and takes it from us; God who lives and reigns forever, who is God from everlasting to everlasting—should that God have made each of us unique and individual for nothing? Are we no more than a blade of grass or a trembling flame, now here, now gone? Is our consciousness of God and of self a mere fantasy and figment of mind?

I phrase these convictions as questions, because to me the answers are self-evident—if beyond this-worldly demonstration. The very nature of our being and our consciousness, the very structure of our conviction and our capacity for caring—these point, in each of us, to something that endures beyond death, that evokes in our being the divine image in which we are made.

If we are in the image and after the likeness of God, then our being comes to an end when God's being comes to an end. Once created, each unique in his and her way, all of us express the image and endure in the likeness of God, who lives forever. If there is a God, if God's image of humanity is in the Torah, then these two facts generate a third: God rules forever, God made us in God's image, and we in the likeness and in the image endure, long after our bodies lie in the dust, and our world has ended in its worldly guise. To hope is to hope for life eternal: nothing less. And for a Jew it is a sin to despair.

Levitas's saying, on the surface, exhibits a certain bitter-
ness. We should be humble, because we die. Akavyah woul
not have been surprised by this saying. Yet a second glanc
tells us that Levitas uses a word we should not expect: hope
What hope is there in the worm, that is, in being buried in th
ground and turning into nothing? The word "hope" in th
context jars us and makes us wonder. For if the hope c
humanity is *not* the worm, then death is *not* the end, since th
worm is the last earthly creature to know us. And, for humar
ity, in the image of God, that cannot be the end. What Levita
must mean is that the true being of humanity begins at deatl
in life with God.

Reflect on how stark and extreme a view the sages too
of their age and their life! They spoke for all time because the
understood and spoke for their own day. Ultimate question
never change. The grave lies open before each of us. Death i
not the end for any one of us.

רַבִּי יוֹחָנָן בֶּן בְּרוֹקָא אוֹמֵר: כָּל הַמְחַלֵּל שֵׁם שָׁמַיִם
בַּסֵּתֶר, נִפְרָעִין מִמֶּנּוּ בַּגָּלוּי.
אֶחָד שׁוֹגֵג וְאֶחָד מֵזִיד בְּחִלּוּל הַשֵּׁם.

ה   רַבִּי יִשְׁמָעֵאל בְּנוֹ אוֹמֵר:
הַלּוֹמֵד עַל מְנָת לְלַמֵּד — מַסְפִּיקִין בְּיָדוֹ לִלְמוֹד
וּלְלַמֵּד.
וְהַלּוֹמֵד עַל מְנָת לַעֲשׂוֹת — מַסְפִּיקִין בְּיָדוֹ לִלְמוֹד
וּלְלַמֵּד, לִשְׁמוֹר וְלַעֲשׂוֹת.

Rabbi Yohanan ben Beroka says: Whoever secretly treat
the Name of Heaven as profane publicly pays the price.
All the same are the one who does so inadvertently and th
one who does so deliberately, when it comes to treatin
the Name of Heaven as profane.

5   Rabbi Ishmael, his son, says:
He who learns so as to teach—they give him a chanc
to learn and to teach.
He who learns so as to carry out his teachings—they giv
him a chance to learn, to teach, to keep, and to do.

The teachings of Yohanan and his son scarcely intersect, .cept in the basic mode of thought. Once more they set up a nsion between opposites. Then they make their point by solving that tension. The father contrasts doing something secret with doing it in public. Heaven has the power to ake public what is done on the sly. Therefore, if in secret ou treat disrespectfully things having to do with God, you ot only will be punished. Making the punishment fit the ime, Heaven treats the punishment as a public matter.

Yohanan's son, Ishmael, asks about the right motive of arning. If you want to learn and that defines your motive, ou gain just what you wanted—but no more. If your motive learning is to enable you to teach, you get to teach. If you ant to learn in order to carry out teachings, you get it all: arning, teaching, keeping, doing. Just as the punishment fits e crime for Yohanan, so the reward fits the good deed for hmael, his son. As I said in regard to the belief in justice, so say here: Would that it were so!

רַבִּי צָדוֹק אוֹמֵר: אַל תַּעֲשֵׂם עֲטָרָה לְהִתְגַּדֵּל בָּהֶן
וְלֹא קַרְדֹּם לַחְפּוֹר בָּהֶם.
וְכָךְ הָיָה הִלֵּל אוֹמֵר: וְדִשְׁתַּמַּשׁ בְּתָגָא חֲלָף.
הָא לָמַדְתָּ: כָּל הַנֶּהֱנֶה מִדִּבְרֵי תוֹרָה נוֹטֵל חַיָּיו מ
הָעוֹלָם.

Rabbi Zadok says: Do not make [Torah-teachings] a crown
in which to glorify yourself or a spade with which to dig.
(So did Hillel say: He who uses the crown perishes.)
Thus have you learned: Whoever derives worldly benefit
from teachings of Torah takes his life out of this world.

Zadok's saying follows Ishmael's because he too is inter-
ated in the motive for which people study the Torah. Just
ow we considered the right motive, which is to learn and to
o. The wrong motive in studying Torah is that you want to
ake a great name for yourself in the world. Zadok uses vivid
mages: a crown for your head, a spade for your digging.

There should be no worldly benefit at all. Yose will present different view in saying 6.

Zadok goes on by saying not to make "worldly use" learning in Torah. The point is the same as before: do t right thing for the right reason. If you study Torah in order become famous or respected, so that people will listen to y and make you feel important, you will be "removed from t world." You must study Torah in order to become like Go in order to know what you are supposed by God to do. If y study Torah for a base motive—not for what you will becom but for what your Torah study will do *for* you—then you w be punished. This notion of being "removed from the worl surely stands with the other statements the sages make indicate how they wish things would be. But, as we kno there are plenty of people who study Torah and are n changed by it, but who would like other people to listen them anyhow. And they are not "removed from the world God's justice, including God's punishment of people who (evil, does not always strike us as being present and effectiv though we wish it were. And when it does not, we have accept—despite it all, against it all—the things we know in t end must prevail.

רַבִּי יוֹסֵי אוֹמֵר:

כָּל הַמְכַבֵּד אֶת הַתּוֹרָה, גּוּפוֹ מְכֻבָּד עַל הַבְּרִיּוֹת.
וְכָל הַמְחַלֵּל אֶת הַתּוֹרָה, גּוּפוֹ מְחֻלָּל עַל הַבְּרִיּוֹת.

רַבִּי יִשְׁמָעֵאל בְּנוֹ אוֹמֵר:

הַחוֹשֵׂךְ עַצְמוֹ מִן הַדִּין, פּוֹרֵק מִמֶּנּוּ אֵיבָה וְגָזֵל וּשְׁבוּעַת שָׁוְא.
וְהַגַּס לִבּוֹ בְּהוֹרָאָה – שׁוֹטֶה, רָשָׁע וְגַס רוּחַ.

הוּא הָיָה אוֹמֵר:

אַל תְּהִי דָן יְחִידִי, שֶׁאֵין דָּן יְחִידִי אֶלָּא אֶחָד.
וְאַל תֹּאמַר: קַבְּלוּ דַעְתִּי! – שֶׁהֵן רַשָּׁאִין וְלֹא אַתָּה.

Rabbi Yose says:
Whoever honors the Torah himself is honored by
people.
And whoever disgraces the Torah himself is disgraced
by people.

Rabbi Ishmael, his son, says:
He who avoids serving as a judge breaks off the power
of enmity, robbery, and false swearing.
And he who is arrogant about making decisions is a
fool, evil, and prideful.

He would say:
Do not serve as a judge by yourself, for there is only
One who serves as a judge all alone.
And do not say: Accept my opinion—for they have the
choice in that matter, not you.

While you should not study Torah in order to gain a
own or a spade, still, there are rewards for study of the
orah and for paying honor to the Torah. Yose makes clear,
nce again, that there is a single just measure. If you honor
ie Torah, you are honored; and if you disgrace the Torah,
ou are disgraced. Still, in the society of Judaism, in which
orah finds honor pretty much everywhere, what Yose says
irns out to be a statement of facts. People generally honor
ie Torah, so if you honor it, you share in the honor naturally
oming to it; and if you disgrace it, no one will respect you.
Ishmael, Yose's son, speaks of the penalties incurred by
ssuming the position of a learned judge. Since a judge judges
ases by the law of the Torah, Ishmael says that enjoying
onor on account of such mastery of the Torah exacts its
rice as well. As a judge, you certainly are honored. But the
enalty is that some people, perhaps many, will hate you. Other
eople—some of them, unfortunately, evil—make choices for
ou, in your own court. As a judge you may become subject
), rather than responsible for, these choices. What honor,
ien, accrues from your honoring the Torah? Returning to
·hat Zadok says, the reward, whatever it is, comes in Heaven
nd not on earth.

Disgracing the Torah

How can someone "disgrace the Torah?" Let me give three examples. First, if a person is known as a learned Jew and cheats someone, that is a disgrace to the Torah which that person is supposed to know. People may reasonably suppose that the lesson of the Torah is how to cheat. Second, if a person asserts things he or she does not believe to be true merely because "the Torah" seems to teach them, that too disgraces the Torah. For the Torah stands for truth, and believing in it must not justify lying—even to oneself. So dissimulation—saying one thing in public and believing another thing in private, suppressing doubts and preserving a double standard of truth— these disgrace the Torah. They indicate to the individual (and the world) that the Torah is a source of disbelief. A third example of disgracing the Torah is pretending that people who do not know what they are talking about when they speak of Torah (or "Judaism") really do know. Jews must not tolerate the pretense of those who know less Torah than they ought, even in the expectation that these people will like us more. Tolerating ignorance is a disgrace to the Torah. Respect for the Torah means respect for learning in the Torah, for the truth of the statements of the Torah, and for the dignity and responsibility of the learning.

ט‎ רַבִּי יוֹנָתָן אוֹמֵר:

כָּל הַמְקַיֵּם אֶת הַתּוֹרָה מֵעֹנִי, סוֹפוֹ לְקַיְּמָה מֵעֹשֶׁר.

וְכָל הַמְבַטֵּל אֶת הַתּוֹרָה מֵעֹשֶׁר, סוֹפוֹ לְבַטְּלָה מֵעֹנִי.

9 Rabbi Jonathan says:
   Whoever keeps the Torah when poor will in the en
   keep it in wealth.

And whoever treats the Torah as nothing when he is
wealthy in the end will treat it as nothing in poverty.

Jonathan makes a lovely promise. But even in his own
ay people who waited for it to come true waited for a long
me. People who kept the Torah when poor may have hoped
ɔ become wealthy. But not many did. The threat is to
ɪe wealthy, who treat the Torah as nothing and then are in
anger of losing it all. I think people always understood—if
nplicitly—that these promises describe the way things should
e. They do not tell us how things really were or ever are. But
ɪose who master Torah are wealthy even if they lose worldly
ealth or if they remain poor. That is the real point.

י   רַבִּי מֵאִיר אוֹמֵר:

הֱוֵי מְמַעֵט בָּעֵסֶק, וַעֲסֹק בַּתוֹרָה.

וֶהֱוֵי שְׁפַל רוּחַ בִּפְנֵי כָל אָדָם.

וְאִם בָּטַלְתָּ מִן הַתּוֹרָה, יֵשׁ לָךְ בְּטֵלִים הַרְבֵּ

כְּנֶגְדָּךְ.

וְאִם עָמַלְתָּ בַתּוֹרָה, יֵשׁ לוֹ שָׂכָר הַרְבֵּה לִתֶּן לָ

0 Rabbi Meir says:
   Keep your business to a minimum and make your
   business Torah.
   And be humble before everybody.
   And if you treat the Torah as nothing, you will have
   many treating you as nothing.
   And if you have labored in Torah, [the Torah] has a
   great reward to give you.

Meir advises Jews to spend as much of their time as they
an in their study of the Torah. The study of Torah should
ecome their principal concern. Meir then repeats that those
gnorant enough to treat the Torah as nothing will end up
reated as nothing, but those who toil at learning in the Torah
vill gain a great reward.

These conventional points require restatement becaus
the point of Avot as a whole is expressed in every detail. Th
purpose of Avot, as we have now recognized, is to establis
the Torah as the principal source of reward, the sage as th
authoritative exponent of the Torah, and the ideal of study c
Torah as the dominant value of Jewish society.

א רַבִּי אֱלִיעֶזֶר בֶּן יַעֲקֹב אוֹמֵר:
הָעוֹשֶׂה מִצְוָה אַחַת, קוֹנֶה לוֹ פְּרַקְלִיט אֶחָד.
וְהָעוֹבֵר עֲבֵרָה אַחַת, קוֹנֶה לוֹ קַטֵּיגוֹר אֶחָד.
תְּשׁוּבָה וּמַעֲשִׂים טוֹבִים — כִּתְרִיס בִּפְנֵי הַפֻּרְעָנוּת.

11 Rabbi Eliezer ben Jacob says:
He who does even a single religious duty gets himse
a good advocate.
He who does even a single transgression gets himse
a powerful prosecutor.
Penitence and good deeds are like a shield again
punishment.

Here again is the emphasis on the importance of a sing
deed. Earlier, the sages insisted that every day should be live
as if it were one's last day. The upshot in joining these tw
ideas is to cultivate an alert attitude of mind. We have t
avoid dull routine. We must remember that everything count
all the time, everywhere. In the system of Judaism fostered b
the sages, with its stress on a lifelong commitment to som
few disciplines of heart, mind, and soul, the reason is clea
The sages understand the importance of rules and disciplin
But they also grasp their danger. If we keep no rules, our live
become wild and vacant. But if we only keep rules, we behav
as robots. To keep things in balance, then, the sages want u
to live by rules, at the same time realizing that each action is
decision; nothing is automatic.

רַבִּי יוֹחָנָן הַסַּנְדְּלָר אוֹמֵר:
כָּל כְּנֵסִיָּה שֶׁהִיא לְשֵׁם שָׁמַיִם, סוֹפָהּ לְהִתְקַיֵּם.
וְשֶׁאֵינָהּ לְשֵׁם שָׁמַיִם, אֵין סוֹפָהּ לְהִתְקַיֵּם.

אֵיזֶהוּ עָשִׁיר. הַשָּׂמֵחַ בְּחֶלְקוֹ.

WHO IS RICH? HE WHO IS HAPPY IN WHAT HE HAS.

יב רַבִּי אֶלְעָזָר בֶּן שַׁמּוּעַ אוֹמֵר:
יְהִי כְבוֹד תַּלְמִידָךְ חָבִיב עָלֶיךָ כְּשֶׁלָּךְ.
וּכְבוֹד חֲבֵרָךְ – כְּמוֹרָא רַבָּךְ.
וּמוֹרָא רַבָּךְ – כְּמוֹרָא שָׁמַיִם.

Rabbi Yohanan Hasandelar says:
 Any gathering which is for the sake of Heaven is going
 to endure.
 And any which is not for the sake of Heaven is not
 going to endure.

2 Rabbi Eleazar ben Shammua says:
 The honor owing to your disciple should be as precious
 to you as yours.
 And the honor owing to your companion should be
 like the reverence owing to your master.
 And the reverence owing to your master should be like
 the awe owing to Heaven.

People in community form parties. It is natural, just as
much as envy, jealousy, strife, and contention often form the
basis for human relationships in an unredeemed world. When
humanity is perfected or saved, there will be no sects, nor
need for orthodoxy or heresy. But here and now, people get
together. For what purpose? Yohanan makes the simple point
that if people get together for a worthy, that is, a holy purpose,
their meeting will produce lasting results. If not, it can serve
only to destroy.

His stress—for the sake of Heaven—hardly invites us to
identify our interests with God's. He means to say the opposite.
Only when we overcome our own concerns and meet to
advance the purposes of Heaven shall we accomplish anything.

We see once more that system of thinking through paradoxes and opposites that characterizes the sages who are the
founders. For when we do meet, quite naturally we assume it
is for a worthwhile purpose of our own. That is why we come
together to work with others, giving up something of our own
in order to get something for ourselves. Yohanan then demands
the opposite: get together with others not for selfish reasons

but for unselfish ones. He tells us to do the opposite of wha
we assume we mean to do in working with others. It is not fo
the (mere) common good, or for the sake of enlightened sel
interest, that Yohanan wants us to work together with other
It is for the sake of Heaven, without compromise, withou
qualification.

Eleazar's saying makes much the same point as Yohanan'
but he says things more directly. If you want honor for yoursel
you must give up honor, paying it over to others. You ge
what you relinquish. The world demands a fair exchange, no
self-aggrandizement. What you want for yourself, you owe t
those nearest at hand, your disciple (in the context of th
teacher-student relationship), your siblings, or your spouse o
children (in our more familiar context). What you want fo
yourself, you owe to your associates, coworkers, friends. Wha
you want for them, you owe to your master, your teache
And why? To bring down to earth, to everyone made in God'
image, what is owing to Heaven. So once more the name o
Heaven is invoked to govern good relationships on earth. W
meet for Heaven's sake. We relate to others on the model o
our way of reaching Heaven.

ג. רַבִּי יְהוּדָה אוֹמֵר: הֱוֵי זָהִיר בַּתַּלְמוּד, שֶׁשִּׁגְגַת תַּלְמוּד
עוֹלָה זָדוֹן.

13 Rabbi Judah says: Be meticulous in learning, for error i
learning leads to deliberate [violation of the Torah].

We know full well that learning is important because
leads to deeds. Thinking matters because it shapes actior
Deeds define us. Judah's point is just that: everything matter
in mind, so learn carefully and critically, because what is i
mind is what ends up in deed.

רַבִּי שִׁמְעוֹן אוֹמֵר: שְׁלֹשָׁה כְתָרִים הֵם:

כֶּתֶר תּוֹרָה,
וְכֶתֶר כְּהֻנָּה,
וְכֶתֶר מַלְכוּת —
וְכֶתֶר שֵׁם טוֹב עוֹלֶה עַל גַּבֵּיהֶן.

Rabbi Simeon says: There are three crowns—
    The crown of Torah,
    the crown of priesthood,
    and the crown of sovereignty—
but the crown of a good name transcends them all.

In the sages' imagination, Jewish society recognizes three estates: the sages, the priests, and the patriarchal ruler. Simeon announces there are three crowns, representing the estates of learning, service, and power. But Simeon then contradicts his opening statement. While there are supposed to be three crowns, in fact there is a fourth which rests outside and above the estates altogether. It is the crown of a good name, of attaining through good deeds and a right attitude the respect of the society at large. There is a real paradox here. We should have expected to find Torah at the top. Yet it is not.

The three crowns really do not matter as much as the nobility of the soul and the spirit. The things people do to distinguish themselves, whether through use of their mind, or through the claim of genealogy and breeding, or through the exercise of lordship over other people, do not really separate people from one another. To wear a real crown of distinction, attain the respect of society. But this must be done under all circumstances, not only in school, synagogue, profession, or center of government. So those who think they gain a crown through the position they hold, err.

יד רַבִּי נְהוֹרַאי אוֹמֵר: הֱוֵי גוֹלֶה לִמְקוֹם תּוֹרָה, וְאַל
תֹּאמַר שֶׁהִיא תָבוֹא אַחֲרֶיךָ, שֶׁחֲבֵרֶיךָ יְקַיְּמוּהָ בְיָדֶךָ.
וְאֶל־בִּינָתְךָ אַל־תִּשָּׁעֵן.

14 Rabbi Nehorai says: Go into exile to a place of Torah, and do not suppose that it will come to you. For your companion-disciples will make it solid in your hand.
And on your own understanding [alone] do not rely.

Learning, we suppose, is something we do all by ourselves. It takes place in our minds—by definition, therefore, in isolation from others. That self-evident proposition is all wrong, Nehorai says. Learning is social, never private. We have to go where Torah is, where great sages locate themselves. Torah is not an inheritance. It will not come looking for us. Where Torah is, there we find the best teachers of all, companions who are also students. We learn Torah more through conversation with them than through passive listening to teachers. Above all, we cannot depend on our own understanding, that is, our own theory of things. Individuals all too often create fantasy-worlds. Life is with people, in community.

טו   רַבִּי יַנַּאי אוֹמֵר: אֵין בְּיָדֵינוּ לֹא מִשַּׁלְוַת הָרְשָׁעִים
וְאַף לֹא מִיִּסּוּרֵי הַצַּדִּיקִים.

15 Rabbi Yannai says: We do not have in hand [an explanation] either for the prosperity of the wicked or for the suffering of the righteous.

Things should make sense, and we know what sense they should make. The good should prosper; the wicked should suffer. Yannai points out that things really are often the opposite. We cannot explain. The sages win our confidence through such simple honesty. Yet Yannai holds out an expectation: the explanation may not be "in hand"; this does not mean that it does not exist.

רַבִּי מַתְיָא בֶּן חָרָשׁ אוֹמֵר:
הֱוֵי מַקְדִּים בִּשְׁלוֹם כָּל אָדָם,
וֶהֱוֵי זָנָב לָאֲרָיוֹת,
וְאַל תְּהִי רֹאשׁ לַשׁוּעָלִים.

Rabbi Mattiah ben Heresh says:
    Greet everybody first,
    and be a tail to lions;
    but do not be a head of foxes.

Mattiah gives sage advice. Many of the sayings in Avot
•ertain to special situations. This teaching applies everywhere
ll the time. First, he says, do not hang back and wait for
•thers to recognize and greet you—that is, to give something
f themselves. Take the first step: greet others. It is an act of
isk, of humility, since you may be ignored or put down. So
•e it: still, greet the other party first, make the connection,
reak the barrier.

Second, Mattiah tells us to seek greatness beyond self,
ather than for self. You never learn if you do not listen. You
ever find a model of something more than yourself if you
pend your time among people less than yourself. So, he says,
: is better to be a tail to lions, that is, to accept a lesser
•osition among greater people, than to be a head of foxes,
hat is, to be the best of a less distinguished crowd. This too is
tern, but apt.

When we analyze the sort of person Mattiah wishes Israel
o produce, we see he seeks the kind of inner strength, confi-
ence, good will for others, humility for ourselves, that can
:ad to greatness.

Yet the majority will be able to endure in the company of
his sort of great person, whose greatness consists in the
pposite of puffery. The one who does not hang back, but
reets others first, takes the lesser role in the transaction. The
ne who accepts a lower status in a distinguished group, rather
han seeking to dominate mediocre crowds, again takes the
:sser role in the transaction. The greatness requires making
pace for others. Once more, therefore, sages recognize that
hings are the opposite of what they seem.

טז רַבִּי יַעֲקֹב אוֹמֵר: הָעוֹלָם הַזֶּה דּוֹמֶה לַפְּרוֹזְדוֹר בִּפְנֵי
הָעוֹלָם הַבָּא.
הַתְקֵן עַצְמְךָ בַּפְּרוֹזְדוֹר, כְּדֵי שֶׁתִּכָּנֵס לַטְּרַקְלִין.

ז' הוּא הָיָה אוֹמֵר:
יָפָה שָׁעָה אַחַת בִּתְשׁוּבָה וּמַעֲשִׂים טוֹבִים בָּעוֹלָם
הַזֶּה מִכָּל חַיֵּי הָעוֹלָם הַבָּא.
וְיָפָה שָׁעָה אַחַת שֶׁלְּקוֹרַת רוּחַ בָּעוֹלָם הַבָּא
מִכָּל חַיֵּי הָעוֹלָם הַזֶּה.

16 Rabbi Jacob says: This world is like an antechamber before
the world to come.
Get ready in the antechamber, so that you can go into the
great hall.

17 He would say:
Better is a single moment spent in penitence and good
deeds in this world than the whole of the world to
come.
And better is a single moment of inner peace in the
world to come than the whole of a lifetime spent in
this world.

Jacob tells us to live a life of preparation, stressing the
importance of what we do, the conviction that our deeds bear
consequences. His contrasts then yield the further judgment
that penitence and good deeds in this world outweigh whatever
is happening in the age for which we prepare: death and
beyond. As if that paradox did not suffice, he further promises
us remission and hope for a life at rest in the world to come.
The consequence, for the good life, seems to me self-evident: a
life of mindfulness, reflection, caring. The deeper outcome
will assure each person of the importance of what he or she
does. That conviction, to be sure, provides the basis for all
else, and is taken as axiomatic.

But it strikes me as paramount in an age, after all, in
which Jews were last and least. For Rabbi Jacob speaks to
Israel, defeated in its last great wars, deprived of its central
modes of cult and rite, wandering in search of a new center for
its national life. The defeated *people* is all that had survived.
Its own small affairs defined all that it controlled. These things,
then, were made to matter most of all.

The lessons of the founders astonish us in their indifference
ɔ appeals to the survival and endurance of the nation, in their
ɪilure to focus upon what is owed to the common good, and
ow to regain what was lost. Jacob speaks to individuals,
ɔrming a community before God, individuals who live and
ho die, and who therefore need to be taught how to live so as
ɔ accept death. These are the critical questions of life, so far
ɪ the sages are concerned. That is why, long after their own
ay, the sages speak so loudly and clearly to us. True, we
ame the issues of our life in different pictures, so "ante-
ɪamber" and "world to come," "penitence and good deeds,"
ɪay require some thoughtful translation. But the message
ɪmains. It must, because it is all there is. The survivors then
ɪeak to the survivors now.

יח   רַבִּי שִׁמְעוֹן בֶּן אֶלְעָזָר אוֹמֵר:
אַל תְּרַצֶּה אֶת חֲבֵרָךְ בְּשָׁעַת כַּעֲסוֹ,
וְאַל תְּנַחֲמֶנּוּ בְּשָׁעָה שֶׁמֵּתוֹ מֻטָּל לְפָנָיו,
וְאַל תִּשְׁאַל לוֹ בְּשָׁעַת נִדְרוֹ,
וְאַל תִּשְׁתַּדֵּל לִרְאוֹתוֹ בְּשָׁעַת קַלְקָלָתוֹ.

8   Rabbi Simeon ben Eleazar says:
Do not try to make amends with your fellow when he is
angry,
or comfort him when the corpse of his beloved is lying
before him,
or seek to find absolution for him at the moment at
which he takes a vow,
or attempt to see him when he is humiliated.

Simeon ben Eleazar's advice presents commonplaces,
ɔod sense framed out of the union of opposites. What amazes
ɪ is that these commonplaces not only must be said, but
ɪrike us as very wise when we hear them. Simeon's advice is
ɔ accept the situation, not to try to change it until the situation
self changes, as it will. So do not confront emotion, absorb
, stand aside, allow it to pass, and then deal with the other

party. When dealing is not possible, do nothing. When some thing can be done, go ahead. All of this is teased out of sequence of opposites: making amends *vs.* anger, comfort *v* grief, regret *vs.* rashness, confrontation *vs.* withdrawal. Onc we recognize *how* Simeon thinks, we of course may compos lists of things to avoid at the wrong time and to do at the righ time. It is good timing that resolves the tensions set up amon these several opposites. Reflecting on what is timely allows t to think just as Simeon does.

Their World and Ours

I believe that the holy writings of Judaism of the first and second centuries demand our attention because we live in that same situation in which, to begin with, lived the sages who wrote the Mishnah in our hands today. Let me be blunt. They were survivors, and so are we. They witnessed the end of a mode of Judaism that had endured for a thousand years. We who look back upon the murder of nearly six million Jews in Europe, we who see the mortal peril in which three million Jews in the State of Israel live out their lives—we too see a world of awful possibilities, many of them realized. So when we hear the sages speak as they do, we have to remember that they knew what we know: a life of tragedy, a world of evil, an age of mass destruction, a time of chaos and disorder.

When they tell us about living life in preparation for a life to come, living a life of penitence and good deeds, they speak not out of some rosy heaven, not out of some academic Eden. Theirs was a world of despair and destruction. If then they could frame the issues of life as they did, so too can we hear their message: a life of goodness in a world of evil; a life of reconciliation in a world of destruction; a life to affirm the abiding value of decency in a world contemptuous of reason and of love. The survivors then have this to say to the survivors now: for a Jew, it is a sin to despair.

יט שְׁמוּאֵל הַקָּטָן אוֹמֵר: "בִּנְפֹל אוֹיִבְךָ אַל־תִּשְׂמָח
וּבִכָּשְׁלוֹ אַל־יָגֵל לִבֶּךָ, פֶּן־יִרְאֶה ה' וְרַע בְּעֵינָיו וְהֵשִׁיב
מֵעָלָיו אַפּוֹ".

9 Samuel the Younger says: *Rejoice not when your enemy falls, and let not your heart be glad when he is overthrown, lest the Lord see it and it displease Him, and He turn away His wrath from him.*

Prov. 24:17

This "saying" may surprise you. The sages of Avot stand in a long tradition of wisdom. True, they contribute to it. But sage defines wisdom as the power to learn from others. Accordingly, Samuel the Younger's saying simply cites a wise statement from Proverbs, one of the Torah's main treasuries of wisdom. Samuel teaches both by *what* he has selected, and also by *how* he provides an example. The wise person does not discover the sun every morning or invent the wheel every night. Wisdom derives from learning and preserving the insight that comes to us as the wisdom of the past.

כ אֱלִישָׁע בֶּן אֲבוּיָה אוֹמֵר:
הַלּוֹמֵד יֶלֶד — לְמָה הוּא דוֹמֶה? לִדְיוֹ כְתוּבָה עַל
נְיָר חָדָשׁ.
וְהַלּוֹמֵד זָקֵן — לְמָה הוּא דוֹמֶה? לִדְיוֹ כְתוּב
עַל נְיָר מָחוּק.
רַבִּי יוֹסֵי בַּר יְהוּדָה אִישׁ כְּפַר הַבַּבְלִי אוֹמֵר:
הַלּוֹמֵד מִן הַקְּטַנִּים — לְמָה הוּא דוֹמֶה? לְאוֹכֵל
עֲנָבִים קֵהוֹת וְשׁוֹתֶה יַיִן מִגִּתּוֹ.
וְהַלּוֹמֵד מִן הַזְּקֵנִים — לְמָה הוּא דוֹמֶה? לְאוֹכֵל
עֲנָבִים בְּשׁוּלוֹת וְשׁוֹתֶה יַיִן יָשָׁן.
רַבִּי אוֹמֵר: אַל תִּסְתַּכֵּל בַּקַּנְקַן, אֶלָּא בַּמֶּה שֶׁיֵּשׁ בּוֹ
יֵשׁ קַנְקַן חָדָשׁ מָלֵא יָשָׁן, וְיָשָׁן שֶׁאֲפִלּוּ חָדָשׁ אֵין בּוֹ.

20 Elisha ben Avuyah says:

He who learns when a child—what is he like? Ink pu
down on a clean piece of paper.
And he who learns when an old man—what is he like
Ink put down on a paper full of erasures.

Rabbi Yose ben Rabbi Judah of Kefar Habavli says:

He who learns from children—what is he like? On
who eats sour grapes and drinks fresh wine.
And he who learns from an old man—what is he like
He who eats ripe grapes and drinks vintage wine.

Rabbi says: Do not look at the bottle but at what is in it.
You can have a new bottle full of old wine, and an ol
bottle which has not got even new wine.

Elisha and Yose have opposed, but complementary views
Elisha says you should learn when you are a child. Yose say
you should not learn from a child. The idea is the same. The
best way is to begin your education when you are young
because learning is cumulative, and one lesson leads to another
deeper one.

Rabbi's saying is separate, but it relates because it carrie
forward the use of the metaphor of wine introduced by Yose
Rabbi's point is that we should not be deceived by appearances
In so stating, Rabbi of course puts into words precisely tha
mode of inquiry—looking beyond the surface—we have many
times observed in Avot.

כא רַבִּי אֱלִיעֶזֶר הַקַּפָּר אוֹמֵר: הַקִּנְאָה וְהַתַּאֲוָה וְהַכָּבוֹד
מוֹצִיאִין אֶת הָאָדָם מִן הָעוֹלָם.

כב הוּא הָיָה אוֹמֵר:
הַיִּלּוֹדִים לָמוּת, וְהַמֵּתִים לְהַחֲיוֹת.
וְהַחַיִּים לִדּוֹן – לֵידַע לְהוֹדִיעַ וּלְהִוָּדַע
שֶׁהוּא אֵל,
הוּא הַיּוֹצֵר,
הוּא הַבּוֹרֵא,
הוּא הַמֵּבִין,

הוּא הַדַּיָּן,

הוּא עֵד,

הוּא בַּעַל דִּין,

וְהוּא עָתִיד לָדוּן.

בָּרוּךְ הוּא, שֶׁאֵין לְפָנָיו לֹא עַוְלָה, וְלֹא שִׁכְחָה, וְלֹא

מַשּׂוֹא פָנִים, וְלֹא מִקַּח שֹׁחַד, שֶׁהַכֹּל שֶׁלּוֹ.

וְדַע, שֶׁהַכֹּל לְפִי הַחֶשְׁבּוֹן.

וְאַל יַבְטִיחֲךָ יִצְרְךָ שֶׁהַשְּׁאוֹל בֵּית מָנוֹס לָךְ.

שֶׁעַל כָּרְחָךְ אַתָּה נוֹצָר,

וְעַל כָּרְחָךְ אַתָּה נוֹלָד,

וְעַל כָּרְחָךְ אַתָּה חַי,

וְעַל כָּרְחָךְ אַתָּה מֵת,

וְעַל כָּרְחָךְ אַתָּה עָתִיד לִתֵּן דִּין וְחֶשְׁבּוֹן לִפְנֵי

מֶלֶךְ מַלְכֵי הַמְּלָכִים הַקָּדוֹשׁ בָּרוּךְ הוּא.

21 Rabbi Eliezer Hakkappar says: Jealousy, lust, and ambition drive a person out of this world.

22 He would say:
Those who are born are [destined] to die, and those who die are [destined] for resurrection.
And the living are [destined] to be judged—so as to know, to make known, and to confirm, that
He is God,
He is the One who forms,
He is the One who creates,
He is the One who understands,
He is the One who judges,
He is the One who gives evidence,
He is the One who brings suit,
and He is the One who is going to make the ultimate judgment.
Blessed be He, for before Him are not guile, forgetfulness, respect for persons, bribe taking, for everything is His.
And know that everything is subject to reckoning.
And do not let your evil impulse persuade you that Sheol is a place of refuge for you.

For despite your wishes you were formed,
despite your wishes do you live,
despite your wishes do you die,
and despite your wishes are you going to give a full
  accounting before the King of kings of kings, the
  Holy One, the blessed.

Eliezer Hakkappar, who lived in the earlier part of the third century, brings to a close the long chain of sayings of second- and third-century sages. Chapters three and four cover the ground of the masters who made the Mishnah as we know it and of their first successors and heirs. We cannot be surprised that at the conclusion and climax is a prayer, a statement of praise of God. We are who we are: in God's image. We give account to God. The deep themes of our tractate—birth, life, death, judgment before God—flow together and form a moving poem. Eliezer lists twelve traits of God: eight positive ones, four negative ones. Then he ends with an implacable and uncompromising judgment of the human condition: we have no choice but to be. We have no alternative but to give a full accounting of what we are. The unstated conclusion, I think, must be: *So let us get on with the work.* The rest of the Mishnah, to which this tractate serves as a prologue (composed at the end, for that purpose, to be sure), then describes the work.

The first message of the survivors of the catastrophe of the destruction of Jerusalem and the end of the Temple cult was a message of Torah. The first message of the survivors of the last hope, when the Temple mountain was plowed over by the Romans and the doors of Jerusalem locked against the Jews, is before us: So take up the work. What a paradox! For what work was left to do, when the old ways in which Israel served God no longer lay open? The paradoxical mode of thought that turns taking into giving, opposites into one another, led our sages to look for the opposite in the thing they saw: Despair? Then hope! Destruction? Then build! The end of all things? Then renew them! No further means of working for God? Then take up the task!

TENS, SEVENS, FOURS, TWOS, AND THREES
Creation and Redemption,
Individual and Society

CHAPTER FIVE
TENS, SEVENS, FOURS, TWOS, AND THREES
Creation and Redemption,
Individual and Society

In the fifth chapter of Avot we have a sequence of lists of things, each in its proper classification, all entries carefully counted. It therefore is an exercise in the simplification and arrangement of facts. What the sages try to do here is to take up a bewildering complexity of unrelated facts and show the order and meaning that inhere in them. The world of experience presents to the sages massive bodies of information, whole carloads of data. What they try to do now is to draw together the world of religious teaching, of Torah, and the world of experience, and to organize all the fragments, all the disjointed facts, into a few well-put-together constructions.

The numbers by themselves—particularly seven and ten—stand for things in Scripture. In the Bible, seven, the number of the known planets, is held by biblical scholars to refer to God's intervention: "look to Heaven." God made the world in seven days; there are seven weeks between Passover and Shavuot; the days of awe, Rosh Hashanah and Yom Kippur, fall in the seventh month; in the seventh year, the fields lie fallow; the jubilee comes seven times seven years plus one year. The ten stands for the number of fingers on our hands—and in nature, only on human hands. The Bible knows ten plagues, ten commandments, ten generations from Adam to Noah, ten generations from Noah to Abraham, the search for ten righteous men in Sodom, ten in a quorum, and the like. Now the Bible knows other important numbers, such as twelve, forty, and so on. But the point is clear. The numbers selected in this chapter are not random, and they also are more than merely aids for memorization.

There may be a thousand thousand types of people, but the sages declare there are four types. There may be any number of groups of tens, or sevens, or fives, or fours. But the sages select the important groups and show the main classifications of things. They execute a kind of natural philosophy of the meaning of Israel's life. This work of arrangement and classification shows the orderliness which lies behind the diverse facets of Torah and of life itself. The sages thus impart the experience of completeness and order. They make sense of all that has gone before by showing the kinds of things that exist, how these may be added up and easily learned. This process of analysis shows the underlying pattern and demonstrates that we can, after all, master and make sense of everything there is to be known, all creation, the whole Torah.

When we draw together the topics of the several compositions in this chapter, we notice something else quite impressive. The lists of tens—sayings 1–6—speak of (1) the creation of the world, (2) the history of humanity from Adam to Noah, then (3) from Noah to Abraham, then (4) the life of Abraham, then (5) ten wonders, (6) ten blows, (7) ten trials of Israel in Egypt and of its redemption at the Sea, and (8) the wandering in the wilderness. Then come (9) ten wonders done in the Temple, matched by (10) ten things created on the eve of the Sabbath at twilight. Thus we end on the theme with which we began. These lists of ten review the entire sacred history of Israel, the Jewish nation, from creation, through the suffering in Egyptian slavery and redemption, the wandering, then the climax of building the Temple. So much for the history of Israel—all captured in the orderly pattern of *ten*.

The sevens—sayings 7–9—proceed to traits of individuals and the possibilities of ordinary life, meaning famine and plenty, poverty and wealth.

There is a transitional unit—sayings 9–15—emphasizing the same kinds of things—pestilence and suffering—all using the number four. But the rest of the lists of four go from

HE WHO BRINGS MERIT TO THE COMMUNITY NEVER CAUSES SIN.

atural calamities as they affect communities to a quite separate
matter: types of individuals.

From four we move on to two—sayings 16–18—and from
considering individuals, we proceed to relationships between
and among individuals, a trilogy of twos. We end up—saying
19—with a final list of three things, now contrasting Abraham
the founder of Israel with Balaam the prophet of the gentiles:
generosity, modesty and humility against pride, arrogance,
and a grudging spirit.

So the composer of the chapter has ended the lessons of
the founders with a complete and encompassing portrait of
Israel: (1) its history, (2) its life together both in community
and (3) between individuals. At the end comes the climax: the
virtues of the founder of it all, Abraham. What we now expect
at sayings 20–23, on the model of the conclusion of chapter
four, will be some final expressions of prayer and exhortation.
The work is complete. At the end, I add my view of what it
can mean to us.

א בַּעֲשָׂרָה מַאֲמָרוֹת נִבְרָא הָעוֹלָם. וּמַה תַּלְמוּד לוֹמַר
וַהֲלֹא בְמַאֲמָר אֶחָד יָכוֹל לְהִבָּרֹאות?
אֶלָּא לְהִפָּרַע מִן הָרְשָׁעִים, שֶׁמְּאַבְּדִין אֶת הָעוֹלָם
שֶׁנִּבְרָא בַעֲשָׂרָה מַאֲמָרוֹת.
וְלָתֵן שָׂכָר טוֹב לַצַּדִּיקִים, שֶׁמְּקַיְּמִין אֶת הָעוֹלָם
שֶׁנִּבְרָא בַעֲשָׂרָה מַאֲמָרוֹת.

ב עֲשָׂרָה דוֹרוֹת מֵאָדָם עַד נֹחַ, לְהוֹדִיעַ כַּמָּה אֶרֶךְ
אַפַּיִם לְפָנָיו, שֶׁכָּל הַדּוֹרוֹת הָיוּ מַכְעִיסִין וּבָאִין עַד
שֶׁהֵבִיא עֲלֵיהֶם אֶת מֵי הַמַּבּוּל.
עֲשָׂרָה דוֹרוֹת מִנֹּחַ עַד אַבְרָהָם, לְהוֹדִיעַ כַּמָּה אֶרֶךְ
אַפַּיִם לְפָנָיו, שֶׁכָּל הַדּוֹרוֹת הָיוּ מַכְעִיסִין וּבָאִין עַד
שֶׁבָּא אַבְרָהָם וְקִבֵּל (עָלָיו) שְׂכַר כֻּלָּם.

ג עֲשָׂרָה נִסְיוֹנוֹת נִתְנַסָּה אַבְרָהָם אָבִינוּ עָלָיו הַשָּׁלוֹם
וְעָמַד בְּכֻלָּם, לְהוֹדִיעַ כַּמָּה חִבָּתוֹ שֶׁלְּאַבְרָהָם אָבִינ
עָלָיו הַשָּׁלוֹם.

עֲשָׂרָה נִסִּים נַעֲשׂוּ לַאֲבוֹתֵינוּ בְמִצְרַיִם וַעֲשָׂרָה עַל הַיָּם.

עֶשֶׂר מַכּוֹת הֵבִיא הַקָּדוֹשׁ בָּרוּךְ הוּא עַל הַמִּצְרִיִּים בְּמִצְרַיִם וַעֲשָׂרָה עַל הַיָּם.

עֲשָׂרָה נִסְיוֹנוֹת נִסּוּ אֲבוֹתֵינוּ אֶת הַמָּקוֹם בָּרוּךְ הוּא בַּמִּדְבָּר, שֶׁנֶּאֱמַר: "וַיְנַסּוּ אֹתִי זֶה עֶשֶׂר פְּעָמִים וְלֹא שָׁמְעוּ בְּקוֹלִי".

עֲשָׂרָה נִסִּים נַעֲשׂוּ לַאֲבוֹתֵינוּ בְּבֵית הַמִּקְדָּשׁ:
לֹא הִפִּילָה אִשָּׁה מֵרֵיחַ בְּשַׂר הַקֹּדֶשׁ;
וְלֹא הִסְרִיחַ בְּשַׂר הַקֹּדֶשׁ מֵעוֹלָם;
וְלֹא נִרְאָה זְבוּב בְּבֵית הַמִּטְבְּחַיִם;
וְלֹא אֵרַע קֶרִי לְכֹהֵן גָּדוֹל בְּיוֹם הַכִּפּוּרִים;
וְלֹא כִבּוּ גְשָׁמִים אֵשׁ שֶׁלַּעֲצֵי הַמַּעֲרָכָה;
וְלֹא נָצְחָה הָרוּחַ אֶת עַמּוּד הֶעָשָׁן;
וְלֹא נִמְצָא פְסוּל בָּעֹמֶר וּבִשְׁתֵּי הַלֶּחֶם וּבְלֶחֶם הַפָּנִים;
עוֹמְדִים צְפוּפִים וּמִשְׁתַּחֲוִים רְוָחִים;
וְלֹא הִזִּיק נָחָשׁ וְעַקְרָב בִּירוּשָׁלַיִם מֵעוֹלָם;
וְלֹא אָמַר אָדָם לַחֲבֵרוֹ: צַר לִי הַמָּקוֹם שֶׁאָלִין בִּירוּשָׁלַיִם.

עֲשָׂרָה דְבָרִים נִבְרְאוּ בְּעֶרֶב שַׁבָּת בֵּין הַשְּׁמָשׁוֹת, וְאֵלּוּ הֵן:
פִּי הָאָרֶץ,
וּפִי הַבְּאֵר,
וּפִי הָאָתוֹן,
וְהַקֶּשֶׁת,
וְהַמָּן,
וְהַמַּטֶּה,
וְהַשָּׁמִיר,
וְהַכְּתָב,

וְהַמִּכְתָּב,
וְהַלוּחוֹת.
וְיֵשׁ אוֹמְרִים: אַף הַמַּזִּיקִין, וּקְבוּרָתוֹ שֶׁלְּמֹשֶׁה, וְאֵיל
שֶׁלְּאַבְרָהָם אָבִינוּ. וְיֵשׁ אוֹמְרִים: אַף צְבַת בִּצְבָו
עֲשׂוּיָה.

1 By ten acts of speech was the world made. And what does Scripture mean [by saying "God said" ten times?[1]] And is it not so that with a single act of speech [the world] could have been brought into being?
But it is to exact punishment from the wicked, who destroy a world which was created through ten acts of speech,
And to secure a good reward for the righteous, who sustain a world which was created through ten acts of speech.

2 There are ten generations from Adam to Noah[2] to show how long-suffering is [God]. For all those generations went along spiting Him until He brought the water of the flood upon them.
There are ten generations from Noah to Abraham[3] to show you how long-suffering is [God]. For all those generations went along spiting Him, until Abraham came along and took the reward which had been meant for all of them.

3 Ten trials were inflicted upon Abraham,[4] our father (may he rest in peace), and he withstood all of them, to show you how great is His love for Abraham, our father, (may he rest in peace).

4 Ten wonders were done for our fathers in Egypt[5] and ten at the Sea.
Ten blows did the Holy One, the blessed, bring upon the Egyptians in Egypt, and ten at the Sea.[6]
Ten trials did our fathers inflict upon the Omnipresent, the blessed, in the Wilderness,[7] as it is said, *Yet they have tempted Me these ten times and have not listened to My voice.*

Num. 14:22

5 Ten wonders were done for our fathers in the Temple:
A woman never miscarried on account of the stench of the meat of Holy Things;
and the meat of Holy Things never turned rotten;

a fly never appeared in the slaughterhouse;
a high priest never suffered a nocturnal emission or
    the eve of the Day of Atonement;
the rain never quenched the fire on the altar;
no wind ever blew away the pillar of smoke;
an invalidating factor never affected the *omer,* the
    Two Loaves, or the Show Bread;[8]
when the people are standing they are jammed
    together, when they go down and prostrate them-
    selves they have plenty of room;
a snake and a scorpion never bit anybody in Jerusalem,
and no one ever said to his fellow, *The place is too
    crowded for me* to stay in Jerusalem.

Is. 49:20

6 Ten things were created on the eve of the Sabbath [or
Friday] at twilight, and these are they:
the mouth of the earth,[9]
the mouth of the well,[10]
the mouth of the ass,[11]
the rainbow,[12]
the manna,[13]
the rod,[14]
the *shamir,*[15]
letters,
writing,
and the tables of stone.[16]
And some say: Also the destroyers,[17] the grave of
Moses,[18] and the ram of Abraham, our father.[19] And some
say: Also the tongs made with tongs [with which the first
tongs were made].

Notes: 1. See Gen. 1–2; 2. See Gen. 5; 3. See Gen. 11; 4. See Gen. 12–22,
5. The ten plagues, see Ex. 7–11; 6. Later explanations cite various verses in
Scripture; 7. See Ex. 14–17, Num. 11; 8. See Lev. 23–24; 9. See Num. 16:32
10. See Num. 21:16–18; 11. See Num. 22:28; 12. See Gen. 9:13; 13. See
Ex.16:15; 14. See Ex. 4:17; 15. A legendary rock-eating worm that hewed
stone for the altar since no iron tool could be used, see Ex. 20:22, I Kings
6:7; 16. Of the Ten Commandments, see Ex. 32:15f. ; 17. Demons; 18. See
Deut. 34:6; 19. See Gen. 22:13.

We leave behind the world of wisdom addressed to ordinary people and take up a wholly fresh sort of discourse. The

ramer of these constructions takes for granted that you and I
vill join in the work. For the framer gives us a model, but
hen not only offers outlines that we must fill in, but also
pells out the purpose of the lists. It is to teach us a lesson.
The lesson is specified, and at each point, we recognize its
depth. Saying 1 tells us there are ten acts of speech, and why
here are ten. Then there are ten generations, to show how
God bears with us. That seems to me to match the ten acts of
peech, both to exact punishment from the wicked. Then there
vere ten more generations, this time to carry through the
ther part of the opening list, namely, the reward for the
ighteous. So the first set of ten items forms a trilogy. Saying
completes the matter of the groups of ten things from creation
o Abraham. The next set, saying 4, does not follow the pattern
stablished in the first. What we have, as I said, are simply
rescriptions for lists, but these are not spelled out, and the
oint that they make is not made explicit. The next sets,
ayings 5 and 6, stand by themselves. The work as a whole
herefore is suggestive.

ז שִׁבְעָה דְבָרִים בַּגֹּלֶם וְשִׁבְעָה בֶּחָכָם.
הֶחָכָם אֵינוֹ מְדַבֵּר בִּפְנֵי מִי שֶׁהוּא גָדוֹל מִמֶּנּ
בְּחָכְמָה;
וְאֵינוֹ נִכְנָס לְתוֹךְ דִּבְרֵי חֲבֵרוֹ;
וְאֵינוֹ נִבְהָל לְהָשִׁיב;
שׁוֹאֵל כָּעִנְיָן וּמֵשִׁיב כַּהֲלָכָה;
וְאוֹמֵר עַל רִאשׁוֹן רִאשׁוֹן, וְעַל אַחֲרוֹן אַחֲרוֹן;
וְעַל מַה שֶּׁלֹּא שָׁמַע אוֹמֵר: לֹא שָׁמַעְתִּי;
וּמוֹדֶה עַל הָאֱמֶת.
וְחִלּוּפֵיהֶן בַּגֹּלֶם.

ח שִׁבְעָה מִינֵי פֻּרְעָנִיּוֹת בָּאִין לָעוֹלָם עַל שִׁבְעָה גוּפֵ
עֲבֵרָה:
מִקְצָתָן מְעַשְּׂרִין וּמִקְצָתָן אֵינָן מְעַשְּׂרִין, רָעָ
שֶׁלְּבַצֹּרֶת בָּא — מִקְצָתָן רְעֵבִים וּמִקְצָתָ
שְׂבֵעִים;

גָּמְרוּ שֶׁלֹא לְעַשֵׂר, רָעָב שֶׁלְמְהוּמָה וְשֶׁלְבַצֹּרֶת
בָּא;

וְשֶׁלֹא לִטוֹל אֶת הַחַלָה, רָעָב שֶׁלְכַלָיָה בָּא.

דֶבֶר בָּא לָעוֹלָם עַל מִיתוֹת הָאֲמוּרוֹת בַּתּוֹרָה,
שֶׁלֹא נִמְסְרוּ לְבֵית דִּין;

וְעַל פֵּרוֹת שְׁבִיעִית.

חֶרֶב בָּאָה לָעוֹלָם — עַל עִנּוּי הַדִּין;

וְעַל עִוּוּת הַדִּין, וְעַל הַמּוֹרִים בַּתּוֹרָה שֶׁלֹּא
כַהֲלָכָה.

ט חַיָּה רָעָה בָּאָה לָעוֹלָם עַל שְׁבוּעַת שָׁוְא וְעַל
חִלּוּל הַשֵּׁם.

גָּלוּת בָּא לָעוֹלָם עַל עוֹבְדֵי עֲבוֹדָה זָרָה, וְעַל
גִּלּוּי עֲרָיוֹת, וְעַל שְׁפִיכַת דָּמִים, וְעַל הַשְׁמָטַת
הָאָרֶץ.

7 There are seven traits to an unformed clod, and seven to a
sage.
A sage does not speak before someone greater than he
in wisdom;
and he does not interrupt his companion;
and he is not at a loss for an answer;
he asks a relevant question and answers properly;
and he addresses each matter in its proper sequence—
first, then second;
and concerning something he has not heard, he says: I
have not heard the answer;
and he concedes the truth [when another person
demonstrates it].
And the opposite of these traits apply to a clod.

8 There are seven forms of punishment which come upon
the world for seven kinds of transgression.
[If] some people give tithes and some people do not
give tithes, there is a famine from drought—so some
people are hungry and some have enough;
[if] everyone decided not to tithe, there is a famine of
unrest and drought;

[if all decided] not to remove dough offering,[20] there is a famine of totality.

Pestilence comes to the world on account of the death penalties which are listed in the Torah but which are not in the hands of the court [to inflict];

and because of the produce of the Seventh Year.[21]

A sword comes into the world because of the delaying of justice and perversion of justice;

and because of those who teach the Torah not in accord with the law.

A plague of wild animals comes into the world because of vain oaths and desecration of the Divine Name.

Exile comes into the world because of those who worship idols, because of fornication, and because of bloodshed, and because of the neglect of the release of the Land [in the year of release].[22]

Notes: 20. See Num. 15:20; 21. When not treated according to Lev. 25:1–7; 22. See Lev. 25:1–7.

From the theme of the history of the world, from creation to the redemption of Israel to the supernatural life of the Temple, we return to the more familiar topics of the good life and the bad life. The sage is contrasted to the clod. The seven traits of a sage are virtues of the mind. If you want to learn how to listen and how to speak to the point, follow these seven rules and you will not go astray. Then, in saying 8, come seven kinds of punishment meant to fit the sin. These are self-explanatory, as are those appended in the first clause of saying 9. So we move through the great issues of the life of Israel, from the national to individual to social.

בְּאַרְבָּעָה פְּרָקִים הַדֶּבֶר מִתְרַבֶּה — בָּרְבִיעִית
וּבַשְּׁבִיעִית, וּבְמוֹצָאֵי שְׁבִיעִית, וּבְמוֹצָאֵי הֶחָג שֶׁבְּכָל
שָׁנָה וְשָׁנָה:
בָּרְבִיעִית, מִפְּנֵי מַעְשַׂר עָנִי שֶׁבַּשְּׁלִישִׁית;
בַּשְּׁבִיעִית, מִפְּנֵי מַעְשַׂר עָנִי שֶׁבַּשִּׁשִּׁית;

וּבְמוֹצָאֵי שְׁבִיעִית, מִפְּנֵי פֵּרוֹת שְׁבִיעִית;
וּבְמוֹצָאֵי הֶחָג שֶׁבְּכָל שָׁנָה וְשָׁנָה — מִפְּנֵי גֶזֶל
מַתְּנוֹת עֲנִיִּים.

At four turnings in the year pestilence increases—in the
fourth year, in the seventh year, in the year after the seventh
year, and at the end of the Festival [of Tabernacles] every
year:

> in the fourth year, because of the poor man's tithe of
> the third year [which people have neglected to hand
> over to the poor][23];
>
> in the seventh year, because of the poor man's tithe of
> the sixth year;
>
> in the year after the seventh year, because of the dealing
> in produce of the seventh year;
>
> and at the end of the Festival every year, because of the
> thievery of the dues [gleanings and the like] owing
> to the poor [but not left for them in the antecedent
> harvest].[24]

Notes: 23. See Deut. 14:28–29; 24. See Lev. 19:9, Deut. 24:19.

Perhaps the opening set of fours, coming in the middle of
saying 9, is meant to complete the interests of the last list of
seven things (of which six are listed). Here too the issue is
natural calamity, affecting towns and villages.

אַרְבַּע מִדּוֹת בָּאָדָם. הָאוֹמֵר:
שֶׁלִּי שֶׁלִּי וְשֶׁלָּךְ — זוֹ מִדָּה בֵּינוֹנִית; וְיֵשׁ אוֹמְרִים:
זוֹ מִדַּת סְדוֹם.
שֶׁלִּי שֶׁלָּךְ וְשֶׁלָּךְ שֶׁלִּי — עַם הָאָרֶץ.
שֶׁלִּי שֶׁלָּךְ וְשֶׁלָּךְ שֶׁלָּךְ — חָסִיד;
שֶׁלִּי שֶׁלִּי וְשֶׁלָּךְ שֶׁלִּי — רָשָׁע.

א   אַרְבַּע מִדּוֹת בַּדֵּעוֹת:
נוֹחַ לִכְעוֹס וְנוֹחַ לִרְצוֹת — יָצָא שְׂכָרוֹ בְּהֶפְסֵדוֹ;

קָשֶׁה לִכְעוֹס וְקָשֶׁה לִרְצוֹת – יָצָא הֶפְסֵ
בִּשְׂכָרוֹ;
קָשֶׁה לִכְעוֹס וְנוֹחַ לִרְצוֹת – חָסִיד;
נוֹחַ לִכְעוֹס וְקָשֶׁה לִרְצוֹת – רָשָׁע.

יב אַרְבַּע מִדּוֹת בַּתַּלְמִידִים:
מַהֵר לִשְׁמוֹעַ וּמַהֵר לְאַבֵּד – יָצָא שְׂכָרוֹ בְהֶפְסֵד
קָשֶׁה לִשְׁמוֹעַ וְקָשֶׁה לְאַבֵּד – יָצָא הֶפְסֵדוֹ בִשְׂכָכ
מַהֵר לִשְׁמוֹעַ וְקָשֶׁה לְאַבֵּד – חָכָם;
קָשֶׁה לִשְׁמוֹעַ וּמַהֵר לְאַבֵּד – זֶה חֵלֶק רַע.

יג אַרְבַּע מִדּוֹת בְּנוֹתְנֵי צְדָקָה:
הָרוֹצֶה שֶׁיִּתֵּן וְלֹא יִתְּנוּ אֲחֵרִים – עֵינוֹ רָע
בְּשֶׁלַּאֲחֵרִים;
יִתְּנוּ אֲחֵרִים וְהוּא לֹא יִתֵּן – עֵינוֹ רָעָה בְּשֶׁלּוֹ;
יִתֵּן וְיִתְּנוּ אֲחֵרִים – חָסִיד;
לֹא יִתֵּן וְלֹא יִתְּנוּ אֲחֵרִים – רָשָׁע.

יד אַרְבַּע מִדּוֹת בְּהוֹלְכֵי לְבֵית הַמִּדְרָשׁ:
הוֹלֵךְ וְאֵינוֹ עוֹשֶׂה – שְׂכַר הֲלִיכָה בְּיָדוֹ;
עוֹשֶׂה וְאֵינוֹ הוֹלֵךְ – שְׂכַר מַעֲשֶׂה בְּיָדוֹ;
הוֹלֵךְ וְעוֹשֶׂה – חָסִיד;
לֹא הוֹלֵךְ וְלֹא עוֹשֶׂה – רָשָׁע.

טו אַרְבַּע מִדּוֹת בְּיוֹשְׁבֵי לִפְנֵי חֲכָמִים: סְפוֹג, וּמַשְׁפֵּן
מַשְׁמֶרֶת, וְנָפָה.
סְפוֹג – שֶׁהוּא סוֹפֵג אֶת הַכֹּל;
מַשְׁפֵּךְ – שֶׁמַּכְנִיס בָּזוֹ וּמוֹצִיא בָזוֹ;
מַשְׁמֶרֶת – שֶׁמּוֹצִיאָה אֶת הַיַּיִן וְקוֹלֶטֶת א
הַשְּׁמָרִים;
וְנָפָה – שֶׁמּוֹצִיאָה אֶת הַקֶּמַח וְקוֹלֶטֶת אֶת הַסֹּל

0 There are four sorts of people. He who says:
What's mine is mine and what's yours is yours—this is

the average sort (and some say: This is the sort o
Sodom.[25]);
what's mine is yours and what's yours is mine—this i
a boor;
what's mine is yours and what's yours is yours—this i
a truly pious man;
what's mine is mine and what's yours is mine—this i
a truly wicked man.

11 There are four sorts of personality:
easily angered, easily calmed—he loses what he gains;
hard to anger, hard to calm—what he loses he gains;
hard to anger and easy to calm—a truly pious man;
easy to anger and hard to calm—a truly wicked man.

12 There are four types of disciples:
quick to grasp, quick to forget—he loses what he gains
slow to grasp, slow to forget—what he loses he gains;
quick to grasp, slow to forget—a sage;
slow to grasp, quick to forget—a bad lot indeed.

13 There are four traits among people who give charity:
he who wants to give but does not want others to
give—he begrudges what belongs to others;
he who wants others to give but does not want to
give—he begrudges what belongs to himself;
he who will give and he wants others to give—is truly
pious;
he who will not give and he does not want others to
give—he is truly wicked.

14 There are four sorts among those who go to the study house
he who goes but does not carry out [what he learns]—he
has at least the reward for the going;
he who practices but does not go [to study]—he has at
least the reward for the doing;
he who both goes and practices—he is truly pious;
he who neither goes nor practices—he is truly wicked

15 There are four traits among those who sit before the sages
a sponge, a funnel, a strainer, and a sifter.
A sponge—because he sponges everything up;
a funnel—because he takes in on one side and lets ou
on the other;

a strainer—for he lets out the wine and keeps in the
lees;

and a sifter—for he lets out the flour and keeps in the
finest flour.

Note: 25. See Ezek. 16:49.

The six sets of fours take up precisely those concerns
dominant in the opening chapter of Avot: first, the way we
should live; second, our lives as disciples of Torah. The first
two lists, sayings 10 and 11, tell us the possibilities of our
relationships to other people. Then come classifications of
disciples, sayings 12–15. But the pattern is uniform throughout,
as we move from bad to good qualities. Thus, at each point,
we see the neutral, but average person (–/+), then the neutral
but bad person (+/–), then the ideal person (+/+), and the
completely wicked person (–/–). Along these lines, meaningful
patterns for any number of other subjects could be constructed.
The powerful effect of the patterns makes it unnecessary for
us to interpret them. The points are clear and apply as aptly
today as they did two thousand years ago.

טז כָּל אַהֲבָה שֶׁהִיא תְלוּיָה בְדָבָר, בָּטֵל דָּבָר בָּטֵל
אַהֲבָה.

וְשֶׁאֵינָה תְלוּיָה בְדָבָר, אֵינָה בְּטֵלָה לְעוֹלָם.

אֵיזוֹ הִיא אַהֲבָה הַתְּלוּיָה בְדָבָר? זוֹ אַהֲבַת אַמְנוֹן
וְתָמָר.

וְשֶׁאֵינָה תְלוּיָה בְדָבָר? זוֹ אַהֲבַת דָּוִד וִיהוֹנָתָן.

יז כָּל מַחֲלֹקֶת שֶׁהִיא לְשֵׁם שָׁמַיִם, סוֹפָה לְהִתְקַיֵּם;
וְשֶׁאֵינָה לְשֵׁם שָׁמַיִם, אֵין סוֹפָה לְהִתְקַיֵּם.

אֵיזוֹ הִיא מַחֲלֹקֶת שֶׁהִיא לְשֵׁם שָׁמַיִם? זוֹ מַחֲלֹקֶת
הִלֵּל וְשַׁמַּאי.

וְשֶׁאֵינָה לְשֵׁם שָׁמַיִם? זוֹ מַחֲלֹקֶת קֹרַח וְכָל עֲדָתוֹ.

יח כָּל הַמְזַכֶּה אֶת הָרַבִּים, אֵין חֵטְא בָּא עַל יָדוֹ.
וְכָל הַמַּחֲטִיא אֶת הָרַבִּים, אֵין מַסְפִּיקִין בְּיָדוֹ לַעֲשׂוֹת
תְּשׁוּבָה.
מֹשֶׁה זָכָה וְזִכָּה אֶת הָרַבִּים, זְכוּת הָרַבִּים תְּלוּיָה בּוֹ,
שֶׁנֶּאֱמַר: "צִדְקַת ה' עָשָׂה וּמִשְׁפָּטָיו עִם־יִשְׂרָאֵל".
יָרָבְעָם חָטָא וְהֶחֱטִיא אֶת הָרַבִּים, חֵטְא הָרַבִּים תָּלוּי
בּוֹ, שֶׁנֶּאֱמַר: "עַל־חַטֹּאות יָרָבְעָם (בֶּן נְבָט) אֲשֶׁר חָטָא
וַאֲשֶׁר הֶחֱטִיא אֶת־יִשְׂרָאֵל".

16 [In] any loving relationship which depends upon something, [when] that thing is gone, the love is gone.
But any which does not depend upon something will never come to an end.
What is a loving relationship which depends upon something? That is the love of Amnon and Tamar.[26]
And one which does not depend upon something? That is the love of David and Jonathan.[27]

17 Any dispute which is for the sake of Heaven will in the end yield results;
And any which is not for the sake of Heaven will in the end not yield results.
What is a dispute for the sake of Heaven? This is the sort of dispute between Hillel and Shammai.
And what is one which is not for the sake of Heaven? It is the dispute of Korach and all his party.[28]

18 He who brings merit to the community never causes sin.
And he who causes the community to sin—they never give him a sufficient chance to attain penitence.
Moses attained merit and bestowed merit on the community, so the merit of the community is assigned to his [credit] as it is said, *He executed the justice of the Lord and His*
Deut.33:21 *judgments with Israel.*
Jeroboam sinned and caused the community to sin, so the sin of the community is assigned to his [debt], as it is said
For the sins of Jeroboam which he committed and where
I Kings 15:30 *with he made Israel to sin.*

Notes: 26. See II Sam. 13:15; 27. See I Sam. 18:1; 28. See Num. 16–17.

From the patterns of fours, we come to three sets of
·inary opposites. This mode of organizing facts presents no
·urprises. Sages set up opposites, each bearing its own inevit-
·ble reward or penalty. The sets then present contrasts not
·nly within, but also between, one another. So we begin, in
·aying 16, with a relationship of love, then proceed to a rela-
·ionship of contention in saying 17. The third binary set con-
·erns social relations, thus completing a trilogy of patterns
·bout the two dimensions of our lives: with other individuals,
·hen with the community at large. The formal perfection of
·he construction matches the encompassing conception of what
·s expressed. So the editor of the chapter moves from the
·ndividual and his or her traits to the individual in community.

יט כָּל מִי שֶׁיֵּשׁ בְּיָדוֹ שְׁלשָׁה דְבָרִים הַלָּלוּ — מִתַּלְמִידָי
שֶׁלְּאַבְרָהָם אָבִינוּ; וּשְׁלשָׁה דְבָרִים אֲחֵרִים —
מִתַּלְמִידָיו שֶׁלְּבִלְעָם הָרָשָׁע.

עַיִן טוֹבָה,

וְרוּחַ נְמוּכָה,

וְנֶפֶשׁ שְׁפָלָה — מִתַּלְמִידָיו שֶׁלְּאַבְרָהָם אָבִינוּ.

עַיִן רָעָה,

וְרוּחַ גְּבוֹהָה,

וְנֶפֶשׁ רְחָבָה — מִתַּלְמִידָיו שֶׁלְּבִלְעָם הָרָשָׁע.
מַה בֵּין תַּלְמִידָיו שֶׁלְּאַבְרָהָם אָבִינוּ לְתַלְמִידָי
שֶׁלְּבִלְעָם הָרָשָׁע?
תַּלְמִידָיו שֶׁלְּאַבְרָהָם אָבִינוּ אוֹכְלִין בָּעוֹלָם הַזֶּ
וְנוֹחֲלִין בָּעוֹלָם הַבָּא, שֶׁנֶּאֱמַר: "לְהַנְחִיל אֹהֲבַי יֵשׁ
וְאֹצְרֹתֵיהֶם אֲמַלֵּא".
אֲבָל תַּלְמִידָיו שֶׁלְּבִלְעָם הָרָשָׁע יוֹרְשִׁין גֵּיהִנָּם וְיוֹרְדִין
לִבְאֵר שַׁחַת, שֶׁנֶּאֱמַר: "וְאַתָּה אֱלֹהִים תּוֹרִדֵם לִבְאֵר
שַׁחַת, אַנְשֵׁי דָמִים וּמִרְמָה לֹא-יֶחֱצוּ יְמֵיהֶם וַאֲנִ
אֶבְטַח-בָּךְ".

19 Anyone in whom are these three traits is one of the
disciples of Abraham, our father; but [if he bears] three

other traits, he is one of the disciples of Balaam, the wicked[29]:

> A generous spirit,
> a modest mien,
> and a humble soul—he is one of the disciples o Abraham, our father.
> A grudging spirit,
> an arrogant mien,
> and a proud soul—he is one of the disciples of Balaam the wicked.

What is the difference between the disciples of Abraham our father, and the disciples of Balaam, the wicked?

The disciples of Abraham, our father, enjoy the benefit [o' their learning] in this world and yet inherit the world tc come, as it is said, *That I may cause those who love Me tc* Prov. 8:21 *inherit substance, and so that I may fill their treasures.*

The disciples of Balaam, the wicked, inherit Gehenna anc go down to the Pit of Destruction, as it is said, *But You, O God, shall bring them down into the pit of destruction; bloodthirsty and deceitful men shall not live out half their* Ps. 55:24 *days; but I trust in You.*

Note: 29. See Num. 22.

What we noticed in the sets of binary opposites we see once more in this set of balanced traits. Generosity, modesty and humility—these are the virtues inculcated through the sages' sayings in the first four chapters. Now they are sum- marized and set in the balance against the bad traits, to be avoided. The model therefore reminds us of a way in which Yohanan ben Zakkai's disciples' sayings are constructed. The message remains constant.

יְהוּדָה בֶּן תֵּימָא אוֹמֵר:
הֱוֵי עַז כַּנָּמֵר,
וְקַל כַּנֶּשֶׁר,
וְרָץ כַּצְּבִי,
וְגִבּוֹר כָּאֲרִי
לַעֲשׂוֹת רְצוֹן אָבִיךְ שֶׁבַּשָּׁמָיִם.

הוּא הָיָה אוֹמֵר:

עַז פָּנִים לְגֵיהִנָּם,

וּבֹשֶׁת פָּנִים לְגַן עֵדֶן.

יְהִי רָצוֹן מִלְּפָנֶיךָ, ה׳ אֱלֹהֵינוּ, שֶׁתִּבְנֶה עִירָךְ בִּמְהֵרָה

בְיָמֵינוּ, וְתֵן חֶלְקֵנוּ בְּתוֹרָתֶךָ.

כא הוּא הָיָה אוֹמֵר:

בֶּן חָמֵשׁ שָׁנִים לַמִּקְרָא,

בֶּן עֶשֶׂר לַמִּשְׁנָה,

בֶּן שְׁלֹשׁ עֶשְׂרֵה לַמִּצְוֹת,

בֶּן חֲמֵשׁ עֶשְׂרֵה לַתַּלְמוּד,

בֶּן שְׁמוֹנֶה עֶשְׂרֵה לַחֻפָּה,

בֶּן עֶשְׂרִים לִרְדוֹף,

בֶּן שְׁלֹשִׁים לַכֹּחַ,

בֶּן אַרְבָּעִים לַבִּינָה,

בֶּן חֲמִשִּׁים לָעֵצָה,

בֶּן שִׁשִּׁים לַזִּקְנָה,

בֶּן שִׁבְעִים לַשֵּׂיבָה,

בֶּן שְׁמוֹנִים לַגְּבוּרָה,

בֶּן תִּשְׁעִים לָשׁוּחַ,

בֶּן מֵאָה — כְּאִלּוּ מֵת וְעָבַר וּבָטַל מִן הָעוֹלָם.

כב בֶּן בַּג בַּג אוֹמֵר:

הֲפֹךְ בָּהּ וְהַפֵּךְ בָּהּ דְּכֹלָּה בָהּ;

וּבָהּ תֶּחֱזֵי וְסִיב וּבְלֵה בָהּ וּמִנַּהּ לָא תְזוּעַ;

שֶׁאֵין לָךְ מִדָּה טוֹבָה הֵימֶנָּה.

כג בֶּן הֵא הֵא אוֹמֵר: לְפוּם צַעֲרָא אַגְרָא.

0 Judah ben Tema says:
    Be strong as a leopard,
        fast as an eagle,
        fleet as a gazelle,
        and brave as a lion
  to carry out the will of your Father who is in heaven.

He would say:
The shameless go to Gehenna,
and the diffident to the garden of Eden.
May it be found pleasing before You, O Lord our God, tha
You rebuild Your city quickly in our day and set out portior
in Your Torah.

21 He would say:
At five to Scripture,
ten to Mishnah,
thirteen to religious duties,
fifteen to Talmud,
eighteen to the wedding canopy,
twenty to responsibility for providing for a family,
thirty to fulness of strength,
forty to understanding,
fifty to counsel,
sixty to old age,
seventy to ripe old age,
eighty to remarkable strength,
ninety to bowed back,
and at a hundred—he is like a corpse who has alread
passed and gone from this world.

22 Ben Bag Bag says [in Aramaic]:
Turn it over and over because everything is in it;
and reflect upon it and grow old and worn in it and d
not leave it;
[in Hebrew] for you have no better lot than that.

23 Ben Hé Hé says: In accord with the effort is the reward.

Judah ben Tema's saying and those of the others at th
end stand in relationship to the chapter, and to the tractate
much as does Eleazar Hakkappar's in chapter four. Separat
and special, the message encompasses the whole of the forego
ing. Judah ends with a set of exhortations, concluding with
prayer. He proceeds to an account of the ages through whic
we pass in our lives. Ben Bag Bag tells us that we should spen
our life reflecting on the Torah. Ben Hé Hé concludes with
simple statement of the reward for doing so. All of this i

acked on to end with prayer, homily, and exhortation, because
Avot to begin with was meant for synagogue study in the
ontext of worship—just as Avot serves even now, even us.

This chapter has presented us with a series of lists. So at
he end we have to ask what is gained by the making of lists.
The answer is at once simple and profound.

The simple side is that in making lists, information is
organized into a useful pattern. By listing diverse things, what
hey have in common becomes clear. We not only remember
hem. We also make a new point, discover a new fact, above
and beyond the points or facts contained in the diverse items
isted. For the sum of the whole is greater than the parts,
when the whole shows the parts in a new way. That is the
imple side.

The profound dimension emerges from the context in
which these particular people made the lists before us. Our
ages of the second and third centuries confronted a world of
haos and disorder. As we now understand, the old regularities
aded, the established certainties lost all credibility. The familiar
ways of organizing the world led to destruction, the reliable
patterns were shattered. For the sages, the work of making a
ist of things sharing a common trait or making a single point
epresents, in intellectual form, the larger task of the age. It is
meant to show that beneath chaos, order yet endures; patterns
an be found; isolated facts can be drawn together, classified,
hown to bear meaning. This work of the mind served a social
purpose. In the life of the mind, the sages lived out the dilemma
of their day—and solved it. So, as I said in the beginning, by
making lists, by thinking in the orderly way in which the
Mishnah's masters pursue thought, we master and make sense
of whatever is to be known.

Chaos and Order

FOUNDERS AND SURVIVORS, THEN AND NOW

EPILOGUE
FOUNDERS AND SURVIVORS, THEN AND NOW

Over and over again I have asked you to read Avot, the Torah from our sages, as a legacy of survivors, the heritage of those who endured disaster and faced a seemingly hopeless world beyond. What I find amazing about our tractate, in the end, is that is exists. For the people who brought together whatever they had preserved from the then-ancient times of Moses and Hillel and composed a message for their own day found the will and strength to do so despite the world.

Nothing that had happened told them Israel, the Jewish people, would go on for even a hundred years more. No precedent out of the past could shine as a beacon now, toward an unknown yet worthwhile future. Quite to the contrary, the lesson of the past was that Israel had been punished because of sin, and had attained restoration and renewal in the aftermath of repentance and reconciliation with God. But the Temple had stood for the final forgiveness, the ultimate redemption. Surely the more than half-millennium from 538 B.C.E., the return to Zion, to 135 C.E., the ultimate disaster—600 years!—testified to something.

For a longer period of time, after all, than Europe has known America, for more years than have passed from Columbus to our own day, Israel knew the security of the cyclical record of Scripture: sin, atonement, reconciliation. Scripture, moreover, had taught that if you sin, you repent in your heart but also bring an offering to God in the Temple. Now the awful events again told Israel that the sin of the age had brought calamity. But how repent without a Temple service? How could they hope without the ancient record of what things meant? Indeed, if the Scripture were to be believed, then nothing now made sense. Everything was over.

The Mishnah, with Avot at its center, tells us about how our sages endured against the world, despite the world. Lacking all, they did not despair. Depending upon God, they turned to what remained of the past, which was the Torah. And so they fashioned their own Torah, the Mishnah.

That, in a few sentences, is the message I derive from this tractate and the book for which it stands. It also is the answer provided by this book to the question I myself bring to Avot.

Mine is the queston of this century and the next, and I do not know how many beyond: how to survive? how to endure? Why that question presses hard upon my consciousness hardly demands much explanation. Every Jew alive in the world today is a survivor. Every Jew who breathes the air was spared the gas. We all live today only because we, our parents or grandparents, had the good fortune not to be in continental Europe from 1933 to 1945, or by some miracle to have been directly spared. Wherever we were, if then alive, we were not *there*. Whoever we now are, we come from someone who was not there. So every Jew today is the brand plucked from the burning. We live by the special grace of God. What happened then happens every day in our hearts and minds, no day without its anguish and its tears. But that means we now live despite the world and against the world in which, in our era and lifetime, our people were burned and gassed and shot and starved to death.

What does it mean to live beyond it all and yet not to despair? We have no answers, only precedents: the legacy and heritage of the enduring people of Israel, hence, this strange and surprising tractate we have opened together.

Challenge and Choice

Well, we ask ourselves, what were the sages' choices? Did other Jews respond differently to the questions confronting the framers of the Mishnah? Yes. There were other, different responses to the catastrophe of that age. To gain a better view of what the sages of the Mishnah accomplished, it is necessary to review rapidly where the heritage of Avot is to be located within the framework of other kinds of Judaism, that is, in the context of other ways Jews thought about the Temple and its destruction. Then, and only then, the message of our tractate will emerge fully—the convictions it rejects, the ones it proposes.

Here then are the might-have-been's, the kinds of Judaism that Israel, the Jewish people, ultimately did not find persuasive. To explain the matter in advance: the other sorts of Judaism looked only backward. Our sages of the Mishnah, and they alone, turned toward the unknown future. That is why we who live in an age still more trying than theirs can turn toward the past they shaped for us, as we too address our unknown future.

Four major responses to the challenges of the destruction of Jerusalem, the end of the Temple, and the cessation of the cult of animal sacrifice may be discerned. These responses confront several crucial social and religious problems, all interrelated:

first, how to achieve atonement without the cult;

second, how to explain the disaster of destructon;

third, how to cope with the new age, to devise a way of life on a new basis entirely;

fourth, how to account for the new social forms consequent upon the collapse of the old social structure.

Here are choices Jews made and here we see the choice made by the sages in context. The four responses are of, first, the apocalyptic writers represented in the visions of Baruch and II Ezra; second, the Dead Sea community of Essenes at Qumran; third, the Christian church; and, finally, the Pharisaic sect, that is, the group from which our sages of the Mishnah derive.

The apocalyptic visonaries were writers who tried to interpret the meaning of events. They expected the imminent end of time, a cosmic cataclysm in which God would destroy evil and establish righteousness. The Essene community at Qumran formed a sectarian monastery, for which the Dead Sea Scrolls articulated a particular view of the meaning of history. The Christian church needs no introduction. The Pharisaic sect does, however, and I shall take some trouble to explain who the Pharisees were, how we know about them, and when we see them as the sages of the Mishnah—and, ultimately, the framers of Avot.

The Apocalyptic View

We begin with the group most interested in the meaning of history, in the coming of the Messiah and the end of time. They were the apocalyptic visionaries, who claimed to interpret the great events of the day and to know where these events were leading. Out of the past, they would discover the future. Two documents, the Apocalypse of Ezra and the Vision of Baruch, are representative of the apocalyptic state of mind. The compiler of the Ezra apocalypse (II Ezra 3–14), who lived at the end of the first century C.E., looked forward to a day of judgment when the Messiah would destroy Rome and God would govern the world. But he had to ask, How can the suffering of Israel be reconciled with divine justice? God's will had been revealed to Israel. But God had not removed the inclination to do evil, so people could not carry out God's will. If such a visionary had written the Mishnah, this is what we should have found in Avot:

> For we and our fathers have passed our lives in ways that bring death . . . But what is man, that You are angry with him, or what is a corruptible race, that You are so bitter against it? [II Ezra 8:26]

Ezra, who took his name from the biblical scribe and so attributed his book to a great man of old, was told that God's ways are inscrutable [4:10–11], but when he repeated the question, "Why has Israel been given over to the Gentiles as a reproach?" he was given the answer characteristic of this literature, that a new age was dawning that would shed light on such perplexities. Thus, he was told:

> . . . if you are *live,* you will see, and if you live long, you will often marvel, because the age is hastening swiftly to its end. For it will not be able to bring the things that have been promised to the righteous in their appointed time, because this age is full of sadness and infirmities. . . . [4:10–26]

An angel told him the signs of the coming redemption, saying:

> . . . the sun shall suddenly shine forth at night and the moon during the day, blood shall drip from

wood, and the stone shall utter its voice, the peoples
shall be troubled, and the stars shall fall. . . . [5:4–5]

And he was admonished to wait patiently:

The righteous therefore can endure difficult circumstances, while hoping for easier ones, but those who
have done wickedly have suffered the difficult circumstances, and will not see easier ones. [6:55– 56]

Ezra thus regarded the catastrophe as the fruit of sin; more
specifically, the result of the natural human incapacity to do
the will of God. He prayed for forgiveness and found hope in
the coming transformation of the age and the promise of a
new day, when the human heart would be as able, as the mind
even then was willing, to do the will of God.

A second, unknown author who attributed his book to
Jeremiah's secretary, Baruch (who lived in the time of the first
destruction), likewise brought promise of coming redemption,
but with little practical advice for the intervening period. The
document exhibits three major themes.

First, God acted righteously in bringing about the punishment of Israel:

Righteousness belongs to the Lord our God, but
confusion of face to us and our fathers. . . . [Baruch
2:6]

Second, the catastrophe came on account of Israel's sin:

Why is it, O Israel . . . that you are in the land of
your enemies . . . ? You have forsaken the fountain
of wisdom. If you had walked in the way of the
Lord, you would be dwelling in peace forever.
[3:10–12]

Third, as surely as God had punished the people, so certainly
would God bring the people home to their land and restore
their fortunes. Thus, Jerusalem speaks:

But I, how can I help you? For He who brought
these calamities upon you will deliver you from the
hand of your enemies . . . For I sent you out with
sorrow and weeping, but God will give you back to
me with joy and gladness forever. . . . [4:17–18, 23]

Finally, Baruch advised the people to wait patiently for redemption, saying:

> My children, endure with patience the wrath that has come upon you from God. Your enemy has overtaken you, but you will soon see their destruction and will tread upon their necks . . . For just as you purposed to go astray from God, return with tenfold zeal to seek Him. For He who brought these calamities upon you will bring you everlasting joy with your salvation. Take courage, O Jerusalem, for He who named you will comfort you. [4:25, 28– 30]

The saddest words written in these times come in II Baruch. This is how Jews felt then—but also in 1945:

> Blessed is he who was not born, or he who, having
> been born, has died;
> But as for us who live, woe unto us
> Because we see the afflictions of Zion and what has
> befallen Jerusalem. . . .
> You husbandmen, sow not again.
> And earth, why do you give your harvest fruits?
> Keep within yourself the sweets of your sustenance.
> And you, vine, why do you continue to give your
> wine?
> For an offering will not again be made therefrom in
> Zion.
> Nor will first fruits again be offered.
> And do you, O heavens, withhold your dew,
> And open not the treasuries of rain.
> And do you, sun, withhold the light of your rays,
> And you, moon, extinguish the multitude of your
> light.
> For why should light rise again
> Where the light of Zion is darkened? . . .
> Would that you had ears, O earth,
> And that you had a heart, O dust,
> That you might go and announce in Sheol,
> And say to the dead,
> "Blessed are you more than we who live."
>   [10:6–7, 9–12, 11:6–7]

The issue before all groups is, What to do now, *today?* We have suffered disaster. What is its meaning and where are we heading? The answer of this sad poem is utter nihilism. Once we are told, "We have no answer but patience," the next step is going to be the end of patience. But there is no new beginning. The apocalyptic writers have nothing to say to those who wait but wait some more. There were Jews who felt that way after World War II. No wonder, then, that they conclude that death is better than life. For those who would live, however, such a message is curiously inappropriate.

Before we proceed, let us consider how a rabbi of the period is portrayed as having responded to the nihilistic message of the disappointed messianists. A leading rabbi after 70, Rabbi Joshua, whom we met in chapter two of Avot, is described as meeting such people. It was reported that when the Temple was destroyed, "ascetics multiplied in Israel" who would neither eat flesh nor drink wine. Joshua challenged them:

> He said to them, "My children, on what account do you not eat flesh and drink wine?"
> They said to him, "Shall we eat meat, from which they used to offer a sacrifice on the altar, and now it is no more? And shall we drink wine, which was poured out on the altar, and now it is no more?"
> He said to them, "If so, we ought not to eat bread, for there are no meal offerings any more. Perhaps we ought not to drink water, for the water offerings are not brought anymore."
> They were silent.
> He said to them, "My children, come and I shall teach you. Not to mourn at all is impossible, for the evil decree has already come upon us. But to mourn too much is also impossible, for one may not promulgate a decree for the community unless most of the community can endure it. . . . But thus have the sages taught, 'A man plasters his house, but leaves a little piece untouched. A man prepares all the needs of the meal, but leaves out some morsel. A woman prepares all her cosmetics, but leaves off some small item. . . ." [Baba Batra 60b]

The response of the visionaries was essentially negative. All they had to say was that God is just and Israel has sinned, but, in the end of time, there will be redemption. What to do in the meantime? Merely wait—not much of an answer.

The Essene Community of the Dead Sea

For the Essene community, the destruction of the Temple cult took place long before 70. By rejecting the Temple and its cult of sacrifice as early as the second century B.C.E., the Essenes confronted a world without Jerusalem even while the city was still standing. The founders of the Qumran community were Temple priests, who saw themselves as continuators of the true priestly line. For them, the old Temple was destroyed in the times of the Maccabees when it fell into the hands of usurpers—namely, the Maccabees themselves! Its cult was defiled, not only by the Syrians, but by the rise of a high priest from a family other than the true priestly family. They further rejected the calendar followed in Jerusalem. They therefore set out to create a new Temple to serve, until God, through the Messiah in the line of Aaron, would establish the true Temple once again. The Essene community believed that the presence of God had left Jerusalem and had come to the Dead Sea. The community now constituted the new Temple, just as some elements in early Christianity saw the new Temple in the body of Christ, in the Church, the Christian community. In some measure, this approach represents a "spiritualization" of the old Temple, for the Temple was the community, and the Temple worship was effected through the community's study and fulfillment of the Torah. But the community was just as much a reality, a presence, as was the Jerusalem Temple; the obedience to the law was no less material and concrete than the blood sacrifices. The Essenes, thus, represent a middle point between reverence for the old Temple and its cult, and complete indifference in favor of the Christians' utter spiritualization of both as represented, for example, in the Letter to the Hebrews.

If the old Temple is destroyed, then how will Israel make atonement? The Essene answer is that the life of the community in perfect obedience to the Law is represented as the true sacrifice offered in the new Temple. The community thus takes over the holiness and the functions of the Temple and so is the

nly means of making atonement for sin and maintaining the
oliness of Israel. The response of the Dead Sea sect, therefore,
/as to reconstruct the Temple and to reinterpret the nature
nd substance of sacrifice. The community constituted the
econstructed Temple. The life of Torah and obedience to its
ommandments formed the new sacrifice.

For a long time the Christian was another kind of Jew.
Moreover, the Christians, whether originally Jewish or other-
vise, took over the antecedent holy books and much of the
·ious life of Judaism, its ethics and religious beliefs. For our
·urposes, therefore, their piety serves as another form of
udaism, one that differed from the others primarily in
egarding the world as redeemed through the word and cross
·f Jesus. But one must hasten to stress the complexity of the
Christian evidence. Indeed, the responses of the Christians to
he destruction of the Temple cannot be simplified and
egarded as essentially unitary.

Early Christianity

Because of their faith in the crucified and risen Christ,
Christians experienced the end of the old cult and the old
Temple before it actually took place, much as the Essene
ectarians had. They had to work out the meaning of the
acrifice of Jesus on the cross, and whether the essays on that
·entral problem were done before or after 70 is of no consequence. The issues of 70 confronted Essenes and Christians
or other than narrowly historical reasons. For both groups
he events of that year took place, so to speak, in other than
nilitary and political modes. But the effects were much the
·ame. The Christians, therefore, resemble the Essenes in having
1ad to face the end of the cult before it actually ended. But
·ecause the Christians did not sequester themselves like the
Essenes, they (like the Pharisees) had to confront the actual
lestruction of the Temple, then and there.

Like the Essenes, the Christian Jews criticized the Jerusa-
·em Temple and its cult. Both groups in common believed
hat the last days had begun. Both believed that God had
·ome to dwell with them, as God had once dwelled in the
Temple. The sacrifices of the Temple were replaced, therefore,
·y the sacrifices of a blameless life and by other spiritual
leeds. But the Christians differ on one important point. To

them, the final sacrifice had already taken place; the perfect priest had offered up the perfect sacrifice, his own body. So for the Christians, Christ on the cross completed the old sanctity and inaugurated the new. This belief took shape in different ways. For Paul, in I Corinthians 3:16–17, the Church is the new Temple, Christ is the foundation of the "spiritual" building. Ephesians 2:18ff. has Christ as the cornerstone of the new building, the company of Christians constituting the Temple.

Perhaps the single most coherent statement of the Christian view of cult comes in Hebrews. Whether Hebrews is representative of many Christians or comes as early as 70 is not our concern. What is striking is that the Letter explores the great issues of 70: the issues of cult, Temple, sacrifice, priesthood, atonement, and redemption. Its author takes for granted that the Church is the Temple, that Jesus is the builder of the Temple, and that he is also the perfect priest and final and most unblemished sacrifice. Material sacrifices might suffice for the ceremonial cleansing of an earthly sanctuary, a sacrifice different in kind and better in degree is required. It is Jesus who is that perfect sacrifice, who has entered the true, heavenly sanctuary and now represents his people before God: "By his death he was consecrated the new covenant together with the heavenly sanctuary itself." Therefore, no further sacrifice—his or others'—is needed.

The Christian response to the crisis of the day was both entirely appropriate and quite useless.

It was appropriate for those who already shared the Christian belief that the Messiah had come and that the destroyed Temple in any case no longer matter.

But this was a message of little substance for those who did not stand within the Christian's circle of faith. To them, the crisis was real, the problem intense and immediate. So far as the Christians formed a small group within the Jewish people, their explanation and interpretation of the disaster was of limited appeal.

What they offered was one messianism in place of another. It was the messianism built upon the paradox of the crucified Messiah, the scandal of weakness in place of strength, suffering unto death in place of this-worldly victory. True, Christian messianism was to speak to millions of men and women hrough the ages. But to people who believed the Messiah vould be a great general, would throw off the rule of pagans, ind would lead the people to an age of peace and prosperity, he Christian Messiah hanging on the cross proved to be an nsufferable paradox. It was not that Christianity was irrelevant. It was that its answers could not be understood by people who were asking a different queston.

We come, finally, to the Pharisees. First, why do we hink they stand at the beginning of that movement that reaches ts climax in the Mishnah? What makes us suppose that such figures before 70 C.E. as Hillel, Gamaliel, and Simeon ben Gamaliel, were Pharisees? The answer, happily, is a matter of record. The Jewish general and historian, Josephus, directly refers to Simeon ben Gamaliel as a leader of the Pharisaic party. The New Testament book of Acts at 5:34, refers to Gamaliel as a Pharisee in the council in Jerusalem. It therefore seems to me reasonable to conclude that the figures on the list at the beginning of Avot were Pharisees. We also know that the sayings of the authorities in chapters two, three, and four come from sages who stand in direct relationship to those listed in chapter one. It follows that Avot is a collection of statements attributed to Pharisees and their successors, heirs, and continuators, our sages of the Mishnah. So the story begins, for Judaism as we know it, with the Pharisees, the masters and disciples before 70.

Who were the Pharisees before 70, and what became of their teachings afterward? More important, why does Avot stand as a document of survival as experienced and explained by people who continue the heritage of the Pharisees in particular? To state the question before us: What has Torah to do with Israel's survival, then and therefore now?

Let us proceed to review what we know about the Pharisees in the context of the destruction of the Temple.

The dominant trait of Pharisaism before 70, as depicted both in the later rabbinic traditions about the Pharisees and in the Gospels, was concern for certain matters of rite. In particular, Pharisees emphasized eating meals in a state of ritual purity as if they were Temple priests, and carefully giving the required tithes and offerings due to the priesthood.

The Pharisees

The Gospels' stories and sayings on Pharisaism also added fasting, Sabbath observance, affirming vows and oaths, and the like. But the main point was keeping the ritual purity laws outside of the Temple. Everyone kept those rules *inside* the Temple, for priests had to observe ritual purity when they carried out the requirements of the cult, and other Jews had to be pure to enter the Temple, too.

The Pharisees believed that one must maintain the purity laws *outside* of the Temple. Following the plain sense of Leviticus, everyone else supposed that purity laws were to be kept *only* in the Temple, where priests entered a state of ritual purity in order to carry out the requirements of the cult, such as animal sacrifice. Priests also had to eat their Temple food in a state of ritual purity. The laity did not have to eat ordinary meals that way. Outside the Temple the laws of ritual purity were not widely observed. The Pharisees alone held that even outside of the Temple, in one's home, one had to follow the laws of ritual purity in the only circumstance in which they might apply, namely, at the table. They therefore held that one must eat secular food—that is, ordinary, everyday meals—in a state of ritual purity, as if those eating were Temple priests.

The Pharisees thus assumed for themselves—and therefore, for all Jews equally—the status and responsibilities of the Temple priests. The table in the home of every Jew was seen to be like the table of the Lord in the Jerusalem Temple. We encountered this idea in chapter four of Avot. The commandment, "You shall be a kingdom of priests and a holy people" [Ex. 19:6], thus was taken literally. The whole country was considered holy. The table of every Jew possessed the same order of sanctity as the table of the cult.

Thus, the Pharisees before 70 revered the Temple and its cult. Afterward, we know, their successors drew up the laws which would govern the Temple when it would be restored. While awaiting restoration, they held that "As long as the Temple stood, the altar atoned for Israel. But now a man's table atones for him" [Berakhot 55a]. This Pharisaic attitude would be highly appropriate to the time when the Temple no longer stood. The Pharisees already had entered that time, in a strange and paradoxical way, by pretending to be Temple priests.

But the pretense contained within itself the germ of a

great religious revolution. For the real issue is the matter of the sacred. Every Jew believed in holiness, in a God who set apart a place, the Temple, for the sacred. Every Jew knew that there was a certain hocus-pocus, a set of rites, that prepared one for the encounter with the sacred. What the Pharisees held before 70 was not merely the fantasy that they would act like priests.

Their message before 70 was that the sacred is not limited to the Temple. The country is holy. The people is holy. The life of the people, not merely the cult of the Temple, is capable of sanctification. How do priests serve God? They purify themselves and offer up sacrifices. How should the holy people serve God? They should purify themselves—sanctifying themselves by ethical and moral behavior. They should offer the sacrifice of a contrite heart, as the Psalmist had said, and they should serve God through loyalty and through love, as the prophets had demanded.

In other words, the Pharisaic message to Israel in the time of crisis was to recover in Scripture those elements that stressed the larger means of service to God than were available in the Temple. Their earlier method—the way of living before 70, as if one were a priest—contained a message concerning all that was left to the Jews in the aftermath of the messianic war of 70: The Temple that remains is the *people*. The surviving holy place is the home and the village. The cult now is the life of the community, of Israel.

Rabbinic Judaism

The response of the heirs of the Pharisees to the destruction of the Temple is known to us only from later rabbinic materials, which underwent revisions over many centuries. The Pharisees and other groups came together in Yavneh, a town near the Mediterranean coast. Yohanan ben Zakkai was their leader. There, over a period of years, the main ideas of what we now know in Avot came to expression. Yavneh therefore serves as a kind of symbol for response to crisis brought on by failed messianism, a symbol of rebuilding. There is another symbol, also a place name, Masada. Masada was a fortress near the Dead Sea, to which the surviving Zealots and messianists retreated for a last stand. As the end drew near, with the Roman fortifications pressing upward on the Jewish castle, the Zealots of Masada committed suicide. Masada stands for bravery, courage, and fortitude. But the end of zealous military courage was nihilistic, not much different from the message of the apocalyptics. Yavneh stands for something else. The people who came to Yavneh did not fight, to be sure; they made their peace with reality through submission to Roman rule. If they were brave, it was not the courage of the battlefield. But, importantly, Yavneh did not end in suicide but in renaissance, the utter revolution in the history of Judaism accomplished by rabbinic Judaism. What is the great gesture of Yavneh, to match the grand, symbolic suicide of Masada? It is in the message that we were created to learn Torah.

A story contained in a fourth- or fifth-century compilation, about Yohanan ben Zakkai and his disciple, Joshua ben Hananiah, tells us in a few words the magnitude of the Yavneh revolution:

> Once, as Rabbi Yohanan ben Zakkai was coming forth from Jerusalem, Rabbi Joshua followed after him and beheld the Temple in ruins.
>
> "Woe unto us," Rabbi Joshua cried, "that this, the place where the iniquities of Israel were atoned for, is laid waste!"
>
> "My son," Rabban Yohanan said to him, "be not grieved. We have another atonement as effective as this. And what is it? It is acts of lovingkindness, as it is said, *For I desire mercy and not sacrifice* [Hos. 6:6]"   [Avot de Rabbi Nathan, chap. 6]

How shall we relate the arcane rules about ritual purity to the public calamity faced by the heirs of the Pharisees at Yavneh, as portrayed four centuries later by fully realized rabbinic Judaism? What connection exists between the ritual purity of the "kingdom of priests" and the atonement of sins in the Temple?

To Yohanan ben Zakkai, portrayed in this story as a rabbi, preserving the Temple was not an end in itself. He taught that there was another means of reconciliation between God and Israel, so that the Temple and its cult were not decisive. What really counted in the life of the Jewish people? For the Zealots and messianists of the day, the answer was

ower, politics, and the right to live under one's own rulers.
For the Pharisees, as portrayed by their heirs, it was Torah
nd piety.

What was the will of God? It was doing deeds of loving-
indness: "I desire mercy, not sacrifice" [Hos. 6:6] meant to
Yohanan, "We have a means of atonement as effective as the
Temple, and it is doing deeds of lovingkindness." Just as
willingly as people would contribute bricks and mortar for the
ebuilding of a sanctuary, so they ought to contribute renun-
iation, self-sacrifice, and love, for the building of a sacred
ommunity.

Earlier, Pharisaism had held that the Temple should be
everywhere, especially in the home. Now, in the mind of fully
leveloped Judaism, as Avot has shown us, Yohanan taught
hat sacrifice greater than the Temple's must characterize the
ife of the community. If one were to make an offering to God
n a time when the Temple was no more, it must be the gift of
elfless compassion. The holy altar must be the streets and
narketplaces of the world, as formerly the purity of the Temple
ad to be observed in the streets and marketplaces of Jerusa-
em. In a sense, therefore, by making the laws of ritual purity
ncumbent upon the ordinary Jew, the Pharisees already had
effectively limited the importance of the Temple and its cult.
The earlier history of the Pharisaic sect thus laid the ground-
work for Yohanan ben Zakkai's response to Joshua ben
Hananiah. It was a natural conclusion for one nurtured in a
movement based on the priesthood of all Israel.

Heirs of the Pharisees, the rabbis of the second, third,
and later centuries, determined to concentrate on what they
believed was really important in Israel's life: study and fulfillment of the laws of the Torah, leading to the sanctification of
the life of the people of Israel, even at home and in the streets,
so that Israel in its everyday life would become the kingdom
of priests and the holy people. True, the Temple was no more.
But the Temple altar in Jerusalem had been the model for the
table of all Israel before. Why? Because what is truly holy is
not the Temple, nor even the Land, nor even the Torah
itself—but the people itself, the people of Israel everywhere
and always. We the survivors are Israel.

PEREK
KINYAN TORAH
Pirke Avot, Chapter Six

APPENDIX ONE
PEREK
KINYAN TORAH
Pirke Avot, Chapter Six
Translated by Howard Schwartz

כָּל יִשְׂרָאֵל יֵשׁ לָהֶם חֵלֶק לָעוֹלָם הַבָּא, שֶׁנֶּאֱמַר, "וְעַמֵּךְ כֻּלָּם צַדִּיקִים, לְעוֹלָם יִירְשׁוּ אָרֶץ, נֵצֶר מַטָּעַי מַעֲשֵׂה יָדַי לְהִתְפָּאֵר".

שָׁנוּ חֲכָמִים בִּלְשׁוֹן הַמִּשְׁנָה. בָּרוּךְ שֶׁבָּחַר בָּהֶם וּבְמִשְׁנָתָם.

א   רַבִּי מֵאִיר אוֹמֵר: כָּל הָעוֹסֵק בַּתּוֹרָה לִשְׁמָהּ זוֹכֶה לִדְבָרִים הַרְבֵּה.
וְלֹא עוֹד אֶלָּא שֶׁכָּל הָעוֹלָם כֻּלּוֹ כְּדַי הוּא לוֹ.
נִקְרָא רֵעַ אָהוּב;
אוֹהֵב אֶת הַמָּקוֹם, אוֹהֵב אֶת הַבְּרִיּוֹת;
מְשַׂמֵּחַ אֶת הַמָּקוֹם, מְשַׂמֵּחַ אֶת הַבְּרִיּוֹת.
וּמַלְבַּשְׁתּוֹ עֲנָוָה וְיִרְאָה;
וּמַכְשַׁרְתּוֹ לִהְיוֹת צַדִּיק וְחָסִיד וְיָשָׁר וְנֶאֱמָן;
וּמְרַחַקְתּוֹ מִן הַחֵטְא, וּמְקָרַבְתּוֹ לִידֵי זְכוּת.
וְנֶהֱנִין מִמֶּנּוּ עֵצָה וְתוּשִׁיָּה, בִּינָה וּגְבוּרָה,
שֶׁנֶּאֱמַר: "לִי־עֵצָה וְתוּשִׁיָּה אֲנִי בִינָה לִי גְבוּרָה".
וְנוֹתֶנֶת לוֹ מַלְכוּת וּמֶמְשָׁלָה וְחִקּוּר דִּין.

וּמְגַלִּין לוֹ רָזֵי תוֹרָה, וְנַעֲשֶׂה כְּמַעְיָן הַמִּתְגַּבֵּר
וּכְנָהָר שֶׁאֵינוֹ פוֹסֵק.
וֶהֱוֵי צָנוּעַ, וְאֶרֶךְ רוּחַ, וּמוֹחֵל עַל עֶלְבּוֹנוֹ.
וּמְגַדַּלְתּוּ וּמְרוֹמַמְתּוּ עַל כָּל הַמַּעֲשִׂים.

ב אָמַר רַבִּי יְהוֹשֻׁעַ בֶּן לֵוִי: בְּכָל יוֹם וָיוֹם בַּת קוֹל
יוֹצֵאת מֵהַר חוֹרֵב וּמַכְרֶזֶת וְאוֹמֶרֶת: אוֹי לָהֶם
לַבְּרִיּוֹת מֵעֶלְבּוֹנָהּ שֶׁל תּוֹרָה.
שֶׁכָּל מִי שֶׁאֵינוֹ עוֹסֵק בַּתּוֹרָה נִקְרָא נָזוּף, שֶׁנֶּאֱמַר:
״נֶזֶם זָהָב בְּאַף חֲזִיר אִשָּׁה יָפָה וְסָרַת טָעַם״.
וְאוֹמֵר: ״וְהַלֻּחֹת מַעֲשֵׂה אֱלֹהִים הֵמָּה וְהַמִּכְתָּב
מִכְתַּב אֱלֹהִים הוּא חָרוּת עַל-הַלֻּחֹת״.
אַל תִּקְרָא חָרוּת, אֶלָּא ״חֵרוּת״, שֶׁאֵין לָךְ בֶּן חֹרִין
אֶלָּא מִי שֶׁעוֹסֵק בְּתַלְמוּד תּוֹרָה.
וְכָל מִי שֶׁעוֹסֵק בַּתּוֹרָה תָּדִיר, הֲרֵי זֶה מִתְעַלֶּה,
שֶׁנֶּאֱמַר: ״וּמִמַּתָּנָה נַחֲלִיאֵל וּמִנַּחֲלִיאֵל בָּמוֹת״.

ג הַלּוֹמֵד מֵחֲבֵרוֹ פֶּרֶק אֶחָד, אוֹ הֲלָכָה אַחַת, אוֹ פָּסוּק
אֶחָד, אוֹ דִבּוּר אֶחָד, אֲפִלּוּ אוֹת אַחַת — צָרִיךְ לִנְהוֹג
בּוֹ כָבוֹד.
שֶׁכֵּן מָצִינוּ בְּדָוִד מֶלֶךְ יִשְׂרָאֵל, שֶׁלֹּא לָמַד מֵאֲחִיתֹפֶל
אֶלָּא שְׁנֵי דְבָרִים בִּלְבַד, וּקְרָאוֹ רַבּוֹ, אַלּוּפוֹ וּמְיֻדָּעוֹ,
שֶׁנֶּאֱמַר: ״וְאַתָּה אֱנוֹשׁ כְּעֶרְכִּי אַלּוּפִי וּמְיֻדָּעִי״.
וַהֲלֹא דְבָרִים קַל וָחֹמֶר: וּמַה דָּוִד מֶלֶךְ יִשְׂרָאֵל, שֶׁלֹּא
לָמַד מֵאֲחִיתֹפֶל אֶלָּא שְׁנֵי דְבָרִים בִּלְבַד, קְרָאוֹ רַבּוֹ
אַלּוּפוֹ וּמְיֻדָּעוֹ — הַלּוֹמֵד מֵחֲבֵרוֹ פֶּרֶק אֶחָד, אוֹ הֲלָכָה
אַחַת, אוֹ פָּסוּק אֶחָד, אוֹ דִבּוּר אֶחָד, אֲפִלּוּ אוֹת
אַחַת, עַל אַחַת כַּמָּה וְכַמָּה שֶׁצָּרִיךְ לִנְהוֹג בּוֹ כָבוֹד.
וְאֵין כָּבוֹד אֶלָּא תוֹרָה, שֶׁנֶּאֱמַר: ״כָּבוֹד חֲכָמִים
יִנְחָלוּ״, ״וּתְמִימִים יִנְחֲלוּ-טוֹב״.
וְאֵין טוֹב אֶלָּא תוֹרָה, שֶׁנֶּאֱמַר: ״כִּי לֶקַח טוֹב נָתַתִּי
לָכֶם תּוֹרָתִי אַל-תַּעֲזֹבוּ״.

ד   כָּךְ הִיא דַרְכָּהּ שֶׁלַתּוֹרָה:
פַּת בַּמֶּלַח תֹּאכֵל.
וּמַיִם בַּמְשׂוּרָה תִּשְׁתֶּה.
וְעַל הָאָרֶץ תִּישַׁן.
וְחַיֵּי צַעַר תִּחְיֶה.
וּבַתּוֹרָה אַתָּה עָמֵל.
וְאִם אַתָּה עוֹשֶׂה כֵן, "אַשְׁרֶיךָ וְטוֹב לָךְ". אַשְׁרֶיךָ —
בָּעוֹלָם הַזֶּה, וְטוֹב לָךְ — לָעוֹלָם הַבָּא.

ה   אַל תְּבַקֵּשׁ גְּדֻלָּה לְעַצְמָךְ וְאַל תַּחְמֹד כָּבוֹד.
יוֹתֵר מִלִּמּוּדָךְ עֲשֵׂה.
וְאַל תִּתְאַוֶּה לְשֻׁלְחָנָם שֶׁלַמְּלָכִים,
שֶׁשֻּׁלְחָנָךְ גָּדוֹל מִשֻּׁלְחָנָם,
וְכִתְרָךְ גָּדוֹל מִכִּתְרָם.
וְנֶאֱמָן הוּא בַּעַל מְלַאכְתָּךְ, שֶׁיְּשַׁלֶּם לָךְ שְׂכַר פְּעֻלָּתָךְ.

ו   גְּדוֹלָה תּוֹרָה יוֹתֵר מִן הַכְּהֻנָה וּמִן הַמַּלְכוּת,
שֶׁהַמַּלְכוּת נִקְנֵית בִּשְׁלֹשִׁים מַעֲלוֹת, וְהַכְּהֻנָה —
בְּעֶשְׂרִים וְאַרְבַּע, וְהַתּוֹרָה נִקְנֵית בְּאַרְבָּעִים וּשְׁמוֹנָה
דְבָרִים:
בְּתַלְמוּד, בִּשְׁמִיעַת הָאֹזֶן, בַּעֲרִיכַת שְׂפָתַיִם,
בְּבִינַת הַלֵּב;
בְּאֵימָה, בְּיִרְאָה, בַּעֲנָוָה, בְּשִׂמְחָה, בְּטָהֳרָה;
בְּשִׁמּוּשׁ חֲכָמִים, בְּדִקְדּוּק חֲבֵרִים, וּבְפִלְפּוּל
הַתַּלְמִידִים, בְּיִשּׁוּב, בְּמִקְרָא, בְּמִשְׁנָה;
בְּמִעוּט סְחוֹרָה, בְּמִעוּט דֶּרֶךְ אֶרֶץ, בְּמִעוּט תַּעֲנוּג,
בְּמִעוּט שֵׁנָה, בְּמִעוּט שִׂיחָה, בְּמִעוּט שְׂחוֹק;
בְּאֶרֶךְ אַפַּיִם, בְּלֵב טוֹב, בֶּאֱמוּנַת חֲכָמִים,
וּבְקַבָּלַת הַיִּסּוּרִין;
הַמַּכִּיר אֶת מְקוֹמוֹ, וְהַשָּׂמֵחַ בְּחֶלְקוֹ, וְהָעוֹשֶׂה
סְיָג לִדְבָרָיו, וְאֵינוֹ מַחֲזִיק טוֹבָה לְעַצְמוֹ, אָהוּב;

אוֹהֵב אֶת הַמָּקוֹם, אוֹהֵב אֶת הַבְּרִיּוֹת, אוֹהֵב
אֶת הַצְּדָקוֹת, אוֹהֵב אֶת הַמֵּישָׁרִים, אוֹהֵב
אֶת הַתּוֹכָחוֹת;
מִתְרַחֵק מִן הַכָּבוֹד, וְלֹא מֵגִיס לִבּוֹ בְּתַלְמוּדוֹ,
וְאֵינוֹ שָׂמֵחַ בְּהוֹרָאָה;
נוֹשֵׂא בְעֹל עִם חֲבֵרוֹ, מַכְרִיעוֹ לְכַף זְכוּת, מַעֲמִידוֹ
עַל הָאֱמֶת, מַעֲמִידוֹ עַל הַשָּׁלוֹם, מִתְיַשֵּׁב לִבּוֹ
בְּתַלְמוּדוֹ;
שׁוֹאֵל וּמֵשִׁיב, שׁוֹמֵעַ וּמוֹסִיף;
הַלּוֹמֵד עַל מְנָת לְלַמֵּד, וְהַלּוֹמֵד עַל מְנָת לַעֲשׂוֹת;
הַמַּחְכִּים אֶת רַבּוֹ, וְהַמְכַוֵּן אֶת שְׁמוּעָתוֹ;
וְהָאוֹמֵר דָּבָר בְּשֵׁם אוֹמְרוֹ.
הָא לָמַדְתָּ, שֶׁכָּל הָאוֹמֵר דָּבָר בְּשֵׁם אוֹמְרוֹ מֵבִיא
גְאֻלָּה לָעוֹלָם, שֶׁנֶּאֱמַר: "וַתֹּאמֶר אֶסְתֵּר לַמֶּלֶךְ בְּשֵׁם
מָרְדְּכָי".

ז

גְּדוֹלָה תוֹרָה, שֶׁהִיא נוֹתֶנֶת חַיִּים לְעוֹשֶׂיהָ בָּעוֹלָם
הַזֶּה וּבָעוֹלָם הַבָּא, שֶׁנֶּאֱמַר: "כִּי־חַיִּים הֵם לְמֹצְאֵיהֶם
וּלְכָל־בְּשָׂרוֹ מַרְפֵּא".
וְאוֹמֵר: "רְפְאוּת תְּהִי לְשָׁרֶּךָ וְשִׁקּוּי לְעַצְמוֹתֶיךָ".
וְאוֹמֵר: "עֵץ־חַיִּים הִיא לַמַּחֲזִיקִים בָּהּ וְתֹמְכֶיהָ
מְאֻשָּׁר".
וְאוֹמֵר: "כִּי לִוְיַת חֵן הֵם לְרֹאשֶׁךָ וַעֲנָקִים לְגַרְגְּרֹתֶיךָ".
וְאוֹמֵר: "תִּתֵּן לְרֹאשְׁךָ לִוְיַת־חֵן עֲטֶרֶת תִּפְאֶרֶת
תְּמַגְּנֶךָ".
וְאוֹמֵר: "כִּי בִי יִרְבּוּ יָמֶיךָ וְיוֹסִיפוּ לְךָ שְׁנוֹת חַיִּים".
וְאוֹמֵר: "אֹרֶךְ יָמִים בִּימִינָהּ, בִּשְׂמֹאולָהּ עֹשֶׁר וְכָבוֹד".
וְאוֹמֵר: "כִּי אֹרֶךְ יָמִים וּשְׁנוֹת חַיִּים וְשָׁלוֹם יוֹסִיפוּ
לָךְ".
וְאוֹמֵר: דְּרָכֶיהָ דַרְכֵי נֹעַם, וְכָל־נְתִיבוֹתֶיהָ שָׁלוֹם.

ח רַבִּי שִׁמְעוֹן בֶּן מְנַסְיָא אוֹמֵר מִשּׁוּם רַבִּי שִׁמְעוֹן בֶּ
יוֹחַאי:

הַנּוֹי,

וְהַכֹּחַ,

וְהָעֹשֶׁר,

וְהַכָּבוֹד,

וְהַחָכְמָה,

וְהַזִּקְנָה וְהַשֵּׂיבָה,

וְהַבָּנִים,

נָאֶה לַצַּדִּיקִים וְנָאֶה לָעוֹלָם, שֶׁנֶּאֱמַר: "עֲטֶרֶת
תִּפְאֶרֶת שֵׂיבָה, בְּדֶרֶךְ צְדָקָה תִּמָּצֵא".

וְאוֹמֵר: "תִּפְאֶרֶת בַּחוּרִים כֹּחָם, וַהֲדַר זְקֵנִים שֵׂיבָה"

וְאוֹמֵר: "עֲטֶרֶת חֲכָמִים עָשְׁרָם".

וְאוֹמֵר: "עֲטֶרֶת זְקֵנִים בְּנֵי בָנִים. וְתִפְאֶרֶת בָּנִי
אֲבוֹתָם".

וְאוֹמֵר: "וְחָפְרָה הַלְּבָנָה וּבוֹשָׁה הַחַמָּה, כִּי־מָלַךְ ה
צְבָאוֹת בְּהַר צִיּוֹן וּבִירוּשָׁלַיִם וְנֶגֶד זְקֵנָיו כָּבוֹד".

רַבִּי שִׁמְעוֹן בֶּן מְנַסְיָא אוֹמֵר: אֵלּוּ שֶׁבַע מִדּוֹת, שֶׁמָנ
חֲכָמִים לַצַּדִּיקִים, כֻּלָּם נִתְקַיְּמוּ בְּרַבִּי וּבָנָיו.

ט אָמַר רַבִּי יוֹסֵי בֶּן קִיסְמָא: פַּעַם אַחַת הָיִיתִי מְהַלֵּ
בַּדֶּרֶךְ, וּפָגַע בִּי אָדָם אֶחָד, וְנָתַן לִי שָׁלוֹם וְהֶחֱזַרְתִּ
לוֹ שָׁלוֹם.

אָמַר לִי: רַבִּי, מֵאֵיזֶה מָקוֹם אַתָּה?

אָמַרְתִּי לוֹ: מֵעִיר גְּדוֹלָה שֶׁלַּחֲכָמִים וְשֶׁלְּסוֹפְרִים
אֲנִי.

אָמַר לִי: רַבִּי, רְצוֹנְךָ שֶׁתָּדוּר עִמָּנוּ בִּמְקוֹמֵנוּ וַאֲנִ
אֶתֵּן לְךָ אֶלֶף אֲלָפִים דִּינָרֵי זָהָב וַאֲבָנִים טוֹבוֹ
וּמַרְגָּלִיּוֹת.

אָמַרְתִּי לוֹ: בְּנִי, אִם אַתָּה נוֹתֵן לִי כָּל כֶּסֶף וְזָהָב
וַאֲבָנִים טוֹבוֹת וּמַרְגָּלִיּוֹת שֶׁבָּעוֹלָם, אֵינִי דָר אֶלָּ

בִּמְקוֹם תּוֹרָה. וְכֵן כָּתוּב בְּסֵפֶר תְּהִלִּים עַל יְדֵי דָוִד
מֶלֶךְ יִשְׂרָאֵל: "טוֹב־לִי תוֹרַת־פִּיךָ מֵאַלְפֵי זָהָב וָכָסֶף".
וְלֹא עוֹד, אֶלָּא שֶׁבִּשְׁעַת פְּטִירָתוֹ שֶׁלָּאָדָם אֵין
מְלַוִּין לוֹ לָאָדָם לֹא כֶסֶף וְלֹא זָהָב וְלֹא אֲבָנִים טוֹבוֹת
וּמַרְגָּלִיּוֹת, אֶלָּא תוֹרָה וּמַעֲשִׂים טוֹבִים בִּלְבַד,
שֶׁנֶּאֱמַר: "בְּהִתְהַלֶּכְךָ תַּנְחֶה אֹתָךְ בְּשָׁכְבְּךָ תִּשְׁמֹר
עָלֶיךָ וַהֲקִיצוֹתָ הִיא תְשִׂיחֶךָ". בְּהִתְהַלֶּכְךָ תַּנְחֶה
אֹתָךְ — בָּעוֹלָם הַזֶּה; בְּשָׁכְבְּךָ תִּשְׁמֹר עָלֶיךָ — בַּקֶּבֶר;
וַהֲקִיצוֹתָ הִיא תְשִׂיחֶךָ — לָעוֹלָם הַבָּא.
וְאוֹמֵר: "לִי הַכֶּסֶף וְלִי הַזָּהָב, אָמַר ה' צְבָאוֹת".

חֲמִשָּׁה קִנְיָנִים קָנָה הַקָּדוֹשׁ בָּרוּךְ הוּא בְּעוֹלָמוֹ, וְאֵלּוּ
הֵן
:
תּוֹרָה קִנְיָן אֶחָד.
שָׁמַיִם וָאָרֶץ קִנְיָן אֶחָד.
אַבְרָהָם קִנְיָן אֶחָד.
יִשְׂרָאֵל קִנְיָן אֶחָד.
בֵּית הַמִּקְדָּשׁ קִנְיָן אֶחָד.
תּוֹרָה קִנְיָן אֶחָד מִנַּיִן? דִּכְתִיב: "ה' קָנָנִי רֵאשִׁית
דַּרְכּוֹ, קֶדֶם מִפְעָלָיו מֵאָז".
שָׁמַיִם וָאָרֶץ קִנְיָן אֶחָד מִנַּיִן? שֶׁנֶּאֱמַר: "כֹּה אָמַר ה'
הַשָּׁמַיִם כִּסְאִי וְהָאָרֶץ הֲדֹם רַגְלָי, אֵיזֶה בַיִת אֲשֶׁר
תִּבְנוּ־לִי, וְאֵיזֶה מָקוֹם מְנוּחָתִי".
וְאוֹמֵר: "מָה־רַבּוּ מַעֲשֶׂיךָ ה', כֻּלָּם בְּחָכְמָה עָשִׂיתָ,
מָלְאָה הָאָרֶץ קִנְיָנֶךָ".
אַבְרָהָם קִנְיָן אֶחָד מִנַּיִן? דִּכְתִיב: "וַיְבָרְכֵהוּ וַיֹּאמַר
בָּרוּךְ אַבְרָם לְאֵל עֶלְיוֹן קֹנֵה שָׁמַיִם וָאָרֶץ".
יִשְׂרָאֵל קִנְיָן אֶחָד מִנַּיִן? דִּכְתִיב: "עַד־יַעֲבֹר עַמְּךָ ה',
עַד־יַעֲבֹר עַם־זוּ קָנִיתָ".
וְאוֹמֵר: "לִקְדוֹשִׁים אֲשֶׁר־בָּאָרֶץ הֵמָּה וְאַדִּירֵי כָל־
חֶפְצִי־בָם".

בֵּית הַמִּקְדָּשׁ קַנְיָן אֶחָד מִנַּיִן? שֶׁנֶּאֱמַר: "מָכוֹן
לְשִׁבְתְּךָ פָּעַלְתָּ ה', מִקְדָּשׁ אֲדֹנָי כּוֹנְנוּ יָדֶיךָ".
וְאוֹמֵר: "וַיְבִיאֵם אֶל־גְּבוּל קָדְשׁוֹ, הַר־זֶה קָנְתָה
יְמִינוֹ".

יא כָּל מַה שֶּׁבָּרָא הַקָּדוֹשׁ בָּרוּךְ הוּא בְּעוֹלָמוֹ לֹא בָרָא
אֶלָּא לִכְבוֹדוֹ, שֶׁנֶּאֱמַר: "כֹּל הַנִּקְרָא בִשְׁמִי וְלִכְבוֹדִי
בְּרָאתִיו, יְצַרְתִּיו אַף־עֲשִׂיתִיו".
וְאוֹמֵר: "ה' יִמְלֹךְ לְעֹלָם וָעֶד".

אָמַר רַבִּי חֲנַנְיָה בֶּן עֲקַשְׁיָא: רָצָה הַקָּדוֹשׁ בָּרוּךְ הוּא
לְזַכּוֹת אֶת יִשְׂרָאֵל, לְפִיכָךְ הִרְבָּה לָהֶם תּוֹרָה וּמִצְוֹת,
שֶׁנֶּאֱמַר: "ה' חָפֵץ לְמַעַן צִדְקוֹ, יַגְדִּיל תּוֹרָה וְיַאְדִּיר".

All of Israel have an inheritance in the world to come, as it is written, *All Your people are righteous. They shall possess the Land of Israel for ever. They are the shoot that I planted, My handiwork in which I glory.* Is. 60:21

The sages taught the following chapter in the idiom of the Mishnah. Blessed be the Holy One who chose [the sages] and their teachings.

1 Rabbi Meir says: Everyone who delves into Torah [study] for its own sake earns many rewards.
Moreover, the entire world is made worthy on his account.
> He is considered an intimate friend;
> he loves God [and] he loves his fellow beings;
> he delights God [and] he delights his fellow beings.
> [Torah] garbs him in humility and reverence;
> [Torah] makes him righteous and pious, upright and honest;
> [Torah] diverts him from sin, but leads him towards merit.
> [Others] profit from his advice and guidance, insight and strength, as it is written, *I [Torah] possess advice and guidance. I am insight and strength.* Prov. 8:14

[Torah] bestows on him kingship, hegemony, and discernment in adjudication.

[When] the secrets of Torah are revealed to him, he is like an overflowing fountain and a river that does not run dry.

[He] is discrete, patient, and forgiving of insult.

[Torah] raises and lifts him above all other creatures.

2 Said Rabbi Joshua ben Levi: Each and every day an echo resounds from Mount Horeb declaring, Woe to those creatures who disregard Torah.

For anyone who doesn't delve into Torah is considered under a ban of excommunication, as it is written, *Like a gold ring in the snout of a pig, is a beautiful woman who lacks taste.*[1]

Prov. 11:22

It is [also] written, *The tablets which were given to Moses were a work of God. The writing is God's writing, engraved on the tablets.*

Ex. 32:16

Do not understand ḥrt [the root for "engraved"] as ḥarut [meaning, "engraved"], but rather ḥerut [meaning, "free"];[2] the only person who is free, is one who delves into Torah study.

Everyone who constantly delves into the study of Torah, lo, he is exalted, as it is written, *From Mattanah to Nahaliel, and from Nahaliel to Bamoth.*[3]

Num. 21:19

Notes: 1. That is, a person who does not study Torah, no matter what other redeeming qualities he or she may have, is like a gold ring in the snout of a pig. 2. That is, understand Ex. 32:16 to read, "The writing is God's writing: freedom through the tablets." 3. These Hebrew words are place names, but if we translate them as words rather than places, the verse can mean, "From the gift of Torah to the inheritance of God. From the inheritance of God to high places."

3 One who learns from someone else one chapter, one law, one verse, one word, or [even] a single letter of Torah, must treat him with respect.

We see this in the case of David, King of Israel, who merely learned two words from Ahitophel, yet called him his master, teacher, and confidant, as it is written, *You are equal in stature to myself, my teacher, and confidant.*

Ps. 55:14

The [general rule] can be deduced *a fortiori* [from the specific case] as follows: If David, King of Israel, who learned from Ahitophel only two words, refers to him as his master, teacher and confidant, then the average person who learns from someone else one chapter, law, verse, word, or only a single letter, how much more so must he treat him with respect.

There is no honor but [through the study of] Torah, as it is written, *The sages will acquire honor* and *the virtuous will acquire good.*   Prov. 3:35; 28:10

There is no good but [through the study of] Torah, as it is written, *A good doctrine will I give to you. Do not forsake My Torah.*   Prov. 4:2

4 The following is the way one lives a life of Torah:
  A morsel of bread with salt is what you eat.
  A minimum of water is what you drink.
  On the ground is where you sleep.
  A life of anguish is how you live.
  In the study of Torah, you labor.
If you do this *you will be happy and [all will go] well for you.* [The words] *you will be happy* [refer to life] in this world; [the words] *[all will go] well for you* [refer to life] in the world to come.   Ps. 128:2

5 Do not seek power for yourself nor long for fame.
Do more than just study.
Do not crave the table of kings, because
    your table is bigger than theirs
    and your crown is greater than theirs.
Your Employer is reliable. He will pay you your earnings.

6 Torah is greater than priesthood and kingship, for kingship is earned on the basis of thirty qualifications, the priesthood on the basis of twenty-four, and [a life of] Torah on the basis of forty-eight. They are as follows:
    through study, attentive listening, careful repetition [out loud], perceptivity;
    awe, reverence, humility, joy, purity;
    apprenticeship to sages, association with colleagues, debates with students, serenity, [knowledge of] Scripture and Mishnah;
    a minimum of business dealings, a minimum of labor, a minimum of gratification, a minimum of sleep, a minimum of idle chatter, a minimum of partying;

patience, a kind heart, trust in sages, and acceptance of one's own suffering;

[one who acquires Torah] knows his place, enjoys his lot, limits his words, downplays his prestige, and is beloved;

he loves the Omnipresent, humanity, justice, even-handedness, and admonishment;

he shuns honor, avoids a swelled head in spite of his knowledge, does not thrive on [the power of] giving legal decisions;

he shares the burden [of living] with his colleagues, he gives others the benefit of the doubt, he insists on truth and peace, he is content with his own level of learning;

he asks questions and gives answers [to the point], he listens and comments [to the point];

he studies so that he may teach, and he studies so that he may carry out [what he learns];

he stimulates his teachers to excellence, and accurately reports what he learned;

when he teaches something, he cites the person's name who said it.

Hence, you can infer that whoever teaches something and cites the person's name who said it, brings redemption to the world, as it is written, *Esther said to the King in the name of Mordecai.*[4]

Es. 2:22

Note: 4. Since Esther observed this dictum, she was able to redeem the Jews of Shushan.

7 So great is Torah that it bestows on those who observe it life in this world and in the world to come, as it is written, *The words of Torah are life to him who finds her, healing for his whole body.*

Prov. 4:22

It [also] is written, *Torah will be a cure for your body, a tonic for your bones.*

Prov. 3:18

It is written, *Torah is a tree of life for those who grasp her, all those who hold her are joyous.*

Prov. 3:18

It is written, *The words of Torah make a beautiful garland about your head, a necklace for your neck.*

Prov. 1:9

It is written, *Torah will adorn you with a beautiful garland, protect you with a lovely crown.*

Prov. 4:9

RE THAN JUST STUDY.

It is written, *Through me [Torah] your days will be leng-
thened and your years increased.*

Prov. 9:11

It is written, *In her right hand is long life. In her left is wealth
and honor.*

Prov. 3:16

It is written, *The words of Torah will grant you length of days
and years of life and well-being.*

Prov. 3:2

It is written, *Her ways are pleasant. All her paths are
peaceful.*

Prov. 3:17

Rabbi Simeon ben Manasia in the name of Rabbi Simeon
ben Yohai says:
> Beauty,
> strength,
> wealth,
> honor,
> wisdom,
> old age and gray hair,
> and children,

adorn the righteous and adorn the world, as it is written,
*Gray hair is a crown of glory. It is attained through
righteousness.*

Prov. 16:31

It is written, *The glory of young men is their strength. The
majesty of older men is gray hair.*

Prov. 20:29

It is written, *The crown of sages is their riches.*

Prov. 14:24

It is written, *Grandchildren are the crown of older men.
The glory of children is their parents.*

Prov. 17:6

It is written, *The moon is embarrassed. The sun is ashamed,
because the Lord of Hosts reigns on Mount Zion and in
Jerusalem. The Presence will be revealed to His elders.*

Is. 24:23

Rabbi Simeon ben Manasia says: These seven qualities that
the sages attribute to the righteous, were found in Rabbi
and his sons.

9 Said Rabbi Yose ben Kisma: One time when I was walking
along a road, I met a man who greeted me. I returned his
greeting.

He said to me: My teacher, where do you come from?

I answered him: I am from a great city of sages and
scribes.

He said to me: My teacher, if you agree to live with us
in our place, I will give you a million golden *dinars*,
precious stones, and pearls.

I answered him: Even if you give me all the gold, silver, precious stones and pearls in the world, I would only live in a place [filled with study] of Torah. So it is written in the book of Psalms by David, King of Israel, *I prefer the Torah* Ps. 114:72 *You proclaimed to thousands of gold and silver pieces.*

Morever, when a person dies nothing accompanies him, not silver, gold, precious stones, nor pearls—rather [his knowledge of] Torah and [his] good deeds [alone], as it is written, *Torah will lead you where you walk, guard you* Prov. 6:22 *while you sleep, and speak to you when you are awake.* [The words] [*Torah*] *will lead you where you walk* [refer] to this life; [the words] *guard you while you sleep* [refer] to the grave; [the words] *speak to you when you are awake* [refer] to the world to come.

As it is written, *Gold and silver belong to Me, says the* Hag. 2:8 *Lord of Hosts.*

10 The Holy One took possession (*qnh*)[5] of five things [for Himself] in His world. They are as follows:

Torah is one possession.

The heavens and the earth are one possession.

Abraham is one possession.

Israel is one possession.

The Temple is one possession.

What is the source [which proves that] Torah [is God's possession]? As it is written, *The Lord took possession of me* Prov. 8:22 [*Torah*] *at the very outset, the first of His works of Old.*

What is the source [which proves that] the heavens and earth [are God's possession]? As it is written, *Thus spoke the Lord: The heavens are My throne, the earth My footstool. Where could you build a house for Me? What place could* Is. 66:1 *serve as My abode?*

It is [also] written, *How great are Your works, O Lord! With wisdom You fashioned them all. The earth is full of Your* Pr. 104:24 *possessions.*

What is the source [proving God's possession of] Abraham? As it is written, *Malchizedek blessed him* [*Abraham*] *and said: Abraham is special* [*an alternate translation of "blessed"*] *to* Gen. 14:19 *the Most High, Creator of the heavens and earth.*

What is the source [proving God's possession of] Israel? As it is written, *Until Your people cross the sea, O Lord, until this people whom You possessed cross over.*   Ex. 15:16

It is [also] written, *The sanctified and mighty people of the land, I desire for Myself.*   Ps. 16:3

What is the source [proving God's possession of] the Temple? As it is written, *The place You made to dwell in, O Lord; the Temple, O Lord, which Your hands established.*   Ex. 15:17

It is [also] written, *He brought them to His holy realm, the mountain which His right hand had acquired.*   Ps. 78:54

Note: 5. The entire verse is a play on the Hebrew root for possession, *qnh*, and God is referred to as the "Creator (*qnh*) of the heavens and earth" in the verse cited from Gen 14:19. The clear intent is to show that everything truly worthy of value is a possession of God.

11 Everything that the Holy One, the Blessed, created in His world, He created only for His own glory, as it is written, *Anything associated with My name, I created for My glory. I fashioned it and made it.*   Is. 43:7

It is [also] written, *The Lord will reign for ever and ever.*   Ex. 15:18

Rabbi Hananiah ben Akashiah says: The Holy One wanted to favor Israel; for their sake, therefore, He expanded the Torah and [increased] the number of commandments, as it is written, [because] *the Lord cares for His righteous [people], he expands and embellishes the Torah.*   Is. 42:21

APPENDIX TWO
SOME FURTHER COMMENTS ON FORM

APPENDIX TWO
SOME FURTHER COMMENTS ON FORM

The opening chapter of Avot presents triplets of sayings assigned to a chain of masters from the men of the great assembly to Simeon ben Gamaliel. There are three singletons (sayings 1–3), then five pairs (sayings 4–15), and, finally, three more singletons (sayings 16–18). This last set of three is achieved by naming the same authority twice. The sayings are addressed in part to judges and in part to disciples. The formal traits of the presentation are clear: *name + attributive + three sayings.* But the formal pattern announced at saying 1 does not predominate throughout, and the introduction of the pairs (sayings 4 ff.) after the singletons (which begin in saying 1 with the men of the great assembly) starts a new unit as well.

Since the formal pattern involving pairs with three sayings each is well established, the set of sayings in Hillel's name is jarring. In this regard, saying 11, the statement of Avtalyon, and the first saying of Hillel at 12 constitute a formal pair, deliberately ignoring the otherwise paramount preference. It is only at saying 14 that the pattern resumes, and then, as we see, it runs on to the end. I am inclined to think that the pair ascription, "Hillel and Shammai received [the Torah] from them," saying 12, is best carried forward as if it were the beginning of saying 14, with what is in between a sizable interpolation; I do not know how to make sense of what Avtalyon says.

Chapter One

The end of the pairs is not without its problems, since saying 17 and saying 18 supply two distinct continuations to saying 16.

Teachings directed to disciples are at sayings 1, 3, 4, 6, 11, 13, 15, 16, and 17. Advice to judges is given in sayings 1, 6, 8, and 9. The remaining sayings are a miscellany of good advice. I have discussed this chapter and its parallel versions in *The Rabbinic Traditions about the Pharisees before 70* (Leiden, 1971), chapter one, pp. 11–23.

Chapter Two

The second chapter is in three units: saying 1 and sayings 2–6—Judah the Patriarch and his sons, Gamaliel and Hillel; sayings 7–14—Yohanan ben Zakkai and his five disciples; and sayings 15–16—Tarfon's sayings. Yohanan's sayings are in fact so framed as to come to a climax with the name of Eleazar ben Arakh who at the end of the three major divisions is given the final and paramount saying.

Most of the sayings given to the several authorities are in groups of threes or fives, though there are a few independent items. It appears that Rabbi at saying 1 has three statements:

I   [A]   Rabbi says: What is the straight path which a person should choose for himself? Whatever is an ornament to the one who follows it, and an ornament in the view of others.

II   [B]   Be meticulous in a small religious duty as in a large one, for you do not know what sort of reward is coming for any of the various religious duties.

     [C]   And reckon with the loss [required] in carrying out a religious duty against the reward for doing it,

     [D]   and the reward for committing a transgression against the loss for doing it.

III   [E]   And keep your eye on three things, so you will not come into the clutches of transgression:

     [F]   Know what is above you:

     [G]   (1) An eye which sees, and (2) an ear which hears, and (3) all your actions are written down in a book.

If I, II, and III are Rabbi's triplet, C and D then amplify B, while contradicting B's claim not to know the precise value of rewards and punishments. E is completed by G, and so is F, so F is surely a secondary interpolation—or, alternatively, E is inserted for redactional reasons.

The two sons of Rabbi—Gamaliel and Hillel—surely are before us. The former has four teachings, the first two in saying 2, as follows:

I   [A] Rabban Gamaliel, a son of Rabbi Judah the Patriarch, says: Fitting is learning in Torah along with a craft, for the labor put into the two of them makes one forget sin.

        [B] And all learning of Torah which is not joined with labor is destined to be null and causes sin.

II   [C] And all who work with the community—let them work with them for the sake of Heaven.

        [D] For the merit of their fathers strengthens them, and the righteousness which they do stands forever.

        [E] And as for you, I credit you with a great reward, as if you had done [all of the work required by the community].

The two statements in saying 2 are divided into two groups— A-B and C-D (E is meaningless). Two further teachings are recorded in sayings 3 and 4. Perhaps saying 2E is part of a fifth entry, but I cannot imagine what it might have been. Hillel has groups of teachings. There are five beginning in the middle of saying 4, as follows:

I   [C] Hillel says: Do not walk out on the community.

II   [D] And do not have confidence in yourself until the day you die.

III [E] And do not judge your fellow until you are in his place.

IV [F] And do not say anything which cannot be heard, for in the end it will be heard.

V   [G] And do not say: When I have time, I shall study—for you may never have time.

Five more are given at saying 5, as follows:

> I [A] He would say: (1) A coarse person will never
> fear sin, (2) nor will an *am ha-Aretz* ever be
> pious, (3) nor will a shy person learn, (4) nor
> will an intolerant person teach, (5) nor will
> anyone too busy in business get wise.

Two singletons are then given, beginning in the middle of
saying 5 and continuing with saying 6. Then four more teachings are given at saying 7.

The formal traits of the set devoted to Yohanan ben
Zakkai are clear. He has the expected three teachings, he
could as well be located in chapter one. Then, the middle of
saying 8, identifying his disciples, begins a long sequence of
units, three in all, in which Eleazar ben Arakh is set as the
climax. If this were not formally obvious, Abba Saul's saying
would have made the point anyhow. At each section of
Eleazar's triplet—beginning at the end of saying 8 with the list
of qualities, throughout saying 9, and in the group of sayings
of the disciples (10–14)—Eleazar is placed at the end and
given the best saying. The opening statement of saying 10,
"They [each] said three things," is misleading. Eliezer has two
sets of three teachings, as follows:

> [A] They [each] said three things:
> I [B] Rabbi Eliezer says: (1) Let the respect owing to
> your fellow be as precious to you as the respect
> owing to yourself.
> [C] (2) And don't be easy to anger.
> [D] (3) And repent one day before you die.
> II [E] And (1) warm yourself by the fire of the sages,
> but be careful of their coals, so you don't get
> burned.
> [F] (2) For their bite is the bite of a fox, and their
> sting is the sting of a scorpion, and their hiss is
> like the hiss of a snake.
> [G] (3) And everything they say is like fiery coals.

But Joshua only gets three teachings by stretching things
(saying 11):

[A] Rabbi Joshua says: (1) Envy, (2) desire of bad things, and (3) hatred for people push a person out of the world.

In saying 13, the section which reads, "But let it be a [plea for] mercy and supplication before the Onmipresent, the Blessed, as it is said, *For He is gracious and full of compassion, slow to anger and full of mercy, and repents of the evil,*" is a major interpolation, extending the thought which precedes it, and the same is true in saying 14 for the last clause, "for your employer can be depended upon to pay your wages for what you can do." In all, we have a remarkably well-constructed unit for Yohanan and his disciples.

Tarfon's two groups are also well formed. In saying 16, the clause reading, "And know what sort of reward is going to be given to the righteous in the coming time," seems out of phase with what precedes it and may be a development of "And your employer can be depended upon to pay your wages for what you do." But it also goes over the ground of the last clause of saying 14, above, so that may be the culprit.

Chapter Three

Seventeen sages are presented in this chapter, some of them with sizable and well-constructed sets of teachings in disciplined form, others given miscellaneous and even scarcely coherent ones. There are some marks of secondary development and expansion, which are fairly easy to discern, for example, the explanation of the scriptural citation given at the end of saying 1. Some sayings tend to concentrate on a single theme, for example, the presence of God where Torah is studied is at sayings 2, 3, and 6. About half the sayings deal with Torah learning: sayings 3, 5, 6, 8, 9, 10 (works more important than learning), 17 (proper conduct is a prerequisite of learning, and vice versa). It cannot be said, however, that the chapter as a whole simply lays out sayings on the importance of Torah study; and some of the moral sayings are rather dubious of Torah study by itself. Hananiah ben Teradyon and Simeon (sayings 2 and 3) cover the same ground, which I assume accounts for the juxtaposition of their sayings.

Chapter Four

There are twenty-five sages represented in this chapter. They comprise two groups: the first group (sayings 1–19) are authorities of the second century; the second, their successors (sayings 20–22). Some of the sayings are sizable and well crafted, for example, Ben Zoma's at saying 1; others are brief and miscellaneous. Eliezer Hakkappar concludes the whole with a very large and strikingly fulsome construction, more substantial than anything else before us. Since what follows in chapter five is long sequences of number constructions, mostly lacking named authorities, it may be that Eliezer's set is meant to mark the completion of the tractate at some earlier stage in its formation.

At sayings 1 and 2, both authorities have statements of paradox, as at saying 3. Ben Zoma hears a gloss in saying 1, "(*Happy will you be*—in this world, *and it will go well with you*—in the world to come)," and Ben Azzai's teaching in saying 2 is given a double amplification in the last two clauses. At sayings 4–8, the sequence of father-and-son teachings is just as miscellaneous as the others. There is in common a certain attitude of mind, favoring deeds over learning, and counseling against serving as a judge. Jonathan and Meir (sayings 9 and 10) go over the same ground; and Eliezer ben Jacob (saying 11) takes up a familiar theme begun by Meir. The other sayings are not cogent with one another. There seems to be a tendency in sayings 15–22 to group teachings in units of two or four stichs. Samuel the Younger (saying 19) is given a scriptural verse as his saying.

Eliezer's materials (sayings 21–22) are out of all proportion to the rest. They also mark a note of finality, exemplified by the barrage beginning in saying 22 with "Blessed be He . . ." and continuing to the end.

Chapter Five

The bulk of the fifth chapter consists of constructions, mostly anonymous, built around an announced number: ten, seven, or four. None of the promised sequences is particularly smooth. All exhibit signs of prior formulation and even agglutination, for example, a set of seven consisting of a group of three matched stichs and another of four. Sayings 1–6 present nine sets of ten-lists; sayings 10–15, five sets of four types, ending with a sixth in the same number but using a

ifferent formal pattern; and sayings 16–18, three sets of
natched pairs built upon the Hebrew word *kl.* Saying 19
resents yet another pair of triplets, also set up on the formal
oining-particle, *kl.* Sayings 20–23 cite three authorities, but
nainly Judah ben Tema, who provides some closing homilet-
cal materials. Surely saying 20 is meant as the conclusion,
ince it ends with a prayer.

At sayings 1–6, it would appear that we have a set of nine
ists of, or references to, ten things, but the items are by no
neans comparable. The distinct units which emerge are saying
  and sayings 2–3—three; saying 4—three; and sayings 5–6, a
ormal pair—two. Obviously, the last list in the judgment of
'some say" should not be *ten* at all.

Sayings 7–9 yield two sets of seven items, one at saying 7,
he other from sayings 8 to 9C, as follows:

I   [A] There are seven traits to an unformed clod,
          and seven to a sage.
     [B] (1) A sage does not speak before someone
          greater than he in wisdom.
     [C] (2) And he does not interrupt his fellow.
     [D] (3) And he is not at a loss for an answer.
     [E] (4) He asks a relevant question and answers
          promptly.
     [F] (5) And he addresses each matter in its proper
          sequence: first, then second.
     [G] (6) And concerning something he has not
          heard, he says: I have not heard the answer.
     [H] (7) And he concedes the truth [when the other
          party demonstrates it].
     [I] And the opposite of these traits apply to a
          clod.
II   [A] There are seven forms of punishment which
          come upon the world for seven kinds of
          transgression:
     [B] (1) [If] some people give tithes and some
          people do not give tithes, there is a famine
          from drought.
     [C] So some people are hungry and some have
          enough.

[D] (2) [If] everyone decided not to tithe, there is a famine of unrest and drought;

[E] (3) [If all decided] not to remove dough offering, there is a famine of totality.

[F] (4) Pestilence comes to the world on account of the death penalties which are listed in the Torah but which are not in the hands of the court [to inflict];

[G] and because of the produce of the Seventh Year [which people buy and sell].

[H] (5) A sword comes into the world because of the delaying of justice and perversion of justice, and because of those who teach the Torah not in accord with the law.

[A] (6) A plague of wild animals comes into the world because of vain oaths and desecration of the Divine Name.

[B] (7) Exile comes into the world because of those who worship idols, because of fornication, and because of bloodshed,

[C] and because of the neglect of the release of the Land [in the year of release].

Following these sevens, the sequences of four begin. The second set of sevens is rather disjointed in its forms since it follows one formal expression for saying 8B–E, above, and a second one for the rest.